SLOW TRAVEL

SLOW TRAVEL

MARI RHYDWEN

A Sue Hines Book
Allen & Unwin

First published in 2004

A Sue Hines Book
Allen & Unwin Pty Ltd
83 Alexander Street
Crows Nest NSW 2065
Australia
Phone: (61 2) 8425 0100
Fax: (61 2) 9906 2218
Email: info@allenandunwin.com
Web: www.allenandunwin.com

National Library of Australia
Cataloguing-in-publication entry:
Rhydwen, Mari.
Slow travel.
ISBN 1 74114 068 4.
1. Rhydwen, Mari – Travel. 2. Voyages and travels –
Indian Ocean. I. Title.
910.9165

Cover design by Cheryl Collins
Text design and typesetting by Pauline Haas
Map by Verity Prideaux
Printed in Australia by Griffin Press

5 7 9 10 8 6 4

For Tony Britchford
Eccentric but Good

CONTENTS

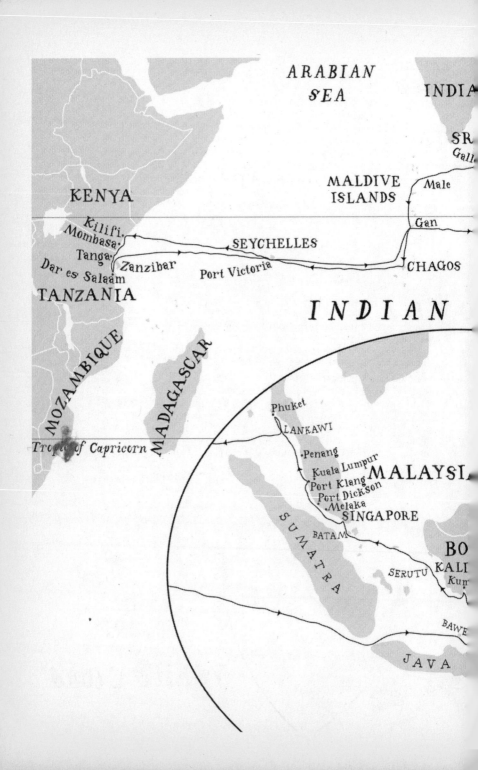

BAY OF
BENGAL

THAILAND

LANKA

MALAYSIA

SINGAPORE

SUMATRA

BORNEO
KALIMANTAN

Equator

OCEAN

JAVA

INDONESIA

TIMOR

Darwin

King George R.
Kimberley

Broome

Dampier

Exmouth

AUSTRALIA

Carnarvon
Shark Bay

Geraldton

Fremantle

EO
NTAN

KANGEAN

BALI

LOMBOK SUMBAWA

KOMODO
RINCA
SUMBA

FLORES

TIMOR

THE
VOYAGE
OF
White Cloud

LETTING GO

Fremantle to Darwin
June 1999–July 2000

GET UP EARLY AND STICK AT IT!
— A wise old woman's response
when asked the recipe for a good life.

Whenever I told people I lived on my yacht, I knew I was going to have to unravel their assumptions. They thought I was rich. They imagined I was on a perpetual holiday, swimming, sunbathing and sipping cocktails at sundown. They knew I was lucky. They were certain I was brave. They took it for granted I must have sailed since I was so-high. They had no doubt I was the kind of person who does things like that. But I'm not, and it wasn't like that. It wasn't like that at all. It takes a while to explain how it really was.

Once, in Africa, I was flipping through a book about creativity, which a friend had insisted on lending me. I have a deep aversion to books that want to fix my inner self, but I was putting off doing the piles of washing-up after the previous night's dinner party, so my totally slack self indulged in synapse-eroding behaviour. The book kept instructing me to 'Imagine a perfect day!' or 'Try something you never thought you could do, take scuba diving or ballroom dancing lessons!' or 'Learn to have fun!' It would be easy to sneer, but not long before, unable to rumba or scuba, I used to sit in an office daydreaming about perfect days. It was not much fun. Now in Tanzania, living aboard the yacht in which I had sailed from Fremantle via many of the countries that fringe the Indian Ocean, I was no longer dreaming. I had scuba-dived off reefs a thousand miles from the nearest dive shop and done the cha-cha on Malaysian television. Every day was a good day.

What happened? 'You met me!' said Allen cheerfully, though he cannot claim all the blame for our fall into grace. Certainly I would never even have learnt to scuba if he had not organised a diving holiday in New Caledonia and in exasperation shoved me cold and kicking into a scuba diving course just days before we left. The dancing is most definitely his fault. Everything else just happened naturally, like breathing, once we crossed over that imaginary barrier we think keeps us in our ruts.

*   *   *

Allen and I and Genghis the cat sailed out of Fremantle one winter Saturday with no idea where we were really going. We knew, or thought we knew, we were heading for Sydney via the north of the country, and we had the charts to guide us there. We knew we were leaving what we think keeps us safe, the things we cling to as children cling to their security blankets: houses, cars, jobs, regular incomes, insurance policies. Freedom is a place for which there are no accurate maps. We were just going to have to wait and see which way the winds and currents took us, note down the positions of dangers and draw mud maps of safe harbours. But that would come later in the voyage;

to start with we were still clinging to the edge of our known world. My main concern was staying alive. I was highly motivated to learn to sail.

Eighteen months earlier, casually, over a drink at the airport, we had made an impetuous decision to buy a boat, leave work, sell the house and sail away into some indeterminate future. I remembered asking my mother when I was on holiday from boarding school, 'Don't you want to do adventurous things? Are you happy? When I'm old I want to ride mules in the Himalayas or something, not be a housewife in North Wales.' My mother never took to mule trekking and, despite my urgings, my daughters had refused to run away and join the circus, but at last I was going to have my own adventure. Luckily I had just married a man who had the combination of practical skill and modulated recklessness to make it happen.

Before we left we joked with the friends who had come to wave us off about leaving so late we might not even reach Cottesloe beach, a couple of miles north, before dark. A few hours later, bobbing around off Cottesloe, we were not laughing. There was no wind, and we had to motor to a marina in the north of Perth to save ourselves from the ignominy of having got nowhere. After several hours of fiddling around tying up at a mooring and then having to move to a different mooring we finally fell asleep only to be woken at around midnight by loud crashes on the deck. We leapt out of bed and struggled into some clothing to glimpse a herd of drunken teenagers hurling rocks at the boat. Why had I abandoned the things any normal person holds dear? Certainly not to be stuck at a jetty on the outskirts of my home town while bored thuglets threw rocks at me. I was tired and miffed but determinedly optimistic. It would all be better in the morning.

Over breakfast the next day we listened to the coastal weather report on the HF radio. If it had not been our first morning cruising we would not have headed out to sea on a day when there were strong wind warnings. We never set off again when there were strong wind warnings. But after nearly two years of bravado we would not have been able to look each other in the face if we had cowered in the marina because of a few waves and a bit of wind. After all, we were supposed to be doing this because we wanted to avoid the false security of urban life. Suburbia was always waiting to beckon with the bewitching seductiveness of the sirens. We finished our muesli, girded our loins and headed out to sea.

Are mountaineers generally people who suffer from vertigo? Do those who suffer from claustrophobia take up caving? Many of the cruising yachties I have met get seasick. On the second day of my new life Allen turned a peculiar pale, glistening grey-green. The strong wind warnings were fulfilled and we battered against them all day before finally giving up and motoring into a private marina. We were a little way north of the one we had left that morning with a miserably sick skipper and a crew member who still had only a sketchy knowledge of how the big white flappy things actually propel thirteen or so tons of plastic tub in the desired direction. The next day Allen was unusually Eeyorish. I was content to sit holed up in the boat listening to the wind howling, waiting until the weather improved and tending my limbfuls of mysterious bruises. After four days of gruelling freedom we had still travelled only about 50 miles in total, arriving at Two Rocks, the remains of Alan Bond's monumental flop of a town.

When we met, Allen and I were both teaching at the same odd little university and neither of us had any serious plans to give up work. About a year later, during a strange time just before our wedding when we were grappling with the usual upheavals of getting married—especially when there are teenagers and labradors involved—lurching between love, war and shambles, Allen flew to Melbourne for a meeting. Trying to grab a few private minutes together we drove to the airport early, sat in the Qantas Club over a glass of wine and talked about dropping out to go travelling.

We talked about where we would like to go and how to get there, the pros and cons of a van or a car and tent. Or a boat, suggested Allen.

'Could we? You never told me you knew how to sail. Do you know how to sail?'

'Course I do.'

'I don't.'

'You can learn. It's easy. I'll teach you.'

'Okay then, let's do it.'

I drove home from the airport feeling madly happy, the way you do after sharing a silly fantasy that perhaps you can escape the drudgery of what passes for normal life.

Within a few weeks of that conversation we bought *White Cloud* from a friend who was leaving the country and anxious to sell. At the time, details of a vessel's construction meant little to me. I just liked the graceful simplicity of the boat's lines and the homely quality of the interior. She was a foam-core fibreglass ketch with a 72-horsepower Perkins engine built by a Geraldton farmer and launched in 1985. As well as replacing the cockpit floor and fixing other problems that are the consequence of salt air and lack of use, we needed to fit her out for long-term cruising, adding a doghouse to protect us from the sun and weather, as well as such things as a new anchor winch, solar panels and an inflatable dinghy. Looking back and recalling all that we did to make her suitable for long-term blue-water cruising—the new uphol-stery, the sail covers, taking off and overhauling both masts, painting and sanding and painting and sanding—I discovered the list went on and on and on. At the time, I had no idea how much work we would have to do. I had no idea what work was. By the time we reached Two Rocks I knew all about drudgery, but I had long forgotten normal life.

At least Genghis the cat was getting used to a world that had suddenly started hurling huge objects at him. The stormiest day, he was on the floor in the forward cabin clinging onto the carpet with his claws and looking tense and petrified. The next time I looked, the spinnaker bag (with the huge sail in it) was in the place he had been sitting. I stumbled around on my hands and knees looking for the squashed remains but there was no sign of cat, dead or alive. Once we stopped he reappeared from some dark hole and sat on the cushion in the cockpit, casual and relaxed, as if he didn't know the meaning of fear. I copied him.

When we put on our wet-weather gear and went for a walk in Two Rocks, it was the coldest and wettest I had been since moving to Western Australia seven years before. I thought, 'This is it! This is what we've been working towards all this time, this oddly uncruisy voyage!' Getting to land and the joy of eating food and having a hot shower bordered on ecstatic. If you know how food tastes when you are truly hungry, imagine that all the pleasures of life on earth are like that. Everything is so gloriously tasty and satisfying after swooshing around reefs and hurtling through waves. I had been led to believe that sailing itself could be pleasurable too and was waiting for the days of lazing in turquoise seas sipping cool drinks and reading. So far it had been hard, tiring, uncomfortable work, though at least I was rapidly learning to navigate quite efficiently. That and the other new skill of assuming the appearance of feline cool whenever possible were reasonable achievements after four days. I just wished it were all a bit less like something designed to be character-building and a lot more like fun.

'How will you cope with being cooped up together, just the two of you, day after day?' a surprisingly large number of people asked when they heard that we were planning to sail away on a yacht. They did not appear to realise it was generally a clue about the wobbly state of their own relationships. Allen would respond, 'How would it be for you?' Apparently happily married people would confess that they could not contemplate the thought of so much intimacy. Some said the only reason their marriages survived was because they were at work all day and had different outside interests in the evenings and at weekends. A local marine scientist on the jetty had caught a female boxfish which looked just like a leopard-skin-patterned box. He explained that she and her blue mate were the most poisonous local fish and their venom would kill themselves and each other if they were confined under stress, so he did not put her in the bucket with the other fish. He told me the blue guys always stay in deep water while their leopard-skinned womenfolk cruise the shallows. There seem to be quite a lot of people with boxfish relationships. Happy couples asked a different question: 'How do you manage to have sex when you are on a long passage and one of you is always supposed to be on watch?'

For the first few weeks, being out at sea with the same person was the least of my worries. Although we had almost weaned ourselves off work and a regular source of income, I was completing a research project and Allen had various work commitments. So, while he went gallivanting off to meetings on the east coast, staying in five-star hotels and sleeping on beds that stayed still, I was stuck in laundromatless Two Rocks, grappling with a supposedly magical pressure washing machine. After several hours I had a searing pain in my lower back and a row of knickers and socks, with that slightly grey hand-washed look, drying on the safety rail. I had spent a morning doing traditional women's stuff with pre-suffragette technology and only myself to blame. With neither sunshine nor glory to bask in I settled for relief at surviving and watching the birds with yellow beaks and nice black hats, crested terns.

Ashamed after making a dramatic exit but not getting very far,

I had resisted communicating with anyone, but finally after a couple of weeks I felt lured by the phone box and rang an old friend to confess my whereabouts. She rushed up to visit me bearing presents of posh bread and decadent cake—a wise precaution when asked to lunch in the culinary wastelands of sub-suburban Western Australia—and we talked about men and children and work.

She was contemplating post-graduate study and after she drove back to the city I mused over my life at university. Many of my friends were leaving academia. 'University is not a pleasure any more. Passion has been replaced by training and everything is stretched tight and lacking in delight,' one lamented. But it was a living though latterly I had been having recurrent nightmares about work, interspersed with occasional sweet dreams populated by wild animals such as koalas and monkeys sitting on the kitchen bench along with the cats. Then I had heard a rumour at work that no one was to have their contract renewed except those few who had been on contract for four years. My three-year contract was due to expire and, soon after buying the boat, I went to the dean, who confirmed that my contract would not be renewed. My ego was bruised. I had wanted to leap, not be pushed, and yet life became much easier and more enjoyable. I had received a grant to participate in a national research project on Aboriginal language-maintenance programs, which was funded through another institution. I would be able to continue to work part-time doing research in an area that I remain passionate about, and still have plenty of time to work on the boat too. I was writing up my results as we sailed towards the Pilbara coast where I had done my fieldwork the year before.

When we finally left Two Rocks, anxious to get north of winter as fast as we could, it was wonderful sailing weather. The sun was shining and the sea and sky were blue for a change. We relaxed with cups of coffee and sandwiches as we took turns at the helm. We saw albatrosses. Ever since schoolroom readings of *The Rime of the Ancient Mariner* I had imagined a creature bordering on the mythological, looming over the boat vast and ominous, but here was the fabulous wandering albatross just sitting on the water like a big white duck. For the first time since leaving Fremantle, I was actually enjoying sailing.

Around mid afternoon I was at the helm, a few miles south of Lancelin, feeling settled and relatively relaxed, when Allen appeared gushing blood to announce that he had mangled his finger while trying to find a way to stop the propeller from rotating. 'Let me see,' I said, knowing that mangled, in the language of the recently injured and slightly squeamish, usually means a bit cut and bruised. It was mangled. It was crushed, broken, severed and squashed. Somehow Allen still took the helm one-handed while I looked for bandages and dressed the wound, and then he called ashore to organise medical help while I steered for Lancelin, the nearest harbour. The only doctor had left town for the weekend, so Allen called his sister Jenny in Perth. Entering the harbour, a sea lion swam alongside. Even a major mishap seems more bearable in the company of other creatures. We anchored and took the dinghy ashore to where Jenny was waiting to take Allen straight to hospital. I went back to the boat. It took a couple of hours to put everything away, by which time it was dark and I was exhausted. Then Jenny rang to say that Allen needed plastic surgery if his finger was to have any chance of being saved and he had been admitted to hospital.

The reality of sailing round the coast of Australia started to sink in. Rural towns do not have doctors at the weekend. They do not have public transport, car hire offices or marinas. I was stuck by myself on board. Alone I could not put out the extra anchors necessary for the boat to be left unattended in the strong winds. Even if I could have left it there was no way for me to get out of town to see how things were progressing at the hospital. After a short thought-burst along the lines of, 'Poor little me, what am I doing here alone in the ocean in the dark on a boat that is too big to handle by myself?' I called the local sea rescue on the radio. The operator on duty was motherly. 'Don't worry, love. I'll sort something out. I'll give some of the boys a call. You just have a good sleep now and I'll make sure someone comes to give you a hand in the morning.'

At nine o'clock three men arrived and, somewhat to my horror, courteously assumed I was in control and knew what to do. I took control. I started the engine and drove where they told me on a hair-raising slalom between large crayfishing boats, trying not to run aground as I monitored depths of zero below me. The men knew the harbour intimately, but little about sailing boats and how cumbersome they are to manoeuvre. It made me aware that seafarers who use engines rather than wind power probably have no idea how vulnerable yachts are when in danger of collision with a motor vessel. But the men were good-natured and dryly jovial.

So, with the help of the local fishermen I had the boat secured on a mooring. Now to get from Lancelin to the hospital to find out whether Allen was still connected to his mangled finger. Though there was no public transport there were some people reputed to have cars for hire, but they, like the doctor, had left town for the weekend. Finally I spoke to someone who offered to let me use his own car and even pick me up in his dinghy. John was an ex-fisherman, and before taking me ashore he helped me lift my dinghy aboard and tie it down. I watched him checking my knots and exclaiming with surprise when he saw my bowlines and half-hitches. My daughter Bee had lamented the replacement of a mother capable of intellectual debate by one obsessed with learning to tie knots, but at last all those hours fiddling with bits of string instead of philosophising were paying off.

Meanwhile Allen had been transferred to hospital in Perth. When I arrived the nurse took one look at me and suggested I take the opportunity to rest on Allen's bed till he returned from his operation. In contrast to my woebegone state he soon appeared in glorious euphoria, announcing to the world how wonderful anaesthetics were these days as he leapt off the trolley and lurched and wobbled around the room trying on his new pyjamas. The operation had gone well. The surgeon had not had to amputate but had inserted a pin through the bone and performed microsurgery to try to preserve the nailbed. The next day they released Allen quite early, having realised there was no way he would stop making a nuisance of himself till they let him go. We went to a chemist to get his antibiotics and something to keep his bandage dry. The female assistant agreed that the finger stalls they had were too small to go over Allen's bandage and she helped him select a packet of non-lubricated condoms. As he walked down the length of the shop to the counter he opened the packet. 'Is it okay if I just try one on to see if it's the right size?' The spotty boy behind the counter looked at Allen with panic and scurried away.

The bad news was we were stuck in Lancelin because of relentless bad weather and it would be weeks before Allen could get the pin taken out of his finger. The good news was my recent epiphany, my conversion to technophilia. I was totally besotted by my new-found faith. If Allen had injured himself even a little more we would have been in serious trouble, as *White Cloud* was not a boat one could sail single-handed. If we had an autopilot, however, I could manage alone. We decided to get one installed as soon as we got to Geraldton. A sailing boat had appealed to the romantic in me and I had resisted high-tech gadgetry when there was a simple low-tech alternative, wind-steering, but it did not work. After the accident I realised how vulnerable we were and gladly abandoned my ideological purity. I knew there would be other problems, but right then the solution seemed clear: I believe in the binary code! I want every electronic doo-dah there is! I want power generators of every kind for Christmas from now on! I sing the boat electric!

Once again we found ourselves wandering the fringes of life in a Western Australian country town. The weather grew worse, with increasing northerly winds making travel impossible, but one long week later we set sail. The winds were a little strong but were at least in the right direction. As we motored out of the harbour, someone on the jetty sang out, 'Do you know the swell is breaking on the leading lines?'

'No! Is it okay?'

'I dunno in a yacht!'

By that stage our fear of the implications of surf on the lines that led out between the reefs, indicated by markers on the beach, was less than the fear of being stuck bobbing and bored in Lancelin any longer, so we went anyway. By sunset we had not reached anywhere we could anchor, so we were committed to sailing through the night.

'My first night-sail!'

'Mine too!' responded Allen.

I did not want to know that. It was why I had never asked.

Allen had never owned a boat, though he had sailed with friends a few times over the years, but he compensated for his lack of experience with a natural affinity for the sky and sea. I had fallen in love with him when he first took me flying. In a small plane, as on a boat, he was in his element, aware of which way the wind blew.

I elected to take the first night shift, to get the fear over with as fast as possible. As darkness fell I knew I was on my own while Allen slept. The prospect of being totally responsible for sailing this lumbering, intractable creature all alone in the dark was awful. My total sailing experience could still be measured in days. But I did not have time to be scared; all I could do was concentrate on keeping on course and maintaining watch. As I took over my second shift I was puzzled by a large, elliptical, orange-red flying saucer over to starboard. Anticipating Allen's likely response to being woken to hear the news of alien invasion, I bided my time, and the flying saucer gradually metamorphosed, becoming silvery, becoming moon.

By morning we were within reach of Geraldton and kept going, though my arms were so tired I could no longer do my share at the helm. It had taken both of us every effort of will to keep steering through that rough night. Each turn of the wheel had needed all my strength. As we entered Geraldton harbour there were people on the jetty waving and shouting directions, and as we came closer we saw it was a couple of cruising yachties with whom we had shared a jetty in Fremantle. I had never been so glad to see someone. I had never been so glad to touch land. Only some vestigial traces of the memory of normal behaviour prevented me from kissing the ground.

When we had left Fremantle five weeks earlier, I had believed that if we could reach Geraldton alive and still talking to each other, everything would be fine. We had heard so many stories of yachts heading north full of optimism and adventure which concluded, 'but they didn't even get as far as Geraldton'. Most ended in divorce or financial ruin but the worst tale was told me by the man who promised to fix my old sewing machine. He boasted proudly that he had done the same for another yachting couple but that they had drowned when their yacht sank a few days later off Cervantes. It was not an irresistible sales pitch. I went next door to his competitor and bought a new sewing machine.

Not only had we reached Geraldton alive and still talking to each other, we were going to get an autopilot installed. The autopilot was delivered and yes, the supplier could install it, but only the electronic components, which Allen was quite capable of doing himself. The complicated bit, which required engineering and boatbuilding skills, was, the supplier told us, our problem. No, the supplier could not do it himself, nor could he give us the name of anyone who could. All the local shipwrights were too busy on the crayfishing boats until November, three months away.

'Well,' said Allen, 'what are we going to do? We've got three choices. We can go back to Fremantle, we can wait until November or we can do without an autopilot.'

We stared at each other glumly across the table.

'Or,' he added eventually, 'I could do it myself.'

Allen had just had surgery on his right hand, his finger was badly damaged, swollen, pinned and bandaged, but having made his decision to install the thingummy our shared gloom lifted. For the next two days he sat in the aft cabin staring at the quadrant and the hydraulic pump. When he had finished staring he began measuring odd angles very precisely with umpteen crisscrossing bits of scarlet string and spirit levels, cutting wood, gluing and fibreglassing, cycling back and forth to engineering shops to get little stainless steel doodahs made-to-measure, drilling and gluing some more. There was sweat and tears but fortunately little blood. At times his finger became so swollen and inflamed that he had to take a long break, and the impact of constant manual work made it necessary for him to be on antibiotics. In the meantime I was doing what I could, cleaning out and repainting the bilge under the shower, putting in a new pump and helping wherever possible with installing the autopilot and extra solar panels. I would also take our washing to the laundromat. It was some way from the boat harbour, so I would wheel it down the main street in an old supermarket trolley. People would sometimes stare and I reassured myself that, even if I looked just like a bag lady, I did not need to feel like one and could thus reject both sympathy and disapproval. Probably bag ladies do not feel like bag ladies either.

It was clear that we would be stuck in Geraldton for far longer than the couple of days we had intended, so we decided we might as well learn to enjoy it. During our three weeks there we went to the opening of an art exhibition and a concert, as well as the regular Friday-night dinners at the local yacht club. People were friendly, except in book-shops. We were even evicted from one by a grumpy man in a cardigan who announced it was closing time—it was 2.30 pm—and waved us out: 'The library is over there.' It was time to move on.

Mary and Trevor, the yachtie friends who had greeted us on our arrival, radioed us from Shark Bay with enticing tales of dugongs and whales, Allen had the pin removed from his finger, and the afternoon came when we could give the autopilot its first sea trial by motoring over to the fuel jetty. Everything seemed fine.

'Let's just keep going, shall we?'

I could think of no good reason not to, except fear, and that could be remedied. 'Just let me have a cup of tea first.'

It was eerie watching the wheel moving by itself. It was like having another person aboard who can steer day and night without ever tiring. The only drawback is an inability to detect obstacles. This miraculous helmsman would run straight through anything in its path, such as uncharted islands or other vessels, so it is still necessary for someone to keep watch. The autopilot can not only steer to a heading, 90 degrees due east, for example, but is connected to the Global Positioning System (GPS) that tells us, via satellite, where we are. The autopilot can therefore be set to steer to any designated point on the planet. For the first day, I could not believe that the invisible helmsman could be trusted and I checked the compass and the charts and the GPS every ten minutes or so. His, I mean its, presence was so real that I found it hard to walk across the space where a human helmsman would be standing.

The night was fairly rough, so neither of us slept very well and by morning the wind was even stronger. The forecast had been for fresh to moderate winds and I kept reassuring myself that they were, therefore, only 25 knots or so. We were pitching through the waves and as it grew dark it was a relief to no longer be able to see the wall-like waves, approaching from behind, sometimes breaking over the aft deck. With the wind behind us the sail was let right out but as we lurched over a wave the boom would too often swing across to the other side. We were putting on our harnesses ready to reef the sail even more when we noticed the boom swinging dangerously. The large block, the pulley through which the mainsheet ran, had snapped in two. We had not heard it break above the roaring of the storm.

'What do we do now?' I asked.

'I'm thinking,' Allen answered, but he did not take long.

We had to release the topping lift and halyard, lowering both the mainsail and the boom completely, and then crawl around the deck and lash them down as waves washed over us. In the raging wind it was a struggle to subdue the sail, which was like an animal battling to get free as the wind caught the folds, but even as I fought it, I could also stand aside and visualise myself looking as I had seen people look in melodramatic seafaring movies. This was not supposed to be happening. I did not want to play a drowning heroine. The weather just got worse, and we battled on past the Zuytdorp Cliffs—named after the Dutch ship wrecked there in 1712—with no sails up by now, taking turns to get a little rest until, just before dawn, we entered Steep Point, between Dirk Hartog Island and the mainland, the south entrance to Shark Bay. Here we could bask and recover in the well-named Shelter Bay.

The next day the wind blew relentlessly from the north, never changing to the forecast southerlies, and we struggled again for a day and a night to reach Carnarvon. Why was it, we wondered, that we never seem to get the light winds and glassy seas that everyone who went a little ahead of us promised were just around the corner? I was questioning the whole silly enterprise. After all, we were only sailing in moderate conditions and I felt that I was pushed to my limits. How would I cope with really rough weather? I was elated to reach Carnarvon and learn from another couple who had battled the same seas that the winds had been a steady 35 knots gusting to 45 knots, not the 25 knots maximum as forecast. I had been almost brave!

In Carnarvon, as at any small harbour, cruising yachties gathered to exchange information about weather, routes, anchorages and local facilities, as well as to socialise if there was time. Most—like the couple who told us the wind speed and who were headed directly for the Red Sea once they repaired the rudder they had damaged in the storm— we never saw again. Yet an American couple, whose tiny yacht had limped into Geraldton after a gale while we were there, reappeared over the horizon one morning while we lay at anchor off Tanga, in Tanzania. Cruising yachts were sparse along the west coast and we were late in the season and so encountered very few before reaching Darwin.

Years ago I had moved to Perth to live with an author who was a name in faint lights. I once dragged him to a Zen weekend retreat—not a formal retreat with hours of meditation, but a social weekend. On the Saturday evening everyone was expected to perform—to recite a poem, or sing, or pull a rabbit out of a hat. Someone read his travel journal. It consisted mainly of detailed accounts of catching trains and catching more trains. My slightly famous author was bored. He whispered a cruel, witty commentary. At the time I still imagined I loved him and I sniggered with him. Now I feel dreadfully ashamed. The train-catcher is a good bloke and the author is long gone to younger pastures. But stories of travel often teeter on the edge of boring,

because much travel teeters there too. There are the tedious practical-
ities, waiting in stations, sitting on buses, queuing for tickets and trying
to find something to eat. Travelling by boat can be similarly frustrating,
but instead of lasting for hours, the delays caused by weather or technical problems can extend for weeks or even months. Yet, oddly,
sometimes what I want is more information about how the personal
complications of travel are managed, the boredom and irritations, and
in particular how we manage aspects of our corporality, the aspects we
do not even talk about in public, like defecating and the disposal of
menstrual blood. Reading Dervla Murphy's account of cycling in the
sixties from Ireland to Delhi through the most remote parts of what
was then Iran, where shops barely had food let alone tampons, I kept
wondering how she coped.

One of my friends at work evidently shared my curiosity about the
intimate details of life in unusual situations and before I left persistently
asked me to record these aspects of life at sea. 'What happens to desire?
How do you deal with it?' I promised to investigate but unfortunately,
given the essentially uneventful nature of an account of sailing from
Fremantle to Carnarvon, there was nothing juicy to tell. Life at sea was
waiting for the moon to rise as anxiously as I ever waited for a lover's
phone call. It was remembering to drink a glass of water every half
hour because it is hard to believe that on a cold, windy night it is possible to sweat to the point of dehydration and that logical routine
drinking must replace reliance on gut reaction. It was feeling utter
gratitude for blue sky, birds and the odd splashes that must mean
something else is living out there. What is most vividly experienced is
both ineffable and prosaic. How could I seriously attempt to describe
the joy of rubbing some talcum powder between my soggy toes in mid
ocean on a stormy night? Small and ordinary pleasures are heightened
to extremes by the sheer discomfort and unease of every other aspect

of existence. I spent years studying Zen with some great teachers, I had taught at an icily cool university department and researched in remote communities in the Northern Territory, but none of this had prepared me for the intensity of delight in the mundane that sailing would bring even when, on an objective level, the voyage seemed to be nothing more than a life of boring activities interspersed by a series of minor disasters. And desire? It would be tempting to enliven my account with some anecdotes about this, but desire lay dormant out at sea in the weather we had encountered. Having only two of us aboard alternating watches meant that only one of us was awake at any time, as we needed all the sleep we could get in order to survive. Perhaps as the voyage proceeded there would be time for extra-curricular activities.

Leaving Carnarvon, Allen tried fishing but caught a tern. After wrestling with the flapping bird he managed to free it, but it must have told all its mates we were okay because from that night on we ended up with about ten terns sitting in a row on our rails.

We carried on, past the reputedly decommissioned spy base at North West Cape with its five towers of red lights, sinister in this lonely place on a tropical night, and arrived for a brief stop at Serrurier Island. As we approached the shore I realised that the numerous partially submerged boulders we were trying to dodge were moving. They were not rocks but copulating couples. We had gate-crashed a turtle orgy. After anchoring in the midst of them we went ashore for a walk on the long sandy beaches, happy, as always after a passage, to be able to use our legs again. Fossicking around the trailing piles of sun-bleached shells along the high tide-line, we found giant clams and a domed rock that revealed itself to be the skull of a whale. It was a private wilderness, known only to a few local fishing enthusiasts who often camp there and the occasional yachties who make the voyage along the lonely west coast of Australia. I did not know at the time how rare such places are becoming.

Inspired by the turtles and the calm, warm weather we abandoned clothing and indulged in a little cuddling ourselves the next morning as we sailed on along the coast, but we were interrupted by a plane that appeared from nowhere to buzz low over us.

'*White Cloud, White Cloud.* This is Coastwatch.'

If they had good enough equipment to read the name of our boat, they must have seen everything. According to yachtie folklore, Australian Coastwatch has a substantial photograph collection none of us would like to see published.

At Dampier, where the iron ore stained everything with rusty dust, we had to stop to be within range of a mobile phone tower so that I could take part in a teleconference about the language project—that last vestige of my working life still clinging to me. I was happy writing up my research report and thinking and talking about language and cultural change but I could see that a life involving fixed schedules was going to be incompatible with serious cruising. This was not because of the work itself—I enjoyed the juxtaposition of intellectual work with the life of a deckhand and navigator—but because of timing. Safe sailing is about going with the weather, not the clock, and when yachts get into difficulties it is so often because they are trying to get somewhere at a particular time or faster than someone else, and not when the conditions are most favourable. Despite feeling frustration about having to hang around a dull anchorage in good sailing weather, the conference offered some compensation: it felt delightfully like transgression. Every other participant was within the four walls of a Canberra government office or a university or state education department, wearing suit and tie or heels and shoulder pads. I participated on deck, staring at the sky. I was in a bikini.

At sea again, heading straight for Broome, we watched the little
sooty terns coming to roost for the night. An annoyed Genghis stalked
them in a wobbly way but could not pounce or he would fall overboard. Later he went below to console himself by stealing his own
catfood. Oblivious to the necessity for rationing aboard ship, or the
concept of weight-watching, he had learnt to get the lid of the plastic
container open, so we had started storing it on a shelf behind the net
that stops the contents flying around in rough seas. That day Genghis
became trapped in the net and was very grumbly-glowery when we
found him in his self-made cage.

Broome was the first tourist town of our voyage and we were
unprepared for it. Everywhere else up the coast of Western Australia
our opening gambit that we had just arrived on a small sailing yacht
led to long conversations with everyone from shopkeepers to volunteer museum guides, taxidrivers to restaurateurs. After days at sea
we were so happy to see people, eager to engage like a pair of friendly
lollopping labradors. But in Broome no one wanted to talk to us.

Leaving, we were cheerfully in the doldrums, becalmed in mists
and thick, glassy seas, and were baffled by what appeared to be a couple
of uncharted black boulders 80 miles offshore out in deep ocean. We
detoured to investigate not stones but a whale dozing with her calf. She
was a humpback, as long as *White Cloud* and two or three times heavier,
so I felt nervous about puttering up so close to a mother of such formi-
dable proportions who might feel the need to defend her baby. Yet
the desire to look was irresistible. It felt like a rare privilege to witness
the intimate scene of these huge wild beasts quietly resting together out
there in the pond-calm ocean.

It was too peaceful; the world seemed eerie and empty. I distracted
myself by reading about Nelson Mandela, how he told a child who asked
him why he wore bright, loose shirts, 'You must remember I was in jail

for twenty-seven years. I want to *feel* freedom.' I was feeling it, but I could have done with the security of walls and floors right then. I was edgy and spent the afternoon watching the towers of cumulonimbus, studying pictures of cloud formations, convinced that trouble was brewing in the stratosphere. And it was. All that night we were savaged by a huge storm that rampaged for hours, surrounding us in dazzling nets of electric light, flying spray and the full force of Thor's hammer. Allen joked about the special effects but I was past cajoling, alone in that quiet place of utter surrender: an unbeliever talking to whatever or whoever might listen to my prayer. I held onto the poor, miserable wet cat who, like us, seemed to feel safer on deck where he could look the monster in the eye.

The next morning Mary and Trevor heard us talking on the radio and called to say they were not far ahead, in Freshwater Bay. They said they would wait so we could all go to King George River and explore it together. We replied that we were thinking of going straight to Darwin because Allen had to attend a meeting. They said we might as well be back at work if we were going to rush around neurotically. 'Change your plans. Start really cruising. We'll expect you the day after tomorrow.'

A couple of days later we arrived at Freshwater Bay and within minutes Mary and Trevor were over for breakfast, bearing hot, fresh loaves. Later we met Stephen and Anna on another yacht. Together we explored and picked oysters as big as saucers, watching nervously for crocodiles. The next day was my birthday and the strains of 'Happy birthday to you' wafted over the radio before we all sailed over to the entrance of King George River and had a movable feast, dinghying to a different boat for each course of the meal, starting with champagne, and oysters that had been smoked over mangrove fires and then marinated in chilli and garlic oil. I do not think any of us remember the rest of the menu.

Nursing six headaches, we set off the following morning in dinghies with plumb lines and floats to find and mark the channel into the river like explorers of old, and at high tide we sailed through the entrance. We motored upstream for about six miles between the steep gorges to the waterfall at the edge of the escarpment, taking Mary and Trevor on *White Cloud*. Trevor was driving me wild. He seemed to think remarks such as, 'This looks like the kind of place you'd expect to see an Abo standing on one leg. Pity I haven't got a gun in case I see one,' are bonding small talk. I am sensitive after living and working with Aboriginal people for years and, torn between the desire to push him overboard and my training as a good hostess, I was speechless. In the end he understood my rigid body language and shut up. After that we had a good day tramping up the escarpment to the top of the waterfall. This late in the season there was nowhere to swim, so we squatted in rock-pools the size of mixing bowls while Stephen told us horror stories about how, a couple of weeks earlier, he and Anna had run aground on some submerged rocks. Caught in the falling tide, his boat was in danger of flipping over.

'I had to get into the water and prop it up with the spinnaker pole and dinghy oars, anything I could find. I knew there were crocodiles everywhere. We'll shine a torch around tonight, you'll see them everywhere, their eyes glow red.' He shuddered.

We were all silent and made our way back to the boats thoughtfully.

We sailed downstream and anchored after dark in the lee of high cliffs just inside the river mouth. Anticipating the usual silence as we turned off the engine, we were assailed instead by the vast rocks singing the song of a million cicadas. We watched the moon rise. It is only now that I have learnt the patterns of the moon's monthly voyage, pulling up the sea as she goes. How she vanished as she waned, rising later and later in the night until she was gone, how she came back early in the night as she waxed and was there for most of the night when she was full. All this regular pattern, there every night of our lives. Watching television in our electrically lit houses, driving round our neon-filled city streets in Britain, in Japan, in Australia, we never see it.

A few days later we arrived in Darwin. We decided to stay there for the six months of the wet, the rainy summer season, because Allen had to go to Singapore to teach for a couple of weeks in late November. By then the cyclone season would be firmly established. We would not have time to sail to Cairns, which was the next place that provided any shelter in a cyclone. When we had left Perth we had hoped to be in Sydney for Christmas and the millennium celebrations, but it was clearly far too late. If we wanted to go to the east coast we would have to wait in Darwin for almost twelve months for the right conditions, so we decided that once the cyclone season was over we would follow the winds to Indonesia. In the meantime we had a long stop in steamy Darwin ahead of us. It was not what we had been hoping for but, as I overheard an exasperated mother tell her wailing child, 'Sometimes you don't get what you want, you just get what happens.'

Stephen made Anna a birthday cake that, in honour of their recent meetings with the world's remaining dinosaurs, depicted a croc-infested swamp of chocolate surrounding a sea of pearl shell on which rode a tiny boat he had fashioned with sails of beaten gold. It was the last meal together for the six of us who had sailed together since meeting in the Kimberley. Mary and Trevor were sailing on to Queensland but Stephen and Anna were continuing with their separate lives after their months of cruising together. Stephen jettisoned the life for which he was apparently destined as a highly paid engineer and instead he lives on his little boat and spends his days fiddling around in rubbish dumps, picking up broken odds and pieces he can transform into

energy-efficient Heath-Robinsonish contraptions. He had just made a
fan out of a 10-cent blade and an old 12-volt motor. It was extremely
efficient, but without the luxury of a guard one risked decapitation in
the confined space of his main cabin. His next plan was to power his
bicycle by solar panels attached to a frame via a bank of mobile phone
batteries, which are the fraction of the size of an equally powerful
deep-cycle battery. He knew that his eccentric passion for making eco-
logically friendly and cheap devices out of the detritus of rampant
consumerism would not allow him to maintain Anna in the comfortable lifestyle to which she had always been accustomed and which, he
believed, she could not live without. 'I can't afford her,' he mused ruefully after she left. I admired Stephen's ability to build his life out of
pieces of string, rubber bands and a secondhand computer chip but
occasionally I secretly coveted Anna's elegant linen shirts and her
necklace of big black pearls. The romantic in me wanted her to stay and
for them to sail the seas with a boatload of babies. I wanted money not
to matter. The pragmatist in me knows that it does. Yet the issue of
money had touched a nerve and it would be a long time before the
twinges of anxiety and regret eased and I grew comfortable with being
one of the nouveaux pauvres.

Some months before setting sail we had moved aboard *White Cloud* at
the jetty in Fremantle to adjust to life on a boat. There were a few other
live-aboards there too, people preparing to cruise soon or sometime,
and we enjoyed the neighbourliness that is characteristic among permanent boat-dwellers. Visiting Sydney during that time, I had begun
to notice the oddness of city life, the way people talked about money
and houses all the time. Disturbed by the shaking hands and shifting
eyes of the teenage children in the house where I was staying, I did the
washing-up just to feel the sudsy water and feel normal again.

Intolerant of urban madness, I was letting go of something, ready to move away, though letting go is a process that is never quite finished.

As we prepared to leave, our lives became an endless shedding. We had sold the house and the cars, and though we put many of our belongings in a container, much did not fit. Everything extra, everything hoarded and saved for sentimental reasons or a rainy day, went.

Nellie, a Rembarrnga woman with whom I worked when I was doing linguistic research in Arnhem Land, had struggled to explain to me how odd the whitefella's view of material possessions is. 'When we die, we can't take them with us. When we die, we die naked. Why do you mob want to do mining? Why do you need more money?' I understood the words but, as she kept telling me, then, I just did not get it.

Letting go was not just about things but more intangible items like security or control. At work parties and other odd occasions when I encountered grown men in dark suits they would sometimes shudder. 'I couldn't do what you are doing. I like to have my life under control.'

'It's never under control,' I told one of them, 'so I prefer not to pretend to myself that it is.' But he did not hear me. He thought I was confessing to a moral disability. He was sure he had his life tightly under control. His words were, 'You are very brave,' but his patronising smile translated their meaning to, 'I think you are very stupid.'

At times I had often wished that I could live more simply and let go of my attachment to possessions. There is a kind of schadenfreude to be derived from those stories of failed attempts. All those friends who went to live in the country and be self-sufficient and came back, five years later, tired of earth-parenthood and gasping for a cappuccino. Or those who returned panting after BMWs, Sydney Harbour views and a sizeable share portfolio, thus proving that trying to be good is actually very bad for you. It provides reassurance that what passes for moderation among the middle classes in the developed world is actually moral. Yet when we had the idea of getting a sailing yacht and going travelling it was not consciously intended as a gesture towards simplicity and, looking back at various jottings, I seem to have thought that it might in fact be choosing hedonism. I had certainly hoped that once the sanding and grinding and painting and sewing and more painting were finished, it was going to be a life of some ease. I was tired of full-time manual labour. At the same time I had become increasingly worried about the actual sailing, which took some of the gloss off my anticipation. Because of the work needed right up until the time we left, we did very little sailing other than occasional weekends to the islands of Carnac or Rottnest. Even before leaving, I suspected that if it were to be hedonism, it was going to be well diluted by fear and mundanity.

I had spent considerable amounts of time in Darwin in the past through my work with Aboriginal languages. I immediately tried to contact a friend who had been both a work colleague and a neighbour when I lived in the Northern Territory. I had not seen her for several years but after a trail of calls I found she was in the psychiatric ward at the hospital. She recognised me immediately. I could not reciprocate. Who was this shrunken, untidy old woman?

'You look great, you didn't know me, eh? I've lost a lot of weight. How is Bee, where is she at uni . . . let me write that down, where's my pen, oh I've got this sandwich in my bag, are you hungry, have a sandwich, oh this fucking cunt, my life's been full of grief, this is a picture of Bob Marley, let me see the label on your dress, oh those letters on the back of your dress, they got a meaning, they got a secret meaning, you know that secret meaning don't you, eh, look at this string I've been making, cocksuckers, where did you say Bee was at uni?'

Where had my old friend gone?

Later I visited another former colleague, who had just been diagnosed with a fatal degenerative disease and could no longer work. She knew that in about four years she would be 'like a vegetable' and have to be in a nursing home. Her husband was taking her south, nearer to both their families. There they could live in the country and enjoy their remaining days together with their beautiful golden retriever puppy, who bounced around cheerfully and helped when words failed us all.

It was a brutal message. Allen had often said he wanted to go sailing 'before it's too late', but I had refused to hear him. I did not want to hear that I would not be young and healthy forever, or at least until I was old, that time that always gets pushed further and further into the future. Too late can happen much earlier than we hope or expect.

Once, at the start of a silent Zen retreat in Fremantle, I was introduced to a cool Scandinavian who has sailed since she was a child. She told me about crossing to England with her father in terrible storms and later marrying a keen sailor. For twenty years they had talked of giving up work, buying a boat and sailing away. Throughout the retreat I was distracted, bursting to ask her about sailing. I was worried too, afraid that she would be scathing about someone so inexperienced presuming they could do it. But, recently divorced and no longer sailing, she was full of encouragement: 'We procrastinated. We were too cautious. It is better just to do it. It is better not to think about it too much.' I did think about it. One Friday I went to the bank unaware it was pension day. I joined the long queue and looked at all the creased necks and yellow-grey hair, the wrinkly armfolds and pair after pair of lumpy, discoloured legs. There is no time to waste. How quickly there is so little time for everything that is waiting until we have enough experience, until the children have grown up, until our invalid parents have died or until the company can do without us. We are waiting until we have more money or more time or we run out of excuses. There is rarely enough money. There is never more time.

Knowing that we would be in Darwin for several months, we both started looking for work. I had read accounts of people who cruised and found work wherever they were. In my romantic enthusiasm I had announced to friends before leaving that I would 'do anything, waitressing or washing up' to finance my life of cruising. It was not so simple. I found that the idea of waitressing—even if restaurant owners did not tend to employ cute young things with hospitality degrees rather than forty-somethings with PhDs—was far less appealing in reality than imagination. I applied unsuccessfully for several jobs but it all seemed difficult and frustrating and much too hot, so I went with Allen to Singapore. He was teaching, so by day I wandered in the botanical gardens and the museums and art galleries and at night revelled in the luxury of coolness at the airconditioned, though otherwise charmless, hotel.

When we returned, restaurants and shops were closed and it was like a ghost town around the marina in Cullen Bay, so we went to Kakadu National Park to watch crocodiles in lotus ponds for Christmas. Back in Darwin we found everything had melted to a stop for a whole month. There were no cruisers around—they had all left before the wet—and we had not yet established contact with people on land. We passed the time reading and wandering vaguely and being hot. Molten, we had put up a notice advertising our services as house-sitters and had an immediate response, the offer of an airconditioned unit for a month, but we would have to part with our trusty pussy cat. We knew that we would not take Genghis with us when we went overseas because of the stringent quarantine laws in Australia that would make it prohibitively stressful and expensive to bring him back into the country. Since we could not take him house-sitting with us, he went to his new home with Allen's stepmother. We would miss him.

Looking back, we were unlucky to arrive in Darwin at the time of the annual exodus. We had not slowed down or softened up enough to respond to doing nothing without resistance. Reading provided some comfort, especially discovering that Charles Darwin had gone through many problems adjusting to a voyaging life, having, in his own words, 'the most ludicrous difficulty' getting into a hammock and suffering miserably from seasickness.

Instead of trying to keep one foot ashore by applying for jobs, we decided to look around for what we could do that complemented rather than competed with our change in direction. Allen enquired about maritime courses in Darwin and found that since leaving Fremantle he had logged enough miles of sailing to sit for his Offshore Yachtmaster Certificate. I enrolled to do an Inshore Skippers course. Before long though, I also had accepted offers of part-time teaching at both the Northern Territory University and Batchelor College.

After years of rubbing shoulders with cultural studies' deconstruction of Grand Theories when I taught in a communications department, I was wholeheartedly enjoying the comfortable certainty of Newtonian physics that I was discovering in my navigation and seamanship courses. I realised too that I had learnt a lot about sailing already and was regarded as an experienced sailor by my fellow students. They might be experienced at day racing in the harbour but were in awe of someone who had done lone night watches in open ocean. All the boring concepts I had found so difficult in school when I did not care how much water I displaced in the bathtub became fascinating and reassuring. I had known for a long time that motivation was an important factor in learning, but I was amazed at how quickly I understood the relationship between centre of effort and centre of lateral resistance when my life could depend upon it. I came to love the way that the world has been cut into segments like an orange by lines of longitude and sliced into circles by lines of latitude. We take such things for granted now, and it is easy to be critical of man's desire to conquer and explain the world, but when I was just about to sail across the Indian Ocean it was good to know that I could describe my exact location in relation to these lines that man has inscribed on the surface of the globe.

The marina in which we first stayed did not allow people to live aboard their boats for more than four weeks, and since we would be in Darwin until July we had to move to another one still under construction, with dust everywhere and temporary and meagre facilities. I overheard a salesman reassuring prospective purchasers of one of the expensive harbourside apartments when he was asked about live-aboards: 'Oh, we'll be getting rid of those as soon as the building work is finished.' I felt peculiarly hurt to hear myself described as something to be got rid of, as vermin. There is an increasing tendency for marinas to be part of harbourside housing developments and, although people like to be able to see well-cared-for yachts from their window, they do not like to have people living on those yachts. Perhaps it is the resentment against those not weighed down by mortgages and work, described over a hundred years ago by RL Stevenson, who wrote:

Idleness so called, which does not consist in doing nothing, but in doing a great deal not recognised in the dogmatic formularies of the ruling class, has as good a right to state its position as industry itself. It is admitted that the presence of people who refuse to enter in the great handicap race for sixpenny pieces, is at once an insult and a disenchantment to those who do . . . And while such an one is ploughing distressfully up the road, it is not hard to understand the resentment when he perceives cool persons in the meadows by the wayside, lying with a handkerchief over their ears and a glass at their elbow.

Or was the lack of welcome a manifestation of that distrust of the nomad, the gypsy, the wanderer? We had become people of 'no fixed address' but we learnt to disguise this from phone companies and banks, who do not do business with hobos who have only post office box numbers and are not quite respectable. I was reminded of my daughter who, throughout her teenage years, had colourful spiky hair and a faceful of piercings. She got very annoyed when shop security guards or police regarded her with suspicion. She had no interest in drug-taking and a strong commitment to social action.

'Why do they always pick on me?'

'Well, they probably think you look like a shoplifter.'

'But they shouldn't label people because of what they look like. Anyway, wouldn't shoplifters try to look inconspicuous?'

'Well, like a thick or drug-addicted shoplifter then.'

'Thanks, Mum.'

But I knew that she was, in her own way, making a stand against people who discriminate against people with labels: Aborigines, women, people with disabilities or green-haired little girls with nose rings. We had no permanent address, no house and no car. That labelled us.

By the end of April we were starting to do serious passage planning for Indonesia. We knew, of course, that we intended to go north and visit the islands of Indonesia bordering the established cruising route west towards Singapore, but passage planning involves several stages. First it is necessary to find out the regulations governing cruising a nation's waters and entering the country by sea, whether visas are required and which ports are official ports of entry. Indonesia is one of the few countries for which it is necessary to apply in advance for a cruising permit, valid for three months. Next there is the detailed planning and plotting, always ensuring that there are several alternatives in case a proposed anchorage proves to be unsuitable or weather conditions force a change of route. We had to make sure we had charts for everywhere we might sail before reaching Langkawi, in Malaysia, where we knew we could buy more. At this stage we did not know where we would go after that, but we did know that regulations made it possible to cruise between Malaysia and Thailand indefinitely, so we would be able to stay there until we decided. We also made sure we had cruising guides for everywhere we might reach within a year of sailing—Africa and the Mediterranean—spares of everything from globes for the mast lights to bilge pumps, and a well-stocked first aid kit including syringes, a range of needles, and such drugs as we were allowed. We also calculated how many weeks it would be before we reached Bali, where we knew we would be able to refuel and buy drinking water in bulk to refill the tanks.

'What about pirates?' wrote my aunty from Wales. 'Aren't you worried about pirates?' emailed someone from Sydney. I found the threat of pirates rather less daunting than the prospect of continuing to cruise the crocodile-infested grey mangrove swamps around the Northern Territory coast. We were no longer bored or lonely in Darwin, but we were still hoping to one day swim in clear blue waters anchored off palm-fringed sandy beaches. Eventually, after what seemed like never-ending weeks of teaching and marking, re-antifouling the hull and doing our respective Australian Yachting Federation examinations, planning, provisioning and farewell parties, we were ready to leave.

Actually, we were not ready to leave. No one is ever quite ready to leave. Moored at the yacht clubs and marinas in Darwin we had met many yachties who had got that far, the place where Australians set off to join the easterly winds around the globe, and stopped. Some were daunted by the difficulty of getting insurance. Some were waiting until things settled down, until there were no wars or political problems in the world. We were supposed to be finding out about insurance and confirming that some last-minute bank transfers had gone ahead, but in the end Allen announced, 'I can't hang around Darwin any longer. We'll work something out. Let's just go.' The day before we left, the crew of another yacht that had been planning to leave at the same time decided to get it shipped as far as Singapore instead of sailing there because, as they told us, the Australian, UK, US and even Indonesian embassies were advising against cruising in Indonesian waters. Right to the bitter end the snares of fear reach out. 'Don't go, there are pirates!' 'Don't go, you aren't insured!' 'Don't go, stay with us in safety!' Oh, the siren songs of the dull and timid. No wonder they drove people mad.

INDEPENDENCE DAY

Darwin to Bali
July—August 2000

YES, WE HAVE NO BANANAS, WE HAVE NO BANANAS TODAY.
— Music hall song from the First World War,
reputedly written by Leon Trotsky's nephew

The first day that dawned after we left Australia was the fourth of July, Independence Day. Sailors are a superstitious tribe, sensitive to signs and omens, and I felt quietly confident when the first night was calm and easy after our wild times up the Western Australian coast. In the dark I sat and breathed and occasionally pondered whether people who do things like sailing through the night on a yacht to Indonesia, having given up work and financial security to do so, spend their twilight years regretfully wishing they had spent more time making money, buying a big safe house on solid land and saving sensibly for their retirement. Probably not.

By day I was reading a biography of the writer Bruce Chatwin and I was fascinated to learn about the shadier aspects of the art world revealed in the book, the relationship between greed and good taste, the games people play to disguise their hollowness, the lengths to which they will go to fill their empty spaces. I sat alone on deck, surrounded by spaces filled with sea and sky. I read too about Chatwin's sensitivity to colours, how he wanted to find a white that was the 'colour of milk' for the walls of his flat, and I started naming the colours around me. Behind, in the east, the sea had turned mauve, reflecting the clouds, and the early-morning sky was the soft yellow of primroses or vanilla custard.

It was our first real ocean crossing and I was determined not to regard these days out at sea as a limbo state, a waiting to arrive. My years at boarding school had been like that, marking time until I arrived at being grown-up and could start really living; I had not yet learnt that it is all real life. Washing with a cupful of carefully rationed fresh water, and afterwards spraying myself with the scent my friend Brigid gave me when I left, became a religiously observed ritual. Having abundant fresh water, or sweet water, as my wonderful Swedish friend in Africa so rightly calls it, is one of many luxuries that I had always taken for granted, but I was to discover that being rationed is the more usual human experience. Over the years to come, experiencing a chronic shortage of sweet water would reveal several mysteries, including the significance of the old saw: cleanliness is next to Godliness.

The days were uneventful. When on watch, I would trim the sails, plot our position on the chart every few hours, listen out for radio calls and stay aware of anything that might change, from the gauges indicating condition of the batteries, to the appearance of the sky. Mostly, during the day, we were reading, chatting or musing but it was important that someone was responsible, was officially on watch, so that we did not collide with another vessel because we were both absorbed in our books.

Each meal was a welcome event that punctuated the days at sea. We were not like those yachties who subsist on tinned beans and bully beef. We ate zucchini cooked with anchovies, raisins and pine nuts, or avocado on cheese muffins with tomato and basil salad, and in between there were cups of flowery tea and bars of Swiss chocolate. And we ate a lot. Before leaving Darwin I had placed an order with a greengrocer who specialised in supplying ships and I had blithely ticked the form: beans 500 g, carrots 500 g and so on. As we were on the jetty about to leave, five boxes overflowing with vegetables arrived and we looked at them in horror. Where would we put all this food? During the first few days of the passage we had to munch unceasingly like manic hamsters just to clear enough room to move around the boat. I seem to have imagined that Australia was the last place I'd ever see a cucumber or an orange whereas, of course, I soon discovered that people everywhere eat and trade in fresh food, even if the range is limited.

There was little wind and we were travelling slowly over sea that was vast, calm and undulating. By day the sky was a fragile pale blue, not like an Australian sky at all. At night I took out my skywatching book and a penlight torch and started to identify constellations: Scorpio and Libra and the one that looks like a teapot. As a celestial illiterate it was hard to find the patterns. This was the sailing I had dreamed of.

Home-built, *White Cloud* is clumpety and sturdy, homely rather than elegant. No amount of make-up or even cosmetic surgery would give her the sleek polish of a modern production boat, but I have always loved ramshackle weatherboard cottages and, though stoutly sea-worthy and well equipped for ocean voyaging, her interior is a mixture of old cottage, hobbit hole and gypsy caravan. The walls and ceiling are timber-panelled, there are tiny bright Oriental rugs on the floor and the upholstery is richly coloured velvet. My favourite small pictures

are firmly stuck on the walls: the Indian dancing girls, the Japanese
Buddhas and the Mexican kitchen. While most of the rooms have
ample height, enough to accommodate tall men with heads unbowed,
the larder is a passageway between main and aft cabin and is entered at
either end through oval doorways that accommodate only children
and elves with ease. We converted much space to bookshelves (thus
raising the waterline by several inches) and had everything we needed
aboard, from laptop computer to lemon zester. It was home, and when
my daughter Bee first visited us onboard she was astonished. 'Mummy,
this is just like the houses we've lived in before!'

After five days we anchored off a corner of Roti, a small island near
West Timor, because it was a weekend and we could not check into
Kupang, an official port of entry, until Monday. We wandered ashore
with no idea of what to expect. We had not even learnt to recognise the
evident signs of habitation. Traditional coastal dwellers do not build
their houses on the beachfront, but a concentration of palms amid the
bush usually signals a settlement and, indeed, villagers were waiting
with fresh coconut juice for us to drink when we went ashore. We were
equipped with phrasebooks that enabled us to say, 'Do you have a double room with en-suite?' or 'Take me to the airport.' I felt like a total
buffoon. How could I have landed myself in this? Surely I had learnt
something from my years of anthropology? What I had not learnt was
to believe I would ever arrive anywhere. The wonder of islands is their
arising in the vast ocean, the little dots on paper charts being matched
in reality by sand and rocks, trees and people. It sounds crazy, but it felt
like a miracle to have sailed somewhere else and for that somewhere
else to actually be there.

   We followed a trail of children who led us on a walk through a
village of dull grey concrete block houses rescued from ugliness by

wooden doors painted in gorgeous colourful designs of hearts and squiggles. We walked along dirt tracks too narrow for any motorised vehicles, past houses surrounded by gardens and enclosed by palm-frond fences to which there were no gates, only wide crooked stiles. This kept the pigs and goats safely enclosed. While the people were evidently poor, the effect was wildly picturesque and bountiful, and the gardens were full of ornamental flowers, rampaging bougainvilleas, as well as vegetables.

But after the first flush of delight I began to wonder: What am I doing here, traipsing uninvited into people's villages, oohing and aahing over puppies and piglets? Relationships are generally founded on trade or passion. I was not sure how curiosity fitted in, but I was glad to feel welcome despite misgivings about our klutziness. Later we went snorkelling on a reef among thousands of tiny electric-blue fishes. It was relaxing. There are no moral dilemmas about staring at fish. But then a swarm of fishermen in little boats became curious about us in our tiny bits of clothing and rubbery webbed feet, so we retreated. We watchers had become the watched.

On Monday we crossed to Kupang to check in. I had been there before when my first marriage was tottering. It was to be our last family holiday. At the time I was not conscious that anything was wrong, yet the world had warped, the air was slightly harder to breathe, every smile had the edge of a grimace hidden in it. I had determinedly enjoyed my visit and taken snaps of bucolic idylls to prove it, smiling goatherd boys and ancient women weavers, which contrast with the sad photos of a family cracking apart. These days I would have been thinking about the exploitation of child labour and wondering if the old women were paid, but, back then, I so much wanted to make everything right with the world that I saw only what was bearable.

From the anchorage, the tall narrow houses teetering on rocks that dropped directly to the sea looked vaguely Mediterranean but without its ice-cream colours. Even grey concrete is eased by trellised vine and trailing ivy, and palm trees mingled with the typically Austronesian-style scrub and new whitewashed buildings that breathed an air of hope. I was glad to be back, to be able see Kupang again differently, without the lens of desperate, hopeless optimism that had forced me to obliterate from view its uglier aspects the first time around.

Crews on visiting ships are obliged by Indonesian regulations to remain at sea while the captain goes ashore to clear in, so I could only listen to the tantalising sound of trumpets and loudspeakers and the hooting of *bemos* (maxi-packed mini-buses) as I waited impatiently on board, yellow quarantine flag flying, while Allen searched for Jimmy. Jimmy did the fixing. We knew about him from some cruising notes we had picked up in Darwin. He acted as our agent and organised our check-in for us. As well as his fee of US$50, Jimmy wanted whisky and some lipstick for his wife. We had neither, so gave him some of the samples of hotel eau-de-cologne Allen had amassed over the years in the thus-vindicated belief that everything turns out to be useful in the end.

As we were to find out, the most stressful part of arriving anywhere is clearing in, especially in places where there is widespread corruption. In Indonesia, officials, and people claiming to be officials, often demanded money even though we had already paid several hundred dollars for a cruising permit. Over the years we developed our skills at haggling and bluffing, bargaining and being doggedly patient, but then, as novice cruisers, we were glad to have Jimmy to do it all for us, especially as there was a slight edge to Kupang. A young man tried to provoke Allen, approaching him on the street. 'You want fight?' He was tiny but he had a gang of friends with him, and it was a relief when he sat down again after Allen good-naturedly declined the challenge.

The few long-term expatriate residents we met had hard faces and reeked of boredom, resignation and stale cigarettes. Tensions were high. It was less than a year since the referendum in which most East Timorese had voted for independence, which led to a rampage of violence and destruction by militia supported by the Indonesian military. A contingent of Indonesian troops was still stationed in Kupang and we heard that someone was shot, a couple of days after we left, on the beach where we had been anchored. We had to beware walking around, especially at night, for Kupang pavements were deadly. On either side, and sometimes unexpectedly in the middle too, were vast stormwater drains. Evidently no one sues the local council when they break a leg. Fascinated as I was by everything happening round me, like the motorcyclist transporting bunches of squawking chickens hanging upside-down like fruit bats at either end of a pole slung across his shoulders, I had to concentrate mostly on not falling down a hole.

Setting off on a sailing boat seems like escaping from the tedious regulations of the modern world, but with yachts limited to only three months cruising through Indonesia we had to keep moving briskly. Our next stop was Ende, one of the few anchorages on the south coast of Flores, a large unstable island comprising a string of restless volcanoes. The town nestles by a bay on an isthmus between volcanoes, and we approached by passing close to one that was smoking and streaked with pretty yellow brimstone. On our arrival we wandered into town looking for a bank and passed a building labelled Flores Universitas. We stopped to look and were approached by a man in a beaten-up 4WD look-alike, a mysterious vehicle that, on closer inspection of the underneath bits, proved to be 2WD. (If in doubt Allen always checks cars the way other people check kittens.) 'My name is Tommy. I am the lector, the boss of the university.' When we told him we had both taught at universities in Australia he immediately adopted us for the rest of our stay. First, he took us to the bank and, while Allen was inside, quizzed me about how many children I had.

'I have two daughters.'

'You and Allen?'

'Well, no, I was married before. Allen was married before and has a son and a daughter.'

'How many children will you and Allen have?'

Disinclined to go into detail about the unlikelihood of a 49-year-old woman and her vasectomised husband having a child, I laughed and explained that I did not think we were going to have any. Tommy was shocked and concerned and fascinated: was it acceptable in Australia for a woman to marry and not to have children?

Tommy told us that Ende was 85 per cent Christian but that Muslims lived around the harbour. We had already heard them; the pre-dawn call to prayer was to become a familiar sound in almost every anchorage we visited in the Indian Ocean, even in countries whose populations were predominantly Buddhist or Christian. Tommy drove us around town, showing us landmarks, the schools and the museums, but mostly he wanted to ask us endless questions. Allen told him we were 'taking a year's holiday' rather than try to explain that we were—were what? We did not feel like rich people swanning around doing nothing but it certainly looked that way to Tommy, and any attempt to explain it otherwise was going to sound, indeed be, a squirming rationalisation.

During our stay, Tommy took us to visit most of his close family and on this occasion he took us to his brother's house for lunch. His brother, the harbourmaster in another town on the island, was at work but his wife was home and cooked us a delightful simple meal of tempeh, a kind of watercress called *kangkung,* and rice. The path to the house took a meandering route along beautifully swept and maintained dirt tracks that seemed to pass through several other people's gardens, up and down twisting stairways, between clipped hedges and past trees where monkeys were tethered and pens where chickens pecked. Like most of the surrounding houses, theirs had woven bamboo walls, a tin roof and concrete floors. The kitchen was outside, where we could see well-used old saucepans hanging on the wall. Inside, in the sitting room, were several sets of enamel and stainless steel saucepans on display in cabinets, unused, still shiny and new. There was a television and video and even a phone, all unusual in a private house. Over lunch Tommy continued his questioning. He wanted to know about education problems in relation to 'narcoba'—narcotics and other drugs—and also BF.

'BF?'

'Blue films.'

Tommy had a disconcerting squint, which gave him a slightly sinister look, especially when the direction of his conversations took these turns. After some time in the predominantly Muslim countries that encircle the Indian Ocean, I too would start to view the West through different eyes. Later Tommy excitedly riffled through some fashion and photography magazines we had on board. It was only then that I noticed how far these magazines went beyond what had passed for pornography in the days when I was an adolescent and had discovered my older brother's stash of rude pictures.

After lunch Tommy drove us along bumpy, muddy tracks through a steamy banana jungle to his house, a decrepit hut built from sheets of woven palm fronds on a timber frame. There were gaping holes between walls and floor big enough for his large dog to run in and out, and for a small burglar too, though the door was padlocked. Inside, we sat in the front room, which was partitioned from the rest of the house by some curtains slung on poles. Paint peeled from the walls, and there was a sad plastic chandelier. There was no television or phone. As well as his job at the university, Tommy ran a private school situated next door to his house with about two hundred difficult pupils who had been rejected by the government education system. Tommy wanted us to meet his staff and so we waited at his house for the school 'headmaster' to arrive. This led to some confusion when two women turned up, one of whom was introduced as the headmaster, and I remained discombobulated for a while, imagining I had a problem with perception rather than with language. The other woman, the one who spoke no English, was the English teacher. Then one of the most camp men I have ever met arrived. It was not just that he was small and delicate and utterly charming, but the way he sat down so primly, flirtatiously primping his beautifully cut trousers and simultaneously swivelling his hips before arranging his hands on his lap. He was introduced as the English teacher's husband. I supposed I was misreading some culturally specific body-language rules, like the one that dictates that sitting European men can confidently cross their legs whereas Aussie blokes who want to signal their blokeness must keep their knees widely apart. But coming so soon after the headmaster confusion I was starting to feel culturally wobbly.

After introducing all his employees, Tommy asked to visit our boat. Over the course of a few days, we took several people to see our boat at Tommy's request: his students, his cousins, in-laws, siblings and all their children. He never tired of displaying it, describing it as 'lux' and 'like being in paradise' and asking how much it cost. Allen doggedly obfuscated, 'I don't know in rupiah.' By Western standards, *White Cloud* was a cheapish boat, but in a place where the average worker was paid a couple of dollars a day, revealing her price would have felt shameful.

One morning Tommy took us to breakfast at his mother's house, where several of his five brothers and five sisters still lived. We sat under a lean-to at the back of the house while further outside, in the kitchen, rice porridge was prepared over a fire fuelled by wood shavings. All the cooking was done on the ground, and dishes were washed from a hose as dogs and cats and chickens mooched around. The television was on but no one was watching. Everyone was either cooking or queuing for the bathroom—a hose rigged up behind a screen—in various states of saronged dishabille to emerge a few minutes later spick and span in Western-style dress.

Later we visited Flores Universitas, which is housed in an old crumbling colonial pile. Each of the four faculties, law, teacher education, technical education and economics, had two small rooms equipped with blackboards. Tommy showed us the computers. There were no printers, and the computers were of a vintage where the disks actually flopped, genuine eponymous $5^1/_4$-inch floppy disks. The library had fewer books than the average Australian primary school. We were introduced to all the lecturers, who seemed extraordinarily friendly—we had not yet become used to Indonesian gregariousness—and told us they would welcome donations of books, but getting them delivered safely was always a problem. Later, from Australia, we sent Tommy a world map, information on AIDS and the details about Australian universities he requested, but we do not know if they ever arrived.

On Saturday, Tommy, his wife and son, and one of his university students came aboard for afternoon tea. I commented on the animals I had seen, the goats being reluctantly washed on the beach and the chickens roaming around town, explaining about battery farming and that we never saw farm animals in towns in Australia.

'Much better, I think,' said Tommy.

'No, here the chickens have a better life. Your chickens are much happier.'

Mad foreigners, judging by the laughter when the exchange was endlessly repeated and translated.

As we sat on deck two girls came over in a dugout canoe from a
nearby prau. They were in their early teens and extremely beautiful,
with strong white teeth, flusters of furry eyelashes and an air of absolute
composure bordering on hauteur, even though they were wearing
what appeared to be yellow face masks, concoctions of turmeric and
rice flour, to protect their skin from the sun. They were sea nomads
whose young womenfolk traditionally free-dive for fish. Tommy
explained that they are the only Indonesian seafarers, apart from the
Macassans, who go on the open sea and, indeed, it is only they and the
Macassans who traditionally visited north Australia. Tommy told us
they practise black magic and people are very afraid of them. We were
afraid of them. Not for their magic but because reputedly it was the
people who sailed the open sea who were pirates and we were still nervous about the pirates. I told Tommy that we did not usually encourage
people on passing boats to come aboard, as we would quickly be inun-
dated with visitors. Tommy was baffled. In any case, I could not
understand why he thought we would welcome aboard people whom
he had just described as dangerous, but perhaps he was already
bewitched by these girls. I could not take my eyes off them. Their
beauty went far beyond ordinary human film-star good looks, more
like that of tigers. Or perhaps it was just that Tommy likes to be inun-
dated, and even the company of dangerous magic women is preferable
to the loneliness we call 'enough personal space'. Everywhere we went
and everything thing we did with him was done with as many people
present as possible. At day's end it was a relief to be just the two of us
again, sitting on deck, looking at the hill behind the beach with its Shar-
pei folds and wrinkles and the perfectly conical baby volcano in the
distance as boatmen paddled home through the silky pink sunset to
join the flock of brightly coloured boats already roosting for the night.
Then we could relax and talk about our confusion and listen to the

music that drifted over the still evening. It sounded as though, somewhere, someone was belly dancing.

On Sunday, Tommy's only day off, he took us to Kelimutu, an excursion to the top of a volcano where, in the caldera, there are three lakes, each a different colour. Tommy picked us up at 5 am, when it was still dark. Then we spent an hour or so collecting sisters and brothers and nieces and nephews and Tommy's wife and, finally, the driver we had hired, before eventually setting off on the long winding drive up to the mountain. It reminded me of when I lived in remote Aboriginal settlements and rarely went far without my car full to the brim. The road was steep and tortuous and washed away in many places. I was glad of our cautious driver because we had already discovered that, despite appearances, Tommy's car was not designed for such difficult terrain. We passed through pretty villages, clusters of woven bamboo cottages, often balanced on the edge of cliffs, their gardens festooned with roses and marigolds amid the corn, eggplants, oranges and coffee, against a backdrop of steep rice paddies and towering volcanoes. The people were quietly elegant with their traditional *ikat* sarongs draped around their heads and shoulders against the early-morning cold. Yet their faces seemed prematurely old and careworn by a life of gruelling work and hardship, and I wondered about their lives. Almost every village had one house with a satellite dish almost a quarter of the size of the house plonked in the dirt yard among the chickens and goats and pigs, so that even here, in such remoteness, people could gather to watch television. What must it feel like to live like this: this hard slog of a life as a subsistence farmer, surviving as your ancestors have done for generations but, unlike them, to be able to see how the rest of the world lives?

The three lakes in the caldera were not only spectacular—circles of milky turquoise, khaki and black right next to each other in a wild

other-planety landscape—but also frighteningly accessible. There was
nothing to stop people scrambling up to the crater edges, no guardrail
and no warning signs. With one slip someone could tumble over into
the lake and there was no vegetation, nothing to get hold of to get out
again, just steep bare cliffs. 'You'd probably dissolve pretty fast anyway,'
Allen said reassuringly, 'so you wouldn't have to swim in desperate
circles for long.' Most of Tommy's family had never visited the lakes
before and were quite terrified and would not walk anywhere near the
top of the volcano. Before heading back to the car, all the women in
the family produced a breakfast picnic of rice porridge and tasty little
dried fish fried with shallots, tomatoes and chilli. The fussing and chattering over the food and being together on a big family outing was
what they enjoyed more than the extraordinary landscape.

When we returned to Ende, Tommy proclaimed he would take
everyone to see our lux boat. When we reached the beach, we could see
that the surf was up and it was rough enough to deter anyone sensible
from taking nervous women and children out in a little dinghy.
Unfortunately, it did not look like impressive surf. A landlubber might
have thought it was merely a bit choppy, so it would have seemed very
mean to refuse to ferry our visitors out. It had evidently not occurred
to Tommy that rich white people might be living in a way that is often
uncomfortable and even potentially dangerous to the point of being
life-threatening. So we took them. The mothers were evidently, and
rightly, terrified as they wobblingly handed their babies up from the
tossing dinghy into the rolling yacht. Once aboard it was chaos. All of
the women wanted to use the loo but knew nothing about Western
lavatories nor about boats. Unwilling to have a discussion of bodily
functions translated by men, they proceeded to cause near disasters
and direct-hit inconvenience as they sploshed precious drinking water
and shit around the floor.

Tommy thought we were exceedingly rich, rich beyond his wildest imaginings, and really we were. We had an electric fridge, a gas stove, shelves full of books, and cupboards crammed with tinned and dried food. It was hard to explain to him that we needed the things we had on board and could not just give them away. For example, the lovely picture books that so tantalised him were actually essential equipment, the pilot books and cruising guides that contain all the information about anchorages, weather and bureaucratic procedures in any particular area. Indeed, on board *White Cloud* we had a kind of rule that everything must have at least one essential function or we could not justify keeping it. (I know, the pictures—but they took up no space!)

Tommy looked at the compass. 'How do you get it to move?' He was fascinated. We did not even try to explain the GPS nor that all these wonderful devices from fridge to sails only worked because we were endlessly fixing and maintaining them. How could I start to explain? It would have been like someone telling me that they needed Porsches and airconditioning and servants. Local fishing boats managed without so much as a chart or a compass, and Tommy himself lived without many of the luxuries we considered essential on board. It started me thinking about what I really need, about what is materially necessary for a good life. It started me thinking there is little pleasure to be had from owning a lux boat in the midst of others' poverty. It started me thinking about the vast gap between rich and poor that I would encounter everywhere I went, and that, as in Tommy's case, it is not only the uneducated or unqualified who are poor by Western standards. It started me thinking again about the parable of the Bugatti.

In the West, the North, the developed world—whatever you want to call the rich nations—we are all living like people who have an uninsurable Bugatti as a nest egg for our old age. One day this Bugatti breaks

down on a railway crossing with a driverless, runaway high-speed train
hurtling down the line towards it. We are near the points and can
switch them so that the train will be diverted onto a siding and the car
will be safe, but there is a small girl playing on the rails there in the siding. Will we sacrifice her for our financial security? Of course not. Yet
the philosopher Peter Unger argues that we do. It is just that we cannot see the consequences of our actions or of our countries' economic
policies, or the tactics of the multinational companies in which our
superannuation is invested.

   We left Flores, hazy with the smoke of thousands of little open
cooking fires, and travelled past looming volcanoes clearly visible, even
at night, by the light of the full moon. Through the three short
watches of each night, I planned education schemes, wanting to solve
what I saw as Indonesia's problems, wanting to cure poverty. We
anchored in the early morning on the south coast of Rinca. This difficult spot of ferocious currents led to tangled anchor chains and
re-anchoring three times before we could go snorkelling in magic coral
gardens and then relax over lunch with a bottle of red wine. The next
morning we went dragon-spotting. Komodo dragons, found, of
course, on Komodo but also on this neighbouring island of Rinca, kill
their prey, including deer and buffalo, by scratching it with their claws
and leaving it to die of infection. They can grow to 3 metres and weigh
up to 135 kilograms. They can run very fast. Having no vorpal swords
to hand, we were armed, English-fashion, with furled umbrellas. Being
automatic-opening, these are also authentic Australian weapons,
mimicking the frill-necked lizard defence strategy. We saw a huge
monster on the beach ahead of us but it wandered off into the nearby
tulgey woods. We continued walking along the beach, jumping whenever there was any rustling from the adjacent trees and ready to race
into the water if necessary. Did dragons swim? We didn't know. I felt

exactly how I did when I was a child playing at knights and dragons. How early we learn to fear the creations of our imagination!

A few days later on Komodo we saw a dragon on the beach where we had anchored and where, during the night, we had heard terrible roaring screams, like a cow or some other large animal in torment. We decided against any more dragon-spotting excursions. The next day the people on another yacht that had joined us in the anchorage told us that the roaring noise was just a heron conversing naturally and not a large animal being savaged. I had not thought of checking in a bird book but found in my field guide that my screaming cow must have been a great-billed heron (*Ardea sumaltrana*) about which was written: 'Voice penetrating (and to the inexperienced) frightening calls including loud guttural roars ("Crocodile like") and groans given by day and night.'

Some days everything goes wrong and, on a boat, this usually means equipment, especially electrical and electronic things, which are particularly susceptible to the corrosive effects of salty air. We had a day with no fridge, no radio and no bilge pump. While Allen fixed each in turn, I vacuumed and made some rather odd chocolate biscuits. It was one of those comfortingly ordinary, puddling days that make us human when miles from home on dragon-infested shores. During that day a couple more yachts flying the stars and stripes arrived at the anchorage, and we were to meet these same boats many times as we travelled through Indonesia and South-East Asian waters. It was our first real involvement with the cruising community. Previously we had been in home waters and were not full initiates, but now we were bona fide yachties and were soon to learn more about the peculiar world of this fluid coterie. Because of the obligation to fly a national flag, we knew the nationality of other yachties even if we never discovered anything more about them. The flags we saw on our travels were predominantly those of Britain, the United States, Canada, Australia, New Zealand and South Africa. Several yachts flew French flags, a few were Dutch and there was an occasional yacht from another Western European country. Seeing four yachts at anchor, some enterprising retailers arrived on a tiny boat selling carved dragons and strings of pearls. The next day the other yachts took off for Bali, but we just slowly moved on to Banta Island where we mostly loafed and did odd chores, like whipping ropes and retrieving lost hats, and dived off the reef, which was calm and shallow and full of fish. There were even some sleeping turtles.

Already there were hints and whispers of 'Why are we doing this? Why do people sail round the world?' They are the sort of questions that arise at night, sailing between islands, and we were on our way from Banta to Moyo. I was yearning for some purpose, already feeling that snorkelling and exploring tropical islands is not quite satisfying. I had not practised Zen meditation for decades without learning, in practice as well as in theory, that suffering is caused by desire and that the way to end it is to be awake to the present moment. There was nothing I could do that was to more purpose than to pay attention to what I was doing: sailing the yacht safely through the dark hours of night while Allen slept. Overnight the wind came up and I was glad because I was able to put up some sails and switch off the engine. I was starting to gain confidence and loved the night-sailing, when I could experiment with sail-trimming with no one watching.

To celebrate our arrival at Moyo we went ashore to the resort for morning coffee. Really we wanted to see what kind of a place costs $A2000 per night. Apparently the owners had shrewdly invited Princess Di to stay there before it opened and after her visit everyone wanted to go. It was very low-key, very tasteful. We sat in an open dining room under a bamboo-shingled roof. The floor was polished timber and there were plain but beautifully crafted teak chairs and tables of varying sizes and shapes, and clusters of casual cotton-covered cream sofas. Outside were coral pebble pathways and simple stone statues and garden ornaments, such as a monkey that doubled as a candle-holder. Even the souvenir shop was subdued and unpretentious and filled with utterly desirable things: exquisite complicated silver jewellery and casual brown cotton clothes that were magically drop-dead elegant. How subtly consumerism can manipulate us into paying pots of money to go a place where we can pretend we have escaped all that. Marie Antoinette played at milkmaid; Princess Di could play at Blue Lagoon. The bill for our two coffees was $A30. We were relieved we had not ordered breakfast.

In the afternoon, we met up with some other yachties anchored nearby, a bunch of people and one King Charles spaniel of happy waggles and smiley face. All of us, except the dog, who is not very welcome in the canophobic world of Islam, went on a long walk to a waterfall through an idyllic island village of prettily painted houses and wallowing buffalo. As we walked, we talked. Mike, an Alaskan with a gentle, deeply creased face, had been a commercial fisherman in the icy Arctic waters before setting off across the Pacific with his wife and their young son. On their arrival in Australia, his wife was found to have cancer, and they stayed there for three years while she grew sicker and died. When we met him he was on his way to India where he wanted to stay for a while so his son could go to school. Jane is English but had lived for years in the US, working as something very high-powered in a successful software company. She and her husband had met Mike and his family when they were all cruising around Mexico, but afterwards her marriage had collapsed. She had kept her boat for a while but, unable to maintain the engine herself, gave up cruising until Mike invited her to act as tutor to his son. Jane had that spinsterish look, tense, with a determinedly thrust-out chin, white shirt and shapeless skirt finished off with tentatively applied lipstick in absolutely the wrong colour. Magnus was thirteen and was so at ease on a boat he seemed part of it, welded to the deck in any kind of weather. Alone on the other boat, except for his dog, was George. He was a hard-core sailor, a single-hander who did not believe in new-fangled devices such as furlers (which allow one to roll up the foresail easily and are now almost de rigueur on cruising boats). He has a PhD in psychology and was a frustrated novelist. He had embarked on his voyage after his divorce and talked bitterly about his ex-wife and money.

Before actually buying *White Cloud*—and typically for someone who, at the time, was much happier in a library than doing something that could remotely be labelled 'sport'—I had done some research, reading my colleague Jim Macbeth's doctoral thesis about the sociology of cruising. The main gist, as I recall, was that cruisers tended to be co-operative, intelligent, adventurous, flexible, competent, independent, interesting people. Naturally I decided that, in theory, I was ideally suited to the cruising life. This was followed by further discussions with Jim himself, who seemed slightly amused by the irony: the work that had opened the doors of academia to him was inspiring two of his colleagues to give up the relative shelter and safety of collegial life for the financial and physical insecurity of cruising.

Now I too wanted to find out more about the lives of this self-selected tribe. How did a good-looking, intelligent woman become so desiccated? How did a boy cope with losing his mother in a strange land far from home? Why did a man carry his anger for so long? And, most mysteriously, why did an Alaskan fisherman want his son to be educated in India? Yachties are indeed always, on the surface, so competent, so cheerful, so able to cope with whatever gets blown at them and so very decent and ordinary. Yet underneath, like the rest of us, they have convoluted lives.

A few days later at Sumbawa Besar, the main town on the island of Sumbawa, one puzzle was solved after we all went ashore together to view the remarkably modest palace of the former sultan. We managed to sneak in through the house next door, a dark warehouse full of furniture, where some elderly women, brewing sticky sweets in one corner, directed us through a hole in the fence. Within minutes a young English-speaking guide arrived to show us inside. The whole place was tatty from half-hearted restoration over the years, and the remains of royal regalia in glass cases looked like circus costumes, gaudy and trimmed with shabby glitter. There was something sad about the palace, the torn remnants of another life, so we all went off to find the markets that are always throbbing and vital. We bought copious supplies of vegetables, and bananas by the tree-load, at ridiculously low prices, but were we being made fools of? Why were the stallholders laughing? I struggled with my phrasebook, but by the time I had looked up the words for things, Allen had already bought them through English and mime.

After the sightseeing and shopping we stopped for a meal together and I was at last able to ask Mike why he wanted to go to India.

'To study.'

'What?'

'Spiritualism.' He was going to study with Sai Baba, a controversial guru worshipped by millions worldwide. 'The universal Christ. The *universal* Christ.'

His interest had developed when his wife was dying of cancer. He learnt reiki from a Japanese master who did not charge any money. 'Everything is an exchange of energy, and I was given reiki for flowers and other gifts. You know, we are entering the Age of Aquarius and the world is going to become more peaceful as we evolve. We are all evolving.'

'I was sorry to hear about your wife.'

'Oh, I'm happy for her,' he responded with hurt surprise, as if I had committed some terrible mistake. 'She had done what she came here for. Everyone is looking for something. Everyone is trying to fill that empty space. Spirituality fills that space.'

He flew a peace flag and gave money to beggars and his mission was to make the world a good place, but he found it hard to deal with the hassles of actual poverty. And it is hard. At anchor off Sumbawa Besar, boatloads of little boys, and later big boys, had swarmed around us on outriggers. We gave biscuits to the first boatload but to the second and the third we gave nothing. We do not know which ones stole some small items, parts of our safety equipment, from the deck. The next place we reached was the kind of rare anchorage you dream of, a beautiful, safe, sheltered natural harbour near a small village. Yet there it was even worse, with boatloads of people coming alongside asking for lollies and cigarettes and pens within seconds of our arrival. It was exhausting; feeling mean, feeling hassled, feeling helpless, wanting to be generous but not being able to make everyone happy, never feeling good. Mike sailed off to find an anchorage with no people, whereas George just announced in pidgin Bahasa, '*Ini bukan toko, bukan rumah makan, bukan bank.*' (This is not a shop, not a restaurant, not a bank.) But I had not yet found a way to be at ease.

We were glad to reach the peace anchorage at Gili Air, a tourist-dependent island, where there were pretty cows with doe-like faces and white kneesocks, the ubiquitous Indonesian ginger cats with stumpy tails, and donkeys pulling carts to convey tourists. We stayed a few nights and walked around the island greeting other visitors we saw but they usually avoided eye contact and did not respond to Allen's cheery 'Hello!' Why were they so unfriendly? Straight from the cities of Europe, people seem suspicious of strangers. Even relaxing on holiday they keep their barriers raised. No wonder then that my journal recorded, as at sea, so many descriptions of animals.

Cruising along the islands of eastern Indonesia, where there is a profusion of sheltered bays, we day-sailed as much as possible. If we found a good anchorage we would stay for a few days but we were glad to move on from those where the current was strong or the holding proved poor. We had to ensure that we left Indonesian waters within three months, before our cruising permit expired, but we did not want to go north of the equator too soon, before the change of monsoon. Since Indonesian tourist visas are valid for only two months, we, like many other cruising yachties, would need to leave the country during our voyage to renew our visas, so we were timing our stop in the marina in Bali to coincide with Allen's mother's birthday.

Our last stop before Bali was Lombok, where there were very few tourists because there had been anti-Christian riots led by Muslim extremists on Senggigi beach earlier in the year. As soon as our dinghy got close enough to shore for wading we were surrounded by people desperate to sell us something, anything. We found ourselves persuaded to take a tour of the island by a persistent and cheerful young Sasak who spoke what he called 'beach English' and used it skilfully to cajole us into the trip on which he would act as guide. The tour proved to be a depressing trail from one tourist souvenir outlet to another during which our guide told us his parents were rice farmers, so he had no education after elementary school as they could not afford even the transport costs for high school, let alone the fees. We ended up buying things we did not really want out of a guilt-ridden awkwardness. Even the temples we visited were decrepit and dull and spoilt by constant harassment for cash after the customary good-natured greetings: 'Oh, bloody Aussies!'

Allen and I talked endlessly about poverty. How long would we be able to look it in the face? Indonesia is very poor. Would Malaysia be different? In a local restaurant we were surprised to see a Channel 9 news program on the television. The owner had been one of the Barnardo's children, unaccompanied child migrants sent from England to orphanages in Australia after the war. (Years later it was found that many of them had been forcibly removed from their parents and separated from siblings.) He knew what it was like to be a poor kid, and there in Lombok he and his Indonesian wife had adopted several children. The first was a relative of his wife's who was sent at the age of ten to work in a cigarette factory. 'I couldn't hack it and asked her parents if I could have her.' The numbers grew, and when we met him he had paid for nine children to go to school. When they finished school he employed them in one of his businesses. He had found a way to live with himself.

We left Lombok for a record-breaking sail to Lembongan, midway to Bali. We raced there at 10.5 knots, double our normal speed, because of the fearfully strong current raging through the strait. Long after dark we were approached by a man in a dinghy who ordered us to move. We refused. People do not move and re-anchor in unknown, reef-strewn waters in the dark when they cannot see the dangers. 'You must,' he said. 'A big pontoon is coming.' It was. We could make out a mass of lights moving rather rapidly towards us, so we moved, tentatively and not very far, though it was against all our instincts. Anchored nearby, George sensibly just stayed below and pretended to be asleep. In the light of morning a vast yellow floating water playground for mega-silly tourists had been parked right next to us.

I felt a bit like a very silly tourist myself. I was happy as anything, partly because of all the bananas and partly because I was finally going to Bali. It seemed everyone in Australia had been there except me. And the bananas? Bananas contain chemicals that work like Ecstasy and

Prozac to stimulate the production of serotonin and dopamine. While I was sceptical about bananas making people happy, in Indonesia almost everyone we met was so cheerful, even if they had no apparent reason to be, that I began to wonder. There were bananas in everything. When you least expected it there was a banana lurking unannounced, even in the middle of a croissant.

TEMPLES AND APES

Bali to Borneo
August—September 2000

THE IDOLS HAVE SEEN LOTS OF POVERTY,
SNAKES AND GOLD AND LICE,
BUT NOT THE TRUTH.
— Wallace Stevens

Bali International Marina provoked much muttering and grumbling among the yachting community. I was just happy to be alive, a feeling that overrode many of the inevitable frustrations of making landfall. During most ocean passage there are ample opportunities for anxiety. In this case the exceptionally strong currents in the Lombok Strait created areas of turbulence: short, steep waves coming from every direction mingled with areas of whirling waters to form what we called washing-machine seas. Though the effects on the boat were generally not as bad as the appearance of the water sometimes led us to expect, there would be moments when everything felt out of control, as in a skidding car. Despite the justifiable complaints, almost every cruising yacht that goes to Bali stops at the marina because it is the only place to safely leave a boat. Before I started cruising I had imagined that the world was full of little bays to anchor in, but safe, sheltered harbours are rare. Bali rises steeply out of the ocean and the local fishing boats can be seen right up on the beaches that slope at about 45 degrees into the sea, indicating that the seabed is far too steep for anchoring. We would regularly have to plot where to stop, and plan our time of arrival to coincide with favourable tides, adequate light and reasonable weather. Cruising is not always about casual spontaneity and hanging loose, rather about working carefully within limits that can be unpredictable. It is about being alert to possibilities, always ready to move at short notice and yet content to wait patiently for as long as it takes.

Being in the safety of a marina gave us unusual freedom to leave the boat, and as soon as we arrived we found ourselves going, unexpectedly and immediately, to Borobudur. George, the single-hander we'd met in Moyo, was going there and had found out about buses and, knowing I had been practising Zen for decades, said, 'Why don't you guys come along too?' Borobudur is one of the most famous ancient Buddhist sites on earth. Of course us guys would go along too. We took an overnight coach and ferry from Denpasar to Yogyakarta. Before night fell, early and suddenly as it always does in the tropics, I looked out of the window trying to grasp some sense of Bali, and what nestled in my mind were the offerings. Outside shops and houses, offices and temples, women in traditional attire had offered thoughtful arrangements of flowers, food and, since Balinese deities evidently smoke, cigarettes. I found it oddly comforting that every day such care and attention was given to the production of an ephemeral work of art, and that the spirits were all around in ordinary places, not sequestered in some other heaven or hell.

During the night, the bus stopped at a large restaurant and we were all given tickets for dinner. The driver told us the bus would be locked up. Allen didn't want to leave our bags on the bus but I resisted him.

I did not want to travel in a state of constant mistrust, clutching my valuables, so we left our bulky backpacks. A few hours later I discovered our cameras had gone from deep inside my pack. 'You're a Buddhist,' said George. 'You can cope with impermanence. See, it's a test for you. You're on your way to see one of the world's greatest Buddhist sites and now you can't even get a photo of it! How's your equanimity? Have you really learnt anything from all that meditation?' But he did let me share his camera when we got there. And I learnt not to dangle temptation in front of people who are very much poorer than me.

Borobudur was magical, a vast stupa enclosing a hill, a three-dimensional mandala, tiers of stone carvings depicting realms of Buddhist existence. At the bottom, and mostly inaccessible, were the walls depicting the lower realms of existence, those of desire. These gloriously erotic scenes were among the most interesting of the carvings. Walking up to the next level we saw scenes from Jataka stories, animal tales such as that in which the Buddha, in his incarnation as a rabbit, offered himself as food to a starving man. At the top, in nirvana, sits a vast circle of life-sized Buddhas in quiet meditation. I found visiting this ancient spiritual site disappointing; it had lost its significance and become a curiosity. I had wanted yellow robes, chanting and gongs, bells and incense, a living religious community. Instead I chatted to endless streams of school children anxious to experiment with their English or have their photographs taken. There we posed, amid gaggles of giggling girls in their uniform headscarves, practising the way of non-attachment—and Borobudur really is a monument to the transitoriness of life. We know almost nothing about the people who built it and what happened to them. What we do know is that this stupendous monument was only used as a place of pilgrimage for about 150 years. It had taken 70 years to build. Like Tibetan sand mandalas, all things pass quickly away.

★　★　★

Soon after returning to Bali we flew back to Perth for Allen's mother's 70th birthday party where I was able to meet many of Allen's relatives for the first time. Everyone reminisced with family stories, evidently repeating the well-known myths that establish one's role. I was hearing them for the first time.

'Oh, Allen was always up to mischief,' said his mother, 'even when he was a toddler he was always in trouble. D'you remember, Allen, down at the river, I'd pushed you there in the stroller and I turned my back. Next thing you were climbing round the outside of the shark net. And there were sharks in that river then and there was a man there, he said, "Don't you shout at that child whatever you do. It'll frighten him and he'll let go. It'll be the end of him." So I had to wait till you come the whole way round. You were always up to something. One day you went down to the airport, the Bankstown airport, and they found you walking down the runway. They thought you were foreign in your little funny boots for your flat feet and you couldn't talk properly, you couldn't say your name, you said your name was Abunaa [Allen Bruce Nash], so they thought you must be a Balt. They went round all the Balt houses first, asking if anyone had lost a little boy. I tried to keep you in.' She turned to me. 'We put up a barbed wire fence, six foot high, but he climbed up it. He threw a sack over the barbed wire so he could get over. He was always doing dangerous things.'

'Pity you didn't tell me he was a reckless maniac before we bought the boat,' I said. But I would have gone ahead anyway.

There were multitudinous celebrations as well as the actual birthday party and we went back to Bali after a week of too much food and drink and talk. After all the frantic activity it was a relief to go back to the soft warmth of Bali, back to fixing things on the boat, back home.

*   *   *

Allen started patiently rewiring the fridge. Explanations of electricity have always bored me—amps and watts and resistance, whether things are wired in parallel or in sequence—and I used to find people who talk about it tedious too. But it would be unwise to even think about going on a sailing boat without at least one person aboard who understands them. Someone needs to be similarly conversant with plumbing, and not just any old plumbing, but plumbing with enough knowledge of hydrodynamics not to accidentally cause an ingress of seawater while, say, removing pipes to unblock the loo. Essentially, on an offshore vessel, the crew needs to be able to deal with any repairs, and electrical and electronic equipment is particularly vulnerable because being exposed to sea air causes rapid corrosion of exposed metals. As the consequences of not keeping a boat in good condition are too awful to contemplate, I was able to generate a fair modicum of interest in most aspects of marine maintenance, though I was happy to trade doing most of the engine maintenance, electrics and plumbing for most of the cooking, sewing and painting.

It was satisfying to be efficiently self-sufficient. We supplied all our electricity through six solar panels. We were able to run everything on the boat—fridge, lights, water pumps—even when the sky was overcast, from the power the panels supplied to two large deep-cycle batteries. Only if we were sailing at night in rough conditions when the autopilot was using an unusual amount of power would we run the engine for an hour or so, to recharge the batteries. Many cruising yachts have more electrical equipment than ours did, for freezers, water-makers and radar, but the more you have, the more difficult it is to generate enough electricity without running the engine or a generator. Freezers are particularly demanding. Allen was rewiring the fridge because the wire we originally used was too thin and so we were losing half a volt of power through resistance over the seven or so metres from fridge to battery. As a consequence, at night, when the battery was lower, the fridge would not get quite cold enough and it would run and run, draining the battery and causing essential equipment like the autopilot to malfunction. Even though it took many days to trace and fix the problem—it involved unscrewing, one by one, each of the boards that lined the cabin ceiling, long discussions with several marine engineers as well as trailing all along the waterfront in search of a supplier of battery cable, as thick as a cigarette, with which to replace the old wires—the experience was not as irritatingly tedious as it sounds. A shift in the psyche transmutes the chronic impatience of urban life to an easygoing diligence. When a home refrigerator runs a little longer than it should—and supposing you even notice—you might ignore it until it becomes very inconvenient and then you would call in a repair person or buy a new fridge. Leaving it for a while is unlikely to be dangerous. On a boat everything is related. If one part of the equipment is not functioning, it affects other parts. The whole system needs to be kept working well or the problems tend to compound. Looking after the boat is about taking responsibility for your life, not in some abstract, metaphysical sense but materially. We could die or we could lose the boat. Taking responsibility was our only insurance or, as another cruiser expressed it, 'We're yachties, we know that once we're out there, we're on our own.'

Once we had done all the regular tasks that have to be done in port—repairs, changing the oil and the filters, checking the batteries, refuelling and refilling the water tanks—we went to Ubud. My friend Brigid regularly used to go there to recharge her muse. I had visions of the Bali she described with gardens, fireflies, peace, massage, meditation, relaxing and drifting, but Allen wanted to hire a motorbike and rush round being what George called an overachieving tourist. We compromised, rushing round on a motorbike from one little oasis of peace to another.

Over dinner at a small garden attached to the home of Han Snel, one of the European painters who had made Bali his home, we sat among the frog ponds and lotuses while a very talkative waiter explained that in Bali people with problems do not go to gaol but must give money to the temple. 'It brings them here,' he said, lunging forward, clutching at his heart, 'closer to the gods.' Being alone, he told us, was terrible to the Balinese who all want to live together in harmony. Brooms with many bristles sweep more effectively than a single bristle. He was interrupted in his poetic account of the nature of the Balinese soul by the arrival of more diners, which meant that he had to jump on his motorbike and go off to buy some more rice.

We went to some rather touristy dancing in Ubud Palace, lit by candles placed up high all around the elaborate gateway. I was content to marvel at this magical lighting but Allen wanted to figure out how it was done. His penchant for translating the apparently magical into the actually do-able explains why we were sailing at all. Meanwhile I was learning survival skills for the over-sensitive traveller. Behind us a young London yuppie mum was explaining to her small daughter how to deal with hawkers, 'Sound tired and resigned at the same time while you look into the middle distance and tell them you are not interested.' She demonstrated, sounding simultaneously dismissive and full of ennui. What a useful mother! I went home and practised.

By late August it was time to move on, to make our way northwards to reach Malaysia and Thailand by Christmas and the change of monsoon. We planned to go to via Kalimantan, in Borneo, because we had heard that it was possible to see orang-utans living in the forests there. At the marina we agreed to travel in convoy with three New Zealand yachts that had been travelling together for months, as well as one American and one English one that also wanted to join up for the Borneo trip. We knew that we would need to hire guides and riverboats to take us to see the wild apes and it would be cheaper if we did it as a group, and also we were still nervous about Indonesian waters. When we had been back in Perth I had bumped into an ex-colleague, a senior academic, who told me he had been doing research on the incidence of piracy in Indonesia and expressed surprise that we were still alive. The yachtie grapevine reported no one experiencing any trouble in the area. It seemed that serious pirates, who used large, well-equipped powerboats and modern weaponry, were uninterested in the meagre returns to be gained from small sailing boats and that, by avoiding major ports, cruising yachts could also avoid the risk of more casual thuggery. However, at that stage in our voyaging, we were still susceptible to pirate tales from the armchair.

We headed north, perilously close to shore to avoid the ferocious southbound current in the Lombok Straits. As we sailed along the coast we could see how the dull greyish-green of older-style Balinese paintings captured the look of the island. Close up, the greens are vivid, but from a little distance the cultivated land, terraced hillsides and palm trees are misty and subdued, both sombre and magical.

The next day at Kangean, a small island between Bali and Borneo that goes unnoticed by guidebooks, Allen received a radio call from our travelling companions to attend a skippers' meeting, men only. The men were going to plan everything; the women were apparently meeting elsewhere but I was not invited. I suspect I may not have joined in enthusiastically enough on a previous occasion when scone recipes were being discussed, or perhaps it was the way my hackles had become visibly erect when Julie had responded to news from New Zealand claiming there had been a call for the renewal of the 'Maori Wars' by saying, 'The sooner the better as far as I'm concerned, then we can shoot them all.' I was happy to sit on my own, listening to *Il Trovatore*, drinking chai, burning incense, writing, and reading an Umberto Eco novel I had just acquired.

We hired a motorbike for a look around, as we had found in Indonesia that people are always happy to rent them out for a few dollars. The island was poor, like Flores, but people were amiable. I had the feeling I was peeping in at the window of another world, a world that was peeping back. Everyone stared at us, and most of them laughed, which, since I was not trying to be funny, made me want to hide. I clung to what another yachtie had told me: 'It's like being a film star, everyone wants to have a look.' It was certainly easier to be gracious, to smile and wave, when I made myself imagine people were staring at me because I was a minor celebrity rather than because I was a big hairy white freak.

I never stopped feeling nervous before setting sail. Usually we left in the mornings, so there was little time to wait building anxiety but the skippers had declared we should leave in the afternoon so I put on the kettle. It is a British habit. Before they rode into the jaws of Death, into the mouth of Hell, you can be sure the six hundred had a cuppa. Intellectually it seemed like paranoia that five boats were all going together via the same waypoints, huddling against pirates. The strategy was to call in our positions over the radio with reference to these undisclosed positions. Thus we would call, 'We are 60 nautical miles from waypoint five', so that pirates would not know where we were but the rest of the convoy, travelling the same route from waypoint to waypoint, would know exactly where we were. It seemed both daft and comforting.

By the next morning we were sailing happily, all fear gone, though we were no longer really travelling together. The American boat had zoomed off first, since it was claimed she was slow, and, though we left next, the rest quickly overtook us, trying to catch up with them I suppose. Ex-racers cannot help racing. We plodded along, hampered as much by our anti-racing attitude, our lazy sailing, as our boat design. We arrived at Kalimantan's Kumai River late at night and anchored until morning when we headed upstream to the town. The river was great, grey-green and greasy, very Limpopo. The town was surrounded by jungle and had a busy frontier-town feeling. There were many small ships at anchor. As soon as we arrived we were approached by a cheerful man in a small boat. He was Jien Joan, one of the recommended guides for trips to see the orang-utans, and he had anticipated our needs. We arranged a meeting with him and all the other yachties to negotiate our visit to the orang-utans.

I should have known it was going to be cringe-inducing from the conversation about the 'Maori Wars'. We met at Jien's house at Julie's insistence.

'We want to have a meeting all together, we'll come to your office.'

'I do not have an office, I have only my house.'

'Well, we'll come to your house then.'

Most of the other women were in skimpy dresses or shorts. For some women this is an act of defiance, a deliberate, considered refusal to conform to the customs of a male-dominated religion, a refusal to hide, but in this case it was a blatant unawareness of cultural sensitivities.

We were welcomed by Jien and his mother and sister, who offered us tea before slipping away. 'White people's meeting,' joked Jien.

'The black people can stay if they want to,' chipped in Narelle.

We agreed to hire Jien and a cook and two of the local riverboats (*kelotoks*) with crew, and arranged to go to the markets with Jien to buy the food for the three-day trip.

Julie then explained that she wanted to do her own cooking. 'Can I plug my rice cooker in on the boat?' she asked.

As in most Indonesian households, cooking on a *kelotok* is done over a charcoal stove. No batteries are needed to start these boats' simple motors which generate no electricity. Kerosene lamps light the night and the bilges must be pumped by hand. No, she would not be able to plug in her rice cooker.

'Never mind, I'll just eat biscuits and vegemite.'

Then she became very agitated when a small cat came into the room and rubbed up against her.

'What's the matter?' I asked. 'Don't you like cats?'

'Oh yes, I like cats but not—' and here her voice dropped to an exaggerated whisper '—Indonesian cats.'

Poor Julie. Her husband was an avid sailor but she hated cruising, not surprisingly since she suffered from chronic seasickness, and she was evidently terrified of all the perceived dangers of the Third World, especially germs and parasites. She travelled in an immaculate boat equipped with every convenience and, when she ventured out of this little outpost of home, was obviously uneasy at any contact with mundane poverty.

The next day Allen and I got subversive. I went with the blokes to the police station in a nearby town of Pangkalanbun to get our police clearances and Allen went to the markets with the women.

'Have you got your passports and cruising permit with you?' asked Neil, Julie's husband.

'No, I'm a woman, I wouldn't have thought of bringing the necessary documents with me.' That's what I wish I'd said, instead of a meek, 'Yes.'

Allen came back to the boat swearing he would never undertake such a painful experience again.

'Why? What happened, what was so awful?'

'Oh, it was boring, endless whingeing about hygiene and lack of choice. What do people expect in a poor country?'

On the morning of our expedition I went with Jien and the other women to do the shopping for the trip and was able to discover what many of the unfamiliar foodstuffs were and what prices to pay. I found out how to buy chickens, that I could expect to pay for the whole chicken and then have it cleaned and cut up how I wanted. We bought raw tempeh and candlenuts, items I had eaten but had never prepared before and would not have recognised. We also bought unripe jack-fruit, for making curries, and some fruit with peel like brown snakeskin, salak fruit.

It is easy to forget we did not come into the world knowing how to push a supermarket trolley, swipe the EFTPOS machine and look on the packet for use-by dates. In unfamiliar places it is very useful to have a shopping teacher, to learn the art of selecting fresh foods in the absence of refrigeration and the highly developed skill of successful bargaining. This, I gradually discovered, is about ensuring that everyone concludes the negotiation feeling satisfied and it is not to be confused with making sure that you get whatever you are buying more cheaply than anyone else.

Later in the morning we set off on our *kelotoks*, leaving the yachts at anchor in the Kumai River. Jien had organised a guard to stay on each yacht. On the American yacht, which had a freezer, the guard had to be taught to start the motor each day and run it for an hour. The skip-per fretted constantly while we were away about whether the guide had understood the instructions, whether he had followed them. At times like that we were glad we were learning to travel simply, to have a boat that could run itself in our absence.

We headed up the Sekonyer River, a tributary that joins the Kumai River almost opposite the town of Kumai and flows along the bound-ary of Tanjung Puting National Park. The banks were lined with nipa palms and the water oddly beautiful, dark but clear, like strong tea. The river grew narrower, stiller, darker, the vegetation more lush and jungly.

Orang-utans, which literally translates as 'forest-people,' are the only great apes outside Africa. I was thrilled with this opportunity to see apes living in the wild. The first stop was a rehabilitation centre for baby orang-utans. Many of them were in cages or being handled by volunteers and rangers. Frustratingly, we were not allowed to initiate contact with these babies who were cuter than anything Disney could create. After months on a boat away from animals or babies, all of us, male and female, were bursting with maternal urges, but the babies were there to learn to be orang-utans and to fend for themselves. They had all been rescued from captivity. Some had been kept permanently caged and their arms were not strong enough for the constant swinging, climbing and hanging-on that is needed to survive in the forest. All of them were used to people and were happy to be cuddled, but they needed to learn the laws of their own jungle.

Late in the afternoon we went upstream to the centre for the rehabilitation of juveniles, but it was getting dark and we saw only Michael, a Hugh Grant kind of gibbon, charming and frivolous and inclined to misbehave, asleep on top of the ranger's hut, and merely glimpsed some orang-utans sleeping in the trees. Nevertheless we had a wild night. Dinner, like all the other meals, was a vast Indonesian smorgasbord—jackfruit curry, fried tempeh, spicy morsels of chicken and umpteen different vegetable concoctions—miraculously produced by Jien and his helper, hunched in the shallow depths of the *kelotok* with the most elemental equipment. Julie stuck to her tins of beans and vegemite and crackers, not tempted by this strange foreign food laced with chilli, garlic, tamarind and deadly exotic germs. After the feast, Allen and I were ready for sleep; it was too dark to read and everyone else had brought copious amounts of alcohol. Yachties, like most seafarers, enjoy their grog. Because of lack of space, some of us would have to sleep on the covered area of the deck, where the others were then sitting. Not wanting to disturb the partying we headed below and, with the help of the crew, discreetly set up a bed in the place they indicated.

It turned out to be a bad idea to claim a sleeping spot, even the only available sleeping spot, when an American princess is getting drunk. Greta rumbled and grumbled, making sotto voce remarks about democracy and taking votes, and eventually exploded in a tantrum. 'How dare you go off and take the best sleeping spot behind our backs? I wanted to sleep downstairs. You have no consideration. You are awful, selfish people. I hate you.' She was not placated by our offer to move, to sleep anywhere, nor by our explanation that we had simply been trying to go to bed without making everyone get up.

Her husband took us aside and apologised, explaining that Greta had not been terribly well and then, exasperated, tried to calm her. 'Greta, you're drunk.'

'I wish I was. You're a first-class creep.'

The bickering continued long into the night, but Greta was no match for Julie in volume and persistence: 'Hon, you know I can't sleep with my legs bent up. I'm nearly six foot, I can't sleep in a four-foot space.'

I lay awake listening to endless human complaints drilling away at the still night. I had come into the jungle to find out about orang-utans, but it was the weird and unpredictable human behaviour that was occupying my attention.

On an early morning walk the orang-utans appeared, young ones who played and demanded to be cuddled. I was led up the path by an orang-utan toddler who then leapt into my arms. Instinctively I supported her, but there was no need. Though orang-utan toddlers are the size of young children, their arms are long and strong like those of a fit young man and they can hold on easily. They can also tussle and fight; one of them wrestled me to the ground, pulling my hair to get me down. It seemed playful but I did not want to annoy even a very young one of these wild creatures. They are generally not aggressive but have a strict hierarchical system and fight whoever they must to maintain their places in it.

Later that day we went to see the orang-utans being fed. Throughout their rehabilitation into the wild, supplementary food is provided in a clearing in the forest away from the ranger station. One of the young orang-utans came with us and clung to me for much of the way. It was tiring on this long walk but it is impossible to put down an orang-utan who is determined to hold on. Not that I wanted to put the ape-baby down. It felt like such a privilege to be allowed so close, to be trusted when, as a species, we have betrayed the trust of so many of our companions on earth. Michael came too, swinging nonchalantly through the trees at high speed and then waiting for us terrestrial plodders to catch up. Because he did not grow up in the community, he is rejected by other gibbons, so lives in a kind of exile in the world of people, playing the fool. When all else fails, keeping people entertained is a useful survival skill.

In the clearing, we waited as the orang-utans gathered for food. Some of them were just as interested in watching us as we were in observing them. They looked on calmly as we sat and chattered and gesticulated. It was what distinguished us, our endless mindless talk. Even if nothing of any significance was being said, we all seemed to need to keep babbling on, while the orang-utans went about their business, eating, copulating, grooming or squabbling without the need to keep up a running commentary. Some simply stood and gazed on us with the expression one expects of bodhisattvas, compassionate detachment.

The first two rehabilitation centres we visited were run by Friends of the National Parks Foundation, a local Indonesian organisation. Eventually we moved on to Camp Leakey where more orang-utans, supposedly wild ones, were being fed. As at the previous location, fruit was set out on platforms in the forest at regular times and orang-utans of all ages would gather to eat. In the wild, orang-utans are normally solitary but these ones were all partially bi-cultural, having been in captivity at some stage or being the offspring of those previously captive. The mothers who had been raised in captivity would allow their children to interact with humans, even though the baby apes had been born free. It seemed the mothers were educating their offspring to be bi-cultural. Camp Leakey was set up as a research centre by Birute Galdikas, one of the triumvirate of female primatologists (the others being Jane Goodall and Diane Fossey) who had been students of Louis Leakey.

There has been criticism of Galdikas and the whole rehabilitation project. Based on the reports of forestry department workers, it was claimed that it was the interests of tourists, rather than those of the orang-utans, that were being best served. Like anyone involved in serious conservation work, Galdikas has made enemies, powerful opponents in government and big businesses. The forestry department itself has been implicated in the continued widespread illegal operations in the national park. While we were visiting the park we could clearly see the logging camps; the presence of tourists does not deter the powerful logging industry from its illegal operations. It is corruption, not tourism, that is allowing the destruction of some of the last remaining orang-utan habitat, the UN Biosphere reserve, Tanjung Puting. Each of the three women primatologists known as Leakey's Angels has been criticised for becoming too involved, for not being objective, not being scientific enough. But it is good to be involved and I was glad I went to see the orang-utans and was reminded so effectively that we are not the only creatures who claim this planet as home.

On our return to Kumai an immigration official suddenly appeared demanding that each yacht pay him a substantial number of US dollars. This was hardly surprising anywhere in Indonesia but particularly in Kumai, which has all the ambience of a centre famous for illegal goldmining and logging. The skippers dressed up in long pants to go ashore and negotiate with officialdom—always a fraught task because it is often difficult to know how official the officials are (people rarely have any ID), and yet we never wanted to irritate officials, or even people posing as officials, who might be inclined to make our lives difficult in some way. While Allen was gone, I started to strip the horrible mock-tile wallpaper off the walls of the bathroom in preparation for painting. It seemed like a good idea at the time but it took hours and made everything look worse. By the time the men returned, after negotiating the bribe down to manageable levels, I was very tired but still needed to bake bread for the next leg of the voyage. Under sail it can be unexpectedly difficult to cook, either because of rough weather or because of the need to do some more urgent task, so I generally prepared food in advance before a passage. The heavy wholemeal loaves I made, following the famous recipe of the Tassajara Zen monastery, kept well and a couple of slices was a substantial meal. Almost as important, kneading dough was a good way to release stress.

Next day we set off together but, as usual, all the other boats were ahead of us. Then, in the middle of the night, we caught up with them all. Neil and Julie were stuck fast in mid ocean, entangled in a driftnet. We dropped anchor along with the other yachts, since it was only 15 metres deep, and Allen went to sleep straightaway so he would be ready to dive to free the trapped boat if necessary. In the morning the fishermen who had set the nets appeared and helped free the yacht and were appeased for damage to their nets by a bottle of rum. Rocky and choppy, it was not pleasant sailing. My arms were so sore I felt like the little orang-utan who had been raised in a cage so did not have the strength in his arms to hang up.

The other boats went ahead to Serutu Island but we were in no rush, knowing they would have to wait till daybreak to anchor. We arrived soon after dawn and crept in the midst of them, the safest option as our depth sounder was, literally, on the blink. There was an extra boat there too: that of Simon and Rachel, whom we had met briefly in Darwin through some French yachtie friends. Because Rachel spoke fluent French, they had many friends among the francophone cruisers, who tended to congregate separately. At anchor there were often clusters of French and Belgians here, British and New Zealanders there. Simon and Rachel had been cruising slowly around remote islands for weeks and were glad of our company. We unloaded the details of our experience of group travel with relief, and they commiserated and reciprocated by telling tales of travelling with an American convoy who had their days totally planned, from aerobics on the beach each morning to quiz shows at night. We were all baffled. A major reason for sailing away on a yacht is to escape from imposed routines, fixed timetables and being told what to do. Even more odd was the way people who travelled in convoy often did so only with others flying the same flag, other people from home.

In retrospect though, I realise that both Julie and Greta had something in common: neither of them was a confident sailor and, though they did watches, they were entirely dependent on their husbands if anything needed doing, from changing sails to re-plotting a course. They were also reluctant sailors. It is not uncommon for one partner in a cruising couple, generally the wife, to be less enthusiastic than the other about sailing but it is rare for anyone on a cruising yacht not to know how to manage the boat single-handedly in an emergency. I can imagine few situations more frightening. No wonder they were angry, for underneath most anger lurks fear.

Simon and Rachel were almost at the end of a circumnavigation with their two young children, Oliver and Emily. Simon grew up in Zimbabwe and had studied engineering in South Africa before leaving to indulge his passion for adventure, delivering yachts from the Mediterranean to the UK and teaching diving. In the Caribbean just after a hurricane, he made enough money through salvaging yachts to buy a ranch in Zimbabwe, adjoining a national park where he had set up a game park. He is one of those men who still look charmingly boyish with tousled, bleached hair and a wicked grin. He was less charmingly allergic to activities like cooking or washing clothes, which he regarded as unmanly. When Rachel saw Allen and I doing the washing together in a stream, she called Simon to look and tried to convince him that this was evidence that real men could help wring sheets too, but he remained determinedly unconvinced and sent Allen glances that made it clear he considered him a traitor. But, as we saw on a promotional video about his safari park, he was great at riding Arab steeds clasping a rifle nonchalantly in one hand like an *Out of Africa* hero. He had an image to maintain. Rachel had studied music, piano and cello in England, and after graduating went on holiday to Zimbabwe where she met Simon and they fell madly in love. She never went home but took a job teaching French and they were married soon after. She was many years younger, dark and lovely and, even scruffy from months at sea, they made a handsome couple. They seemed to have it all: good looks, beautiful, healthy children, zebras on the lawn at home and cruising the world. There was just one problem. They could not go home. Since leaving, the situation in Zimbabwe had changed and they were drifting around this side of the Indian Ocean, waiting to see what would happen.

While Rachel and I talked and talked about men and mothers and other affairs of the heart, Allen and Simon went hand-spear fishing and Allen caught four fish. We were impressed. Man-the-hunter suddenly becomes rather more attractive when the only things left in the larder are onions, cabbage and more red kidney beans. Adding to the primal experience we did our washing in a stream on the island, bashing the clothes on rocks as I had seen in films, and getting them coated with slime and grit, which is not usually shown on screen.

The regular convoy of yachts moved on but we stayed. We got into a habit of eating together, muffins or cake and coffee in the morning on *White Cloud* and a dinner of fresh fish with lime zest and ginger and garlic, whatever we had left for flavouring, over with Simon and Rachel. I had a huge box of crayons and felt pens and reams of paper, so Emily and Oliver always drew pictures for hours, digging up to their elbows for new colours. Rachel was surprisingly strict and was always cautioning the children about their manners but in a playful way: 'Emily! Don't be so rude!' in the tone of voice somebody would use if she were a child herself. We explored the island, paddled round the bay in the afternoon, watched a snake swimming in the water and saw monitor lizards ashore. We found a creek in a tropical glen, all dappled light and boulders, and little running waterfalls in lush jungle full of liana and palms. There were even macaques on the beach at nightfall; the whole picturesque caboodle.

We had to move on. We travelled with Rachel and Simon so that we could follow them into anchorages, because our depth sounder continued to do nothing but blink. We crossed the equator in the rain, motor sailing through the endless grey of the doldrums and a long night to a tiny island. It was inhabited by just a few fisherfolk living in a stilt house and subsisting on a diet of fish, rice and coconuts. Rachel had a knack for languages and seemed to find out all about the local inhabitants wherever she went. She had already discovered that there was a family of four living in the house and that, as she recounted with the dismay, 'They never eat vegetables at all, just fish and rice and coconuts.' I saw a couple of people in the far distance paddling their dugout laboriously towards me. A man and a woman had rowed the length of the island with their transistor radio in the hope of getting some batteries. As always on a small cruising vessel, we could not carry large supplies of anything in excess of our own needs but we were able to give them enough batteries. They paddled away slowly but some hours later I saw them again making their way across the water towards us and I wondered what they wanted. They wanted only to give us a couple of coconuts in return.

The next day Allen had gone fishing and I was below reading when I heard the slap of waves on the stern and a voice calling out. Another local fisherman was there in his small, narrow dugout, clinging to *White Cloud* and struggling to maintain his precarious balance in the choppy water. On board he had a collection of caged birds, sulphur-crested cockatoos and lorikeets. He grinned at me and held up the cage. 'No, no!' I waved it away. He wanted roti, bread, but we had eaten the loaves I had made. He asked what we ate if we had no bread. *Ikan* and *nasi*, I told him, fish and rice, and I gave him some nuts. I think I explained that I could not take birds back into Australia—I certainly thought I made it clear I did not want to buy one, but he didn't want to go and so we struggled on with one of those conversations where there is much smiling and nodding but where one suspects much mis-information is being exchanged. I pointed at a sea eagle hovering above us, but was his enthusiastic reply some information about this bird or did he think I wanted one in a cage? Then he pointed at a speck in the distance. It was Allen returning. He arrived at speed, trailing a wake that rocked the dugout so unexpectedly one of the cages slipped straight over into the water. The man grabbed it before it sank and retrieved the cockatoo, which was dripping and fussing, and set off, having finally realised he was not going to make a sale.

These were good days. Simon and Rachel had been cruising for years, avoiding marinas and crowds, happy to linger around remote islands eating rice and fish and coconuts like the local people, and we relaxed too and stopped worrying about pirates, the lack of news and the fact that we had run out of vegetables and wine. Instead we spent our days where we were. We were living on the sea and exploring its surfaces and depths. We watched turtles, and rays like giant butterflies, read poetry and listened to music and ate fish straight from the sea. There was nothing I wanted. Nothing I craved or missed.

RUNNING THE
MILK RUN

Singapore to Malaysia to Thailand
October 2000–January 2001

HOW SAD THAT PEOPLE IGNORE THE NEAR
AND SEARCH FOR TRUTH AFAR.
— Hakuin Zenji

I did not want to cross the Singapore Straits. I wanted not to go
so much that I fell overboard as we were leaving. We had travelled to
Batam, the last port of call in Indonesia, so that we could check out of
the country and find out about getting our depth sounder fixed. There
we discovered we would have to go to Singapore to be hauled out. The
idyll of the simple life was shattered. Staying at a marina in Singapore
while we had the boat lifted would be horribly expensive and disrupt
the low-key, anti-urban lifestyle we were starting to enjoy. But there
was no choice, a depth sounder is vital. This was not reason enough to
fall overboard; it was the horror stories that pushed me over the brink.
The Straits are one of the most congested waterways in the world, and

even before leaving Fremantle I had heard how trying to cross them, dodging tankers and bulk carriers, was the stuff of nightmares—those ones where you are trying to cross a multi-lane freeway and run and run but your legs refuse to move.

I told Allen I didn't want to go that morning. The visibility was poor and the currents were against us, but it was too late, he had already checked out of the country. I was casting off the bowline when I fell into the water. Allen was steering and couldn't see me, nor hear my cries: 'I'm in the water!' But he could see I was not occupying any of the empty space where I should have been, and so he waited until I clambered dripping onto the jetty and jumped aboard again. Then he motored off, instructing me to fish for the penguins I'd dropped overboard in my wet bad temper. (The torpedo-shaped rubbery things that dangle over the side of moored boats are usually known as fenders but a hard-of-hearing early visitor aboard called them penguins, which they resemble to some extent, and the name stuck.)

I stayed spitting mad and miserable, yet crossing the shipping lanes turned out to be easy. In busy areas everyone is cautious, big ships are highly visible and it is just a matter of taking care. Luck interferes too. Approaching Singapore I was baffled by the number of ships coming up from behind and overtaking us and I went to check the chart. We had made a mistake keying in a waypoint and were actually going along the middle of a shipping lane, but we had survived even that horrible navigational error. I relaxed and we continued towards our destination through the main anchorage, where I counted 72 ships. Allen went to the loo. When he came back on deck he looked behind at the ship I had just narrowly missed colliding with. 'Wow, that was close!' And then, puzzled, 'Why aren't you panicking?' I had not even seen it. Wending my way through all the ships at anchor, ecstatic that we'd crossed the Straits unscathed, I had not noticed the one that was actually moving. A thunderstorm blew up and we inched up the Johor Straits and into Raffles Marina in blinding rain. There, oh bliss, were uniformed men waiting to take the lines; for once I did not have to leap across the abyss.

Following my example with the wallpaper, Allen ripped the bed apart as he had established we could get a new mattress made to order in the odd shape we specified 'by tomorrow'. The next day on the phone we learnt, 'Sorry, it is not possible to make ones that shape.' Meanwhile we hauled the boat and had a new transducer, which bounces a signal from the hull to the seabed to gauge the depth, installed. When we got back in the water it still did not work and it was clear it was the depth sounder, not the transducer, that was the problem. There had been no need to take the boat out of the water at all. We found someone to make a new mattress but when it was eventually delivered it was much too short. I was going crazy. It was like being stuck in a horror taxi: every minute we were spending hundreds of dollars but not only was nothing fixed, everything was in a worse state than before.

I went on a book-shopping binge in an attempt to make sense of what I was doing. Allen did not need to make sense of it. He expects things to go wrong and never takes frustrations and setbacks as omens of divine wrath. I know he is probably right and his attitude is much healthier but his unbotheredness about the Why? of life sometimes enraged me. Despite decades of Zen meditation I would still search for an answer when I thought no one was looking. Born atheists have it easy: they do not have to disentangle themselves from a relationship with god and a belief that the meaning of life must be something more than a mattress that doesn't reach one's toes.

So, we were stuck at Raffles until we sorted out our depth sounder and mattress problem. When I could ignore the ticking meter that was

eating money at an alarming rate, it was an embarrassingly nice lapse
into luxury. The papers were delivered to the boat each morning, we
were not allowed to carry anything—efficient men in motorised shopping carts took everything from our hands, and addressed us as 'Sir'
and 'Madam' even though we looked disgracefully shabby alongside
them in their neat nautical uniforms. There were several swimming
pools and restaurants and a fabulous marble shower room supplied
with hairdryers and fluffy white towels. The former naval officer who
ran the marina even hosted a magnificent Chinese banquet, an abundance of delicacies (including braised shark's fin soup, Beijing duck,
soft-shelled crabs, black mushrooms and sea cucumbers in brown
sauce) accompanied by fine French wines, for all visiting yachties. The
majority of cruising yachties do not stay at marinas as a rule, visiting
them only when repairs or a trip home are necessary. It is not simply a
matter of cost but of lifestyle. It feels like sneaking into a hotel when
you are supposed to be on a camping holiday in the bush.

We travelled up Melaka Strait (between Sumatra and the Malaysian
Peninsula) via a series of awful anchorages. A combination of poor
holdings and furious 'sumatras'—line squalls that emanate from the
mountainous island that gives them their name—made for edgy
nights. The anchorages were rolly too, with strong winds against
strong currents, so we fled to another marina, Port Dickson, where we
found several other yachties-who-normally-anchor holed up too,
alongside the usual marina crowd. The monsoon winds further north
had not yet changed, so we all hung around, taking advantage of being
there to do maintenance work that is difficult to do at anchor, such as
painting and engine repairs. Most days everyone worked on their boats.
I painted the bathroom walls. Day after day of bubbling walls. The
nano-bits of glue remaining from the wallpaper continued reacting with
the two-part epoxy paint. Days afterwards my handiwork remained

lumpy despite all the care and patient sanding and re-sanding. In the late afternoon everyone would meet in the swimming pool to play team ball games. Having spent most of my childhood avoiding team sports whenever possible, since they usually entailed being trampled by herds of stampeding stick-wielding girls with looming pink thighs in minimal clothing on frosty Welsh sportsfields, I was a reluctant participant. Spending several hours each day playing catch in a swimming pool seemed like an oddly boring way to fritter away a better life.

Some evenings the yachties put on a film show at the club room in the marina. We went once, when *Magnolia* was on, but after about half an hour, when several people had walked out in disgust at this uncompromising look at American society, it was turned off. 'Crap,' it was decided, so they watched *Rambo* and *The Patriot* instead. Apparently violence was okay but not the word 'fuck'. I went back to the jetty in a blaze of fury. I had been enjoying the film, but my rage was bigger than that. I had landed in the wrong world.

I was used to mixing at work, as well as socially, with people who were committed to social justice, supported Aboriginal land rights legislation, unionism, gay rights—the typical educated, left-wing conglomeration of attitudes. These yachties seemed a different breed altogether and my cross-cultural communication skills were severely tested. I struggled to remain calm when the Aryan goddess on her second circumnavigation arrogantly complained about Poles: 'They all steal cars', and Yugoslav refugees: 'They should go back and build up their country, that's what my husband's parents had to do.' I told her about the woman I had met in Australia who had returned to Croatia after the war and found no one she knew left in her village. 'Well, I wouldn't want to go back either,' said Linde. It is our own desires and weaknesses that we are so intolerant of in others, I know. I was grappling with the paradox of my own intolerance of intolerance. I seemed to have joined a band that kept sailing from one tourist ghetto to another, staying at grandiose palaces protected from local culture in order to swim, drink and eat more cheaply than at home. Allen called it marina fatigue. I put it down to being caught in the bottleneck of the milk run, the name for the route most commonly followed by circumnavigators. I wished I could stop judging the world and just be aware of it: the cool breeze and the enormous seed pods on the white frilly agapanthus flowers.

It seemed that people at Port Dickson would go into automatic dole-bludger or racist-story mode, unless kept safely on the topic of engine maintenance or sailing. We were regaled with such tales by some people who swanned in on an expensive catamaran.

'Australia's full of bludgers. Met one, a painter, lived like a bloody king on taxpayer's money. Said he couldn't get a job. "Why not?" I asked him, "There's plenty of bloody painting jobs around." "Yeah, but I'm a specialist, see. I only do flagpoles." I only do flagpoles, I ask you! They shouldn't give the dole to people like that.'

If I had wanted to pass my time hearing conversations like that I could have stayed home and tuned in to talkback radio. Even so, much as I had hoped for divine retribution, this particular group's punishment seemed overly harsh. They were robbed by armed pirates on their way into the Red Sea.

Why do we travel? Travel is supposed to be a Good Thing. It is supposed to broaden the mind and thereby make us better people. That was my justification for travelling but I was starting to wonder. After all, there is plenty of evidence that people often travelled to other places to see who lived there, and then killed them, raped them and stole everything they had, before bossing around whoever was left— activities collectively known as colonisation. Even if today's tourists are not engaged in quite such antisocial activities, it is hard to know what lying on the beach for two weeks getting frizzled by day and sozzled each night does for the body, let alone the mind. And if we diligently visit art galleries, great heritage sites both religious and historical, pretty villages, people with different customs and food, are we changed? Are we better? Does travel provide succour to the soul?

Allen and I had an agreement before we left that we would not keep going just for the sake of it and I was starting to wonder if we should go on when our marina-induced gloomy introspection was gloriously relieved by Mr and Mrs Teh. We had met them a few days earlier when we were walking down the road and they offered us a lift. They owned one of the high-rise apartments at the marina at Port Dickson as a weekender. The Tehs wanted to show us everything and after proudly showing us around their apartment, decorated with ducks in every form—duck pictures, duck cups, ducks flying across the wall—they drove us inland to their hobby farm. Before we could drive through the gate, Mr Teh had to deal with the four fierce dogs whose huge jaws I could just glimpse as they leapt at the fence. He locked them up and led us to the enclosure for the chickens and ducks, an area the size of a tennis court, surrounded by wire fencing. We went in and started to wander round the edge of the duck pond, collecting eggs. 'Hey, look at this!' said Allen enthusiastically before making a noise that sounded like that of enthusiasm draining out. At his feet was curled a huge diamond-patterned python, its tummy bulging with the twin peaks of two chickens. Despite the snake being protected—it was a reticulated python and it's beautiful skin would make shoes to kill for—the Tehs said they were going to get their revenge by inviting all their friends around to eat it. Mrs Teh was obviously used to this for she scurried away and quickly returned with a snake-catching device like a pair of very long-armed forceps, grabbed the snake round the neck and stuffed it into a sack. 'We Chinese people eat anything whose backbone faces the sun,' explained Mr Teh, though later he revealed that, after they had stopped being so cross, they had let the snake go.

After taking us for a long walk around the orchard that covered the rest of the property—organically grown durian, jackfruit, mangosteen, pineapple, bananas and avocadoes—the Tehs took us to where they actually lived, about half-an-hour's drive away. They had planned to build a house and live on the farm, they told us, but decided it was too isolated. I looked around at the dwellings that surrounded their land and caught Allen's eye: this was isolation? Their house in Seremban was tightly packed in among others. It looked like any modern two-storey suburban house from outside but we entered into a stiffly formal room lined with sombre, ornately carved black timber and marble furniture of overwhelming proportions. Then the Tehs led us past a traditional black lacquered and gilded shrine displaying the usual pantheon of mysterious gods I had seen in Buddhist temples in Malaysia. They had declared themselves to be free-thinkers and hurried us past it into the kitchen, the dry kitchen, to sample some of their home-grown durian. I had managed to avoid eating this fruit, famed for its foul smell, like the forgotten bag of vegetables left in the boot of the car, but the plates were on the table and Mr Teh was already cutting into a green thorny football. He was an aficionado; I got the impression the reason for the farm was to grow organic durian to perfection. I smiled, tried not to breathe, and it tasted no worse than mildly rotting hay. As well as the dry kitchen, which was just like any contemporary Western kitchen-dining room, there was a wet kitchen, smaller and full of well-seasoned pots and pans and a heavy-duty stove. This was evidently where the real action took place. Upstairs, along with the bedrooms, there was a cosy family room furnished with casual, comfortable sofas. Later that day the Tehs drove us to Melaka and, horrified by the price of tourist accommodation, would not leave until they had installed us in a guest house that they thought was good value.

The next day, we followed Mrs Teh's advice and ordered *kaya* toast at a small Chinese cafe she recommended. 'Sorry. We don't have any toast, only bread, but I can burn it for you, it's nicer that way.' Afterwards we visited some of the Peranakan houses, the houses of the Malaccan people formerly called Babas and Nonyas, who were the offspring of the original Chinese settlers who had married local Malay women. We learnt about the typical arrangement and function of the rooms in such houses, how the entrance hall was traditionally used as a place to formally entertain visitors and was filled with expensive, uncomfortable Chinese furniture behind which was an inner room containing the family shrine. The family living areas were located behind this public space. Seeing this, the apparently odd aesthetics of the Teh house made sense.

We invited Mr and Mrs Teh to sail with us as far as Port Klang, the port of Kuala Lumpur. We had told them we needed to make an early start but they surprised us by arriving in the dark at 5.30 am, before our alarm had even gone off, and we scrambled into our clothes and tried to look conscious while they clambered aboard. Both were nattily dressed to go to sea with nautical striped jumpers and immaculate boat shoes and were terribly excited about the trip. They sat down at the table in the main cabin and spread out a row of packets and pills and busily dosed themselves, attaching their medication-dispensing patches, while we took off the sail covers and checked the instruments and charts ready to set sail.

Once we were clear of the marina Mr Teh nervously took the wheel but Mrs Teh looked pale and went below. A few minutes later he followed her and when I looked down through the hatch I could see they were sitting in the cabin, their heads resting on the table, fast asleep.

I wanted to give them a good time after all their hospitality, so when Mrs Teh woke up I offered her a cup of tea. She looked around and smiled bleakly before curling up to sleep again. They only looked happy and regained their normal skin colour when we arrived at Klang, where they insisted on taking us out to celebrate.

We had anchored in the river along with the other yachts at Port Klang. To get back aboard after saying goodbye to the Tehs, we had to go through the clubhouse of the Royal Selangor Yacht Club, a sprawling building, all timber panelling and columns and tons of silver racing trophies. It had an air of colonial grandeur, though the 'royal' in the name referred not to the kings and queens of the British Empire but to the patronage of Sultan of Selangor. The first sultanate of Selangor was established in the middle of the seventeenth century by a Bugis from Sulawesi, maritime trading people. Their influence was felt throughout South-East Asia to as far as north Australia where, to this day, Bugis words are found in the languages of the Aboriginal people of the region. A senior official of the club, an elderly dato (a kind of Malay knight), insisted on buying everyone round after round of gin and tonics. There was a band playing the kind of music to which couples dance holding onto each other and, unable to resist, Allen and I headed for the floor and soon everyone, including the dato and his young wife— 'I'm half Malay, half-Wimbledon'—waltzed, jived and cha-cha-ed for hours. Meanwhile a South African member apologised for the lack of email facilities, telling us he believed the Indians in the bar had sabotaged the computer and VHF. 'A good whipping would sort them out.' I think Great-uncle Jack would have recognised this Malaysia.

My Great-uncle Jack had built railways and wharves, grown rubber and acted as a correspondent for the *Financial Times* in the Federated Malay States before the First World War. His letters home tell of a trip up a river: 'the trees had sunk into grotesque and hideous shapes, the tomtoms in the jungle sounded hollow and eerie, the demoniacal evolutions and familiarity of the great bats made our blood run cold'. Other missives warn his brothers to 'avoid the evil associated with the heathens', advising them to 'get to a civilised country'. He told Tom, his younger brother, not to follow him to the tropics: 'you would ruin yourself and your prospects for life'. Evidently those words had little effect since Tom subsequently spent most of his life in what is now Bangladesh and his youngest brother went to Singapore. Presumably Jack's description of entertaining the Prince of Wales on board a boat and the attendant difficulties of ensuring the intoxicated prince did not fall overboard, as well as accounts of adventures like having to deal with elephants on the train line he was building, tantalised his younger brothers more effectively than his admonitions to stay away from the East.

It has always seemed inevitable that, like Jack's siblings and several of his nephews and nieces, I too would be drawn to the tropics he had warned us against. Nothing is more alluring than what is forbidden. My father and mother were not travellers. During his entire six years as a medical officer aboard ship during the Second World War, my father went ashore overseas only once, while anchored in Cape Town, to climb Table Mountain. He claimed everything one needed was contained within the borders of Wales. My mother would have liked to travel but did not venture abroad until after my father's death. But by telling the family tales, my mother made sure she put temptation in my path.

When you are on a yacht, everyone wants to come and visit. Allen's daughter, Kathy, and her family were arriving in Langkawi in November. My daughters were due there the week after that and we planned to sail with them to Thailand where Allen's sister and her husband were to join us for Christmas. Langkawi is a duty-free island off the north-west coast of Malaysia where yachties stock up on grog before the long haul across the Indian Ocean. It also has a marina where repairs can be done and parts can be imported quite easily. Again the boring gritty of boat life. It is not like a romantic holiday; it is like being a manual labourer. A major obsession of most yachties is how to get hold of the essential spare parts on which to labour without having to bribe a string of officials and battle through weeks of entangling bureaucratic red tape. Langkawi is probably the easiest place in the Indian Ocean to fix a boat because customs and immigration procedures are straightforward, and there is a marina where refuelling and re-watering can be done quite simply. It is a dull holiday destination compared with cosmopolitan Penang or the relaxed Thai islands nearby, but for yachties it is a true haven.

Langkawi was given duty-free status over Penang as a way of boosting the economy of Bumiputra, the indigenous Malays, who tend to do less well financially than the Chinese. Government support of tourist development has poured into the island since the mid eighties, and Dr Mahathir, who was then prime minister, worked there as a young man and is reputed to own tourist resorts on the island. Yet there is something a little odd about the juxtaposition of Islamic Malaysia and tourism. We stayed at the marina for a few days to have easier access to shore while we had a new baby granddaughter as well as an eight-year-old and four adults on board. The marina was designed to be an international tourist resort and had a swimming pool with a bar in the middle of it. Sometimes we would treat ourselves to a margarita at sundown, but it was inhibiting to have to order drinks from a barmaid who was covered from head to toe while we sat at the bar in bikinis feeling underdressed. The barmaid, or bartender as she might be more aptly termed, would then go in search of an Indian employee, a non-Muslim, to actually handle the alcohol.

In Langkawi I started meditating again. Despite the mystique surrounding it, Zen simply means meditation, following the example of the historical Shakyamuni Buddha. He realised his essential nature when the morning star appeared while he was sitting in meditation. There is nothing magical about this. With diligent practice, attachment to our habitual thoughts and chattering opinions, which we tend to think constitute who we really are, drops right away, to be replaced by the vastness of moment by moment awareness. A star appears. The wind gusts cold and strong. It is time to let out some sail.

One morning, I was browsing through a book by Joko Beck, a Zen teacher I had worked with when she visited Australia in the eighties. She referred to a sutra dedication: 'Unceasing change turns the wheel of life, and so reality is shown in all its many forms. Peaceful dwelling as change itself liberates all suffering sentient beings and brings them to great joy.' Living on the ocean I was learning about unceasing change. I rarely slept in the same place for more than a few nights, and even overnight, swinging at anchor, one's point of view is ceaselessly changing. Waking up, the whole world is seen from a new perspective. The weather comes and goes as fast as a mood. There are cultures, languages, rules and new bureaucratic oddities to wrangle with as well as the movement of currents, tides, the moon and, of course, the sun. Nights are so much closer and darker; they determine one's lifestyle when there is no electric light to maintain busy urban daytime activity long after the sun has gone. As well as being aware of change, I was deliberately trying to change: practising steering in nonchalant pose with one leg on the seat instead of standing rigidly gripping the wheel, in the hope that I could trick myself into being a calm helmsman by relaxing my body, just as deliberate gentle smiling can trick us into happiness.

At the time we were debating whether to stay around Malaysia and Thailand for another year or whether to head for Europe via the Red Sea after Christmas. I was feeling jaded with Zen, not the practice itself so much as the politics, and thought that sampling another Buddhist meditation tradition, that of the Therevadan forest masters of Thailand, might shift something. Vipassana practice is not unlike Zen *shikataza*, just sitting in moment by moment awareness, though the tradition has developed a greater abundance of detailed and sophisticated techniques for developing mindful awareness and loving kindness and places less emphasis on enlightenment, though awakening experiences are common to students of both. And I was enjoying moozling around Malaysia. Marinas made me want to give up cruising; anchorages were making me want to keep doing it forever.

Sometimes we went to the Lake of the Pregnant Maiden for a swim in fresh water. The story of its name seemed to have lost something in translation. It described how a woman had disposed of her baby in the lake after it had died and seemed to have nothing to do with her pregnancy, though subsequently it has become a place of pilgrimage for women seeking to conceive. We called it the Lake of the Dead Baby. Once, while there, I was chatting to a teenage girl who was visiting from England. Her father was Malaysian and she was being shown around the country by her relatives. She asked what I was doing and when I told her she said, 'Fantastic. A boat. Did you just wake up one day and think "Let's get a boat and sail round the world"?'

'Yes, more or less.'

Adults never ask a question like that. They never think it could be that simple.

After Kathy and her family left we were at anchor and began to reconnect with some of the other yachties. Book-swapping is a favourite activity when yachties get together but it involves delicate negotiation, as tastes vary widely. The novice cruiser may find her offerings—an almost-new collection of recent fiction, a couple from the Booker shortlist, a Pat Barker gem, the latest Ben Elton—eagerly accepted and yet offered in return is a selection of exhausted airport fiction. Skilled book-swappers have mostly trash on display and wait to see what is on offer before revealing they may have 'something you might be interested in' down below. We met a couple of Canadian bibliophiles, one an ex-English teacher, 'I'm one of the rare people who still reads', with whom we concluded some mutually satisfactory negotiations. She told a story of asking some fellow yachties somewhere out in the mid Pacific whether they had any books to swap. They thought for a minute, looking puzzled, and then said, 'Oh yes, I think we do have a book somewhere—but we haven't finished it yet.'

We met some other yachties, Peter and Heather. Peter had worked as a computer consultant but could not bear to be away from the sea. He had bought his first boat while at university and had later worked on commercial ships simply to be at sea: 'It was a low, low life,' he said, 'not at all romantic.' He was the first yachtie I had ever met who used the word *romantic* of sailing, or still used it, after actually doing it. They were heading home though; Heather was missing her high-powered job on the stock exchange. This was so often the story we were told, the man happy to sail forever, the woman hankering for home. I hated the way it always seemed to be the woman who played the spoilsport: the girl who didn't want to play rough games any more, the mother who said it was time to tidy away the toys and do some homework.

While we were in Langkawi waiting for the arrival of my daughters and an alternator, we enjoyed encounters with the local fauna, especially the shy spectacled langurs. When people flew out to visit they never seemed as entranced by the wildlife as I was. Ho-hum, another monkey. Being at sea and being at the mercy of the elements makes us more aware of what we share with other animals, how alike we are. The geneticist Steve Jones, explaining the new logic informing organic creation that has arisen as a consequence of DNA analysis, argues that recent changes in taxonomy show how closely related we are to plants too and put 'humankind in its place, near bananas'. Bee, Lucy and the alternator arrived on the same day and, after installing all of them, we set off for Thailand, the island of Lipe just 20 miles away.

'So, what are the plans for today?' asked Bee, fresh from Sydney. Plans? We had no plans. We would get up and swim if we felt like it, and then sail to somewhere else. Or not. Probably not. We would think about food now and then, see what was in the fridge and wonder what to cook. Or perhaps we would take the dinghy ashore and explore the little restaurants on the beach. We would see how we felt later. Right now? What about a cup of tea?

Over the two weeks that Bee and Lucy stayed, we island-hopped up the coast to Phuket, visiting phallic shrines on Ko Rok Nok, playing petanque on Racha Yai and feeling ancient on Phi-Phi, an island overwhelmed by Western twenty-somethings. We snorkelled and pottered round rock pools, and Allen took Bee and Lucy scuba diving in turn. Bee had started smoking and I had optimistically imagined that since smoking on board was banned for safety reasons, being in a different environment and away from temptation might help her kick the nicotine habit. I was wrong. Bee found ways. Even though I disapprove of manipulative, interfering mothers I am sorry my plan failed. Bodies are so fragile and precious, and I love her to bits.

Two weeks later we had to drive down to Satun, on the south-west coast of Thailand, so that Bee and Lucy could catch a ferry to Langkawi for their flight home. On the way back we stopped at a temple where we walked in a dipterocarp forest in a hidden valley surrounded by sheer cliffs. This was a stand of meranti trees, a thousand years old, and tucked in among them were *kuti*, the little huts in which the forest monks live, each about the size of a sleeping mat. I had yearned for this place, unchanged over the centuries, cool and secret, free from cars and speedboats and hurly-burly.

When I next checked my email I was shocked to get one from the forest monk at the monastery where I had planned to do a retreat. Instead of the enthusiastic response I was expecting came a circumspect warning: 'I have not been there for over a year and do not know what the situation is but I have my suspicions and cannot vouch for the retreats.' It does not matter how far we travel, how deeply we escape behind walls or into the woods, we are still political beings, still in the world, and we have to deal with the intrigues, the one-upmanship, the jealousies and squabbling that naturally arise in any community. After the initial disappointment, and the realisation that I now had no particular reason to stay around Thailand and Malaysia for another year, it was a relief that I was not going to find a more perfect meditative tradition here in the heartland of Buddhism than I had found already at home.

Jenny, Allen's sister, and her husband, Kevin, joined us a few days later. It was liberating to be on a boat for Christmas because, since it already was odd, I did not feel obliged to maintain any established tradition. We started by eating plum pudding with brandy custard for breakfast and found it tastes better then than after a large heavy roast dinner. After that we headed off for another island-cruising holiday.

To the casual observer, the person in the bikini lying on the front deck who comments, 'Oh, you have such a busy life, deciding whether to snorkel before or after lunch', sailing a boat looks like nothing much, but it is always mildly stressful, especially in areas with many reefs where navigation and anchoring have to be done with great care. There were times when Allen and I were twitchy all night, checking if the anchor was holding, disturbed by noises we could not explain, while our visitors slept. We were beginning to realise why people who ran charters charged so much money, and so by the time our last visitor arrived we had abandoned the attempt to be perfect hosts.

The day Kathleen arrived we had her helping us to lug 400 litres of water in 20-litre drums across the beach, into the dinghy and out to *White Cloud*. Kathleen had emailed me in December saying she was feeling bad about a relationship that was going nowhere. 'Come to Thailand,' I emailed back impulsively and the next day she emailed me her flight details. An experienced traveller, Kathleen had also crewed on a yacht so arrived expertly prepared. Her baggage contained copious amounts of peanut butter and maple syrup, jars of pesto and myriad containers of delicacies from our favourite Italian deli, and just the few essential items of clothing. She even bore good tidings—unexpected tax refunds—which was a very good way to make an entrance.

We had planned to go inland to visit some temples but it was proving difficult to find somewhere to leave the boat without going into a marina, and Kathleen, a Buddhist from way back, began to melt into cruise mode and decided she would rather hang out on board instead. The days were starting to blur. We swam and hauled water, we varnished the bright work and rowed ashore singing to eat at beach-hut cafes. Easy days of work and play. One day Kathleen and I went ashore to visit the *wat*, the local temple, behind the beach. I had initially meditated at a Zen temple in Japan in the seventies but Kathleen's initiation had been in Thailand and she knew the etiquette, bowing and scurrying past the monks with bended knees. I could not do it. A kind of low-key but implacable rage came over me; I did not want to kow-tow. I especially did not want to kow-tow to someone who regarded all women as subordinate to men and who believed that only men were capable of attaining enlightenment. I was intrigued by the temples, could admire the artwork and enjoy the curious mixture of busy activity and relaxing serenity that often characterises residential religious communities, but something was shifting. After 25 years as a practising Buddhist I was clear about the benefits of meditation, but I was becoming increasingly disillusioned at how easily it became entangled with the familiar trappings of organised religion, those manifestations of human frailty such as the hierarchies, the idolatry, the sexism and the gold leaf. Buddhism is not a religion in the ordinary sense—there is no god, no transcendent being to worship—but after a visit to a Buddhist temple one could easily be forgiven for assuming there is. It seems more wonderful that we are close to bananas, than to some gilded idea of perfection.

After visiting the temple, Kathleen went for a walk inland to escape the heat. I went to a beach cafe and listened to some sleazy German men chat up local women and watched my waiter casually put his finger into my drink to fish out an insect that had landed as he was pouring it. I was going to miss fingers in my drink and cats and dogs on tables when I returned to Australian cafes.

People with no emotions, whose emotional responses have been damaged by trauma, cannot make even simple decisions like whether they want to drink tea or coffee, according to a book I was reading. The world is brimming with so many curious facts that I cannot understand how people worry about boredom so much. You can think about things like this for hours. Another thing to think about is cross-species interaction. One evening Kathleen and Allen and I were at our favourite beach-hut cafe. We were getting quite friendly with the proprietors—so far as one could with their minimal English, our non-existent Thai, and a lot of goodwill, smiles and gestures—and they showed us their photo album, which included pictures of their dog suckling kittens. I had just read about a tiger farm in Thailand where pigs acted as foster mothers to tiger cubs. Was it a Thai thing? Why did I regard it as so odd? We seem to draw the line at such inter-species intimacy, and those who have transgressed, like witches with their familiars, are punished.

Sometimes Allen and I would go for a walk by ourselves to meet up with other yachties. Yachties and non-yachtie visitors do not mix. I was puzzled by this for a while. We had initially invited yachties over for sundowners when we had visitors but the two groups never seemed to get on together. It took a while to figure out that yachties are not so much friends as work colleagues. When yachties get together they talk about work matters, how to stop garlic from rotting, the best place to buy fuel, why the weather fax does not work—all the kind of conversation that most normal people find utterly boring. As with work colleagues, some people do form very close friendships, but more often one maintains extremely cordial, but not very intimate, relations. The social networks between yachties are essential. It is through them that crucial information about weather, anchorages, sailing routes and provisioning is circulated. Also, travelling through foreign countries it is rare to form social relationships with local people and so one's social life is with other cruisers and, in times of crisis—aground on a reef, stuck at sea with a broken engine—other yachties will inevitably offer aid. They are, of necessity, resourceful people, problem solvers, bricoleurs, who can fix a problem with a piece of string, three nails and a multimeter. I have rarely encountered any community whose members can so dependably be relied upon to be so helpful and generous. They may be people you would not want to talk to about politics, and most of them did not share my taste in books but, when push came to shove, you could depend on them to be there with lines and winches, pushing and shoving. Yachties also have endless gossip about other yachts. Heather told us how she and Peter had met the crew from a big posh yacht anchored nearby and were invited aboard for dinner. They learnt that the airconditioning had to run day and night to stop the 24-carat gold taps in the bathroom from tarnishing. Later the rumour was that one of the English princes, Edward or Andrew, was aboard.

On Kathleen's birthday we started the day visiting a local temple where there was some kind of festival. I was in the hall viewing the Buddha's relics from Sri Lanka when one of the guards pointed his finger and shouted at me, 'You!' I was wearing long sleeves, a long skirt and no shoes. I was the most demurely attired tourist in the entire complex. I had been censoriously eyeing the other Westerners in skimpy, bun-revealing shorts and cleavage-emphasising tops. 'Take off your hat!' How easy it is to offend. How arbitrary are the rules. How unfair and how mortifying to be singled out when I had gone to such effort to respect local customs.

We went in search of a waterfall next but stopped at another temple on the way. A local man had seen us wandering round, and Kathleen made appropriate bowing and scurrying movements and carried on an animated conversation. She then beckoned me to follow as the man led us across the garden. 'I think we're being taken to see the abbott,' whispered Kathleen. 'Apparently he's resting.' Indeed he was, in a glass box, just like Snow White's.

The waterfall was disappointing. So disappointing that I can remember nothing at all about it, though my diary tells me I went there. The elephants nearby were a birthday treat though. Kathleen insisted on treating me to a giggly ride. 'You can set this as an essay for your pupils next term,' I told her. 'Write a story that starts, "Two old ladies went for a ride on an elephant."' I did not really approve of elephant rides but I enjoyed it so much, the size and power and intractability of an elephant that wants to stop to munch on a particular branch. We have so little to do with other animals. We know our cars more intimately than we know the slow-swaying, sure-footed gait of enormous beasts, or even the nimbler one of horses. A ride gave me time to watch those ears, like laden clothes hangers, fanning back and forth, and feel those giant shoulders moving beneath me, edging their way tentatively down slippery, muddy streambanks.

After Kathleen flew home it was time for us to sail back to Langkawi, since our Thai visas were due to expire. As we made our way slowly back down through the islands, stopping at Ko Lanta, where we walked along the beach and saw the same cheap souvenirs we had seen at Patong beach and on Ko Phi-Phi, I felt a bit disgruntled at the thought of a whole year meandering around more of the same island beaches, reading novels, passing time. I wanted a real life. I was tired of being on holiday. Allen was having problems with his knee, which, since a skiing accident several years before, was held together with metal pins. He was thinking of flying back to Australia, and so we discussed our options: to sail back to Australia, stay in Thailand or continue to the Red Sea. I dismissed the first option. I may have been tired of being on an aimless holiday but I was not ready to go back to Australia. I wanted to feel I had really done something before that. I did not know what, but I had not done it yet. Staying put though the wet season seemed like a re-run of a wet season in Darwin. We were veering towards going to the Red Sea.

Fed up with Thailand we stopped at an island we had not visited before, Ko Muk, and of course it was the ultimate tropical island dream-come-true. We anchored off a deserted small bay and took the dinghy to a cave that led deep into the cliff, paddling it slowly by torchlight into the cold dark. After a while a glimmer of light appeared, then opened up to a small beach inside the island. This was a *hong*, a flooded sink hole connected to the ocean by a cave. Stepping from the cool green water we were encircled by steep cliffs. They enclosed the small sandy beach and an area of level ground filled with mossy trees festooned with epiphytes, ferns and elephant's ears, plants that I had seen as little pot plants but here were so gigantic that Allen, standing among them, looked like a garden fairy. Later, on the reef, we went snorkelling around abundant coral, luminous apple green, pink and vivid blue, and long-armed pink sea-anemones (though, as usual, there were few edible fish). We stayed. We slowed right down. I made bread and swam and pondered. This was different from being on holiday. This was cruising.

LIMES AND
LOTUS LANDS

Thailand to Sri Lanka
January—March 2001

YOU DON'T REACH SERENDIB BY PLOTTING A COURSE FOR IT.
YOU HAVE TO SET OUT IN GOOD FAITH FOR ELSEWHERE
AND LOSE YOUR BEARINGS SERENDIPITOUSLY.
— John Barth

The fly buzzed around while I was drinking my tea. I flapped it away, irritated, but Allen chirped, 'It's our good-morning fly. We always have a good-morning fly when we take down the mozzie screens.'

I looked at him. The way you do.

'It's good to be cheerful and positive.'

Without Allen's good-natured optimism we would never have been there, two Librans in a boat off the Thai coast wondering what to do next.

We had hopped down the islands to Ko Lipe where we had been six weeks earlier with Bee and Lucy. There had been a frenzy of building activity in the meantime, and the number of beach bungalows had already multiplied. Deserted beaches are fast becoming figments of the imagination, but at least the development was still on a small scale, small family-run cafes and huts. Anchored nearby was a big traditional Indonesian wooden boat where Philippe lived. Allen had met him the night before and, while we were meditating in the early morning, he arrived to talk about charts.

'I'm Philippe, but don't worry, I never remember names. Australians do. And Americans. You meet them once and then three months later you see them again and they say, "Hello, Philippe!"'

'That's because they've looked at their list. We all write down the names of the people and boats we meet.'

'Really?' His eyes became saucers. 'A list?' Amazement. Then suspicion. 'No, no, you are joking, non?'

'It's true. I'm not teasing you. I couldn't understand how people always remembered my name when I didn't have a clue what theirs was. Now I can retaliate. Look!' I grabbed our list off the corkboard by the navigation table.

'I don't believe it. I don't believe it.' He was silent for a while. 'Oh, that's okay then. It's not my memory. I just don't have a list. Next time someone says, "Hello, Philippe," I can just say, "Hello, I don't remember your name, sorry. I don't keep a list."'

We pottered around, watching videos, swimming and waiting for bread to rise. Allen was getting fidgety. He had taken to pulling pens apart and getting covered in splotches of indelible blue ink. Often we went ashore for dinner at one of the cafes on the beach where, at night, plastic tables and chairs were set out on the candlelit sand and everyone would gather to eat the ridiculously cheap prawn soups, green mango salads and chicken curries, and swap stories or glean snippets from the lives of tourists who didn't ever get round to telling you their names. 'My brother's just bought a boat. It was very expensive, it cost him hundreds of thousands of pounds but it's got everything. He's very rich, he works in computers. Actually he's a total shit. I can't stand him but I really want to go on his boat.'

By day we exercised by snorkelling for hours in the perpetually warm water. Once Allen dived down, grabbing at a coral outcrop to peer under a ledge at a crayfish. Just next to his hand I could see a strange, knobbly lump. I pointed it out to him and, signalling with my thumb, urged him to the surface. 'Just a lump of coral,' he said, but we dived down again to look. It was *Synanceja horrida*, the estuarine stonefish. Fatally poisonous. It had been worryingly inconspicuous, but living at sea hones the senses. I'd had a not-quite-right feeling about that rock. Actually I was delighted to see the stonefish. I had seen so many pictures of them and heard dire warnings, but I had never seen one before, and it is easy to become blasé about snorkelling, to forget to be vigilant. Life had become disturbingly hedonistic and easy; I needed the encounter with a stonefish to maintain my illusion that I was having an adventure and not a holiday.

It was late January and we were still undecided about where to spend the coming year. There was to be a Hindu festival at Penang the following week. Thaipusam, a festival which is banned in India, celebrates Lord Muruga and runs for several days. We left *White Cloud* on a mooring in Langkawi and travelled by ferry. Anxious not to miss anything on the first morning, we got up at 5 am and set off for the temple where crowds of people were piling offerings of flowers, fruit, money and incense into a silver carriage ready for the procession.

While most people took offerings of fruit and flowers to the temple, some walked barefoot along the entire route to another temple across the city, from before dawn until after midnight, carrying offerings of milk and honey in brass pots on their heads. The reason Thaipusam is nowadays forbidden in India soon became apparent. Young males, their bodies pierced with hooks attached to ropes, were driven like beasts through the streets by other young men. As well as the rope reins, some had limes and other offerings dangling from the hooks on their bodies. Apparently in a trance, they danced and performed wildly all along the route of the procession. The way was piled with coconuts which devotees threw into the path of the silver chariot as it approached. The streets were lined with temporary shrines and painted with Hindu symbols, while from the speakers came music strange and plangent. Despite claims that the point of the festivities was to subdue the ego, the pierced young men played to the crowds and cameras, along with their entourages of entranced and bopping dancing boys. They all gyrated to a kind of Indian reggae while girls in saris crowded round in giggling admiration. The whole Indian population of Penang seemed to be there, dressed in their finest clothes, bright silks and lots with gold. Only the tourists were in Western-style dress, looking drab and hot.

On the motorbike we'd hired it was possible for us to zip back and forth during the festivities. When we realised that the processions were going to continue for days, we took some time off to go to the hospital for Allen to get his knee checked. It is never advisable to set sail with any crew member injured, especially a chief engineer who has become unable to do the contortions necessary to maintain the engine. I sat in the hospital waiting room watching Bollywood movies while Allen had an MRI scan. Within a couple of hours and without an appointment, Allen had walked in and been examined by an orthopaedic surgeon familiar with his condition. The doctor reassured him that there was nothing seriously wrong, to take it easy, and that his knee would recover untreated within a few weeks. I was glad we were not going to have to go home ignominiously defeated by aging joints.

As well as the Hindu festival it was also Chinese New Year, and the fifteenth night was Chap Goh Meh, when maidens throw oranges into the sea and wish for a husband. We went to the esplanade for the orange-throwing ceremony and entered an enclosed area by the stage near the beach. It became evident that everyone, except VIPs and people with press cards, was being turned away. 'Look confident,' Allen whispered. 'We'll just pretend we belong.' I assumed an air of uncharacteristic sangfroid and eventually we were ushered to some seats overlooking the beach.

The festival involved young women on the shore throwing oranges to young men in boats. The girls were terrible shots and the boys were inexpert boatmen, so it was not a thrilling courtship display but it was bearably short. Then people again moved to the enclosed area near the stage. Once more we managed to get into the non-public enclosure, but there was trouble marching towards us in the form of a tough policeman wearing a jaunty red beret and a villainous moustache. Our moment had come. 'Dance!' he ordered. 'Enjoy yourself!' Allen whispered, 'It's a cha-cha,' and off we went, dancing for our lives. Allen's varied life experiences often come in handy and this time I was grateful for his incarnation as a teenage ballroom-dancing champion. Not only can he dance, but he can steer a partner in a manner that suggests a modicum of ability on her part too. Everyone else had just been shuffling vaguely and soon a circle formed around us, cameras arrived, and we performed for television and the press. We were interviewed, invited to dance onstage and the next day our pictures were all over the papers.

After the night of dancing we had our usual dimsum breakfast and then headed back to an intriguing shopfront we had seen the night before. It was run by the Penang branch of Tzu Chi, a Buddhist organisation founded by a Chinese nun and funded by local businessmen. Although it was called a cafe and served tea and coffee, it was really more like an urban spiritual oasis. The style was designer Zen: expanses of polished wooden floor were partitioned by driftwood lattice screens set in channels of white pebbles, silk calligraphy scrolls hung on the white walls, and the handbasins in the loos were like large versions of the priceless crazed-porcelain bowls one sees in oriental museum collections. We found, through conversation with the quietly efficient employees, that the organisation funded a dialysis centre on the island. Other projects included disaster relief, and, that week, some volunteers were setting off to Gujarat to help with earthquake relief. We wondered if it might be an avenue for us to get involved in some community work, to meet local people and do something useful. We arranged a meeting with one of the organisers for the next day.

I mulled over whether the whole approach of Tzu Chi was a bit like old-fashioned charity organisations, and the photographs of the Faith Corps—armies of Taiwanese volunteers in uniform—were daunting but Mr Koay was encouraging. The only problem was the boat. Was there anywhere we could safely anchor around Penang? There was nowhere near the main town, but Mr Koay made some enquiries and we went off immediately to look at a marina towards the south of the island. It proved totally unsuitable for yachts, being both shallow and completely isolated. It was disappointing. We had finally found a way to become engaged in a local community but it looked as if there was no way for us to live aboard in Penang. It seemed the fortunes predicted for us at the temple we visited were right. Allen's read: 'You who get this are not good for everything. Your present condition is like a big tree receiving no wind and rain and its main roots have been entirely cut off. It is better if you are able to remove your present residence to some other place. Your property which had been lost can hardly be found. You have very little hope in love affairs. On case of prosecution, you will perhaps be the loser. Your aim for other things is rather poor.' Mine was almost as bad, so we had crossed the road to a Burmese temple full of monks and good feelings where we attempted to reshape our karma by donating money in exchange for ice-creams and coffee.

Back in Langkawi we faced the reality of ten and a half more months dangling around through another wet season. A few days earlier, before visiting Penang, we had briefly met our Zimbabwean friends, Rachel and Simon, again. Like most of the few remaining yachties in Langkawi, they were about to head off across the ocean, in their case to South Africa. We told them we had missed our opportunity to make it to the Red Sea this year, particularly as we wanted to visit Sri Lanka on the way.

'Go to Africa,' Rachel insisted. 'You'd love it.'

'And you'd have time to stop in Sri Lanka,' added Simon.

We were not so sure. The cruising guides warned of ferocious currents along the East African coast and this, combined with warnings about the inaccurate charts, the rapacious officials, and umpteen nasty diseases including yellow fever and burrowing parasites, was not enticing.

Back in Langkawi we spent one hot and bothering day doing a few simple tasks like posting letters and then watched *The Beach*, a film that was far too close to the bone for comfort, a tropical paradise as a virtual hell, a prison of pleasure. We lay awake in the heat until we both said what we were thinking: 'Let's go to Africa.'

Just three days after our middle-of-the-night decision, we were underway. It was these sudden leaps into the unknown that I loved: the moment we decided to buy a boat after a few minutes discussion, the decision to head west to Indonesia instead of east to Sydney when we arrived so late in Darwin, as well as the constant less dramatic changes of plan because of a shift in the wind or a change of mood. They established an ease with the fickleness of the universe.

This was our first big ocean crossing. Sailing to Malaysia we had never been more than a couple of days away from land. From Langkawi to Sri Lanka is nearly 1200 miles and it takes at least ten days. Although we had been living on board and sailing for eighteen months, the prospect of crossing the Indian Ocean frightened me but was tempered by people applauding our courage. Many people do things that require far more— invisible acts of constant bravery, such as dealing with chronic pain or refusing to compromise personal integrity for a pay rise or job security— but rarely win applause for that. The fear of crossing oceans is clean and clear, life and death. Much later, an experienced yachtswoman in the last long painful stages of cancer said to me, 'I hope when your time to die comes it will be quick and easy—a blow to the head from the boom.'

Crossing from Thailand to Sri Lanka was lovely. It was easy. Time is experienced differently away from the world of clock-regulated time. From now on we abandoned our previous night-shift pattern. Allen watched from dusk to midnight and I took over until sunrise, which worked much better. Midnight to dawn did not seem any longer than each of my shorter night shifts had previously. The lack of stimulation out at sea made the world much more interesting. I could sit for hours, not reading or doing anything, just gazing. Days would pass, and I would have to look at my diary to see if it was Tuesday or Wednesday.

All the time at sea, day or night, we would be on-watch or off-watch. Off-watch during the day we tended to sleep or read or do odd jobs down below. The first couple of days I made a Sri Lankan flag. It is required that one not only flies one's own national flag on board but, as a courtesy, the flag of the country one is visiting should be flown higher up. Allen and I ate meals together but spent most of the time apart. Normally our watch patterns would revolve around radio schedules or weather reports but, during this voyage, we had no radio contact with anyone and our weather fax system—a system for downloading a weather map onto computer via the HF radio—continued to produce nothing but visual static. It was the north-east monsoon, when the trade winds generally blow steadily at around 10–15 knots, and for the first few days we sailed the trades fast on a broad reach, but as we drew south there was scarcely a whisper of air, and the last three days we were in classic doldrums. The sea was molten heavy metal, and it was comforting to have a 72-horsepower diesel engine. We rarely saw another ship. The only signs of life were dolphins playing in the clear deep ultramarine, our first spinner dolphins. They leap from the water and spin in the air, performing airborne pirouettes like a voluntary and spontaneous circus act. They even put on night shows. Dozens of them would frolic around the boat leaving three-dimensional trails of inter-weaving phosphorescence, criss-crossing tunnels of flashing light like underwater fireworks across the bows.

During the crossing I read books I had picked up from Mr Sam's shop in Penang, which had the best collection I'd seen since Singapore although the cataloguing system was unusual and challenging. All the books were shelved alphabetically according to the author's first name. Naipaul? Oh yes, look under V, he's there with Vikram Seth. I picked up Theroux's book about his friendship and his tiff with Sir Vidia, which was gloriously gossipy, as well as Conrad's *Lord Jim*, which seemed like the book one should read when crossing the Indian Ocean. I don't read to escape but to help me be where I am.

After ten days I went on deck after my early morning nap to see we were about five miles from Dondra Head lighthouse, shining white and proud, at the southernmost tip of the teardrop of Sri Lanka. We could therefore expect to arrive at Galle—where according to the BBC World Service we were just missing a test match against England—later in the day. It was wonderful to see land after more than a thousand miles of open ocean. For once, I gave thanks to the American military-industrial complex. It brought the Global Positioning System to the world. Our GPS had directed us safely to this beautiful island coast, shimmering emerald and sapphire in the morning sun.

Galle and Colombo were the only harbours at which a yacht was permitted to stop in Sri Lanka and we had to approach in the daytime to avoid the risk of being mistaken for a Tamil vessel making a surprise attack. Coastal cruising was prohibited because of the civil war, which had been continuing for so long that most of the rest of the world had forgotten about it. We announced our arrival over the radio and were ordered to moor outside the port itself. As we arrived an ominous dark grey Sri Lankan naval cutter drew alongside. Solemn uniformed officials came aboard to check our papers. We had become used to the system in Malaysia, Thailand and even Singapore, where we would anchor, shower, have something to eat and then, at our own pace, make our way ashore to find the immigration and customs authorities in order to check in to the country. We were terribly tired after eleven days at sea and we had not expected to have to deal with officialdom before we even had time to stop and have a cup of tea. All we felt like doing now was sleeping but we were expected to respond like efficient professional mariners, not like a pair of dozy wombats.

Allen went below to get the passports the navy demanded. I could hear him scrabbling through the shelves above the navigation table where we kept our documents but he came back with empty hands. The officials shook their heads. Allen and I considered our situation in befuddled anxiety: what were we going to do? If we had no papers, we could not enter the country. If we could not enter the country, we could not contact our embassy and organise replacement passports. We could not return to Australia, since there was no way to sail back eastwards against the prevailing monsoon winds, and if it was bad being in Sri Lanka without passports, it was going to get worse if we continued sailing to Africa or the Red Sea. We also needed some vital parts—the bilge blower that extracts potentially dangerous fumes from around the engine was broken and we also needed food and, more crucially, water and fuel. We were not in a happy situation and the officials looked grim. There was evidently no way we would get ashore without our papers.

I had once been on a small plane which Allen was flying with some nervous friends aboard, and the only clue to the fact that we were dangerously low on fuel was the dampness I could see on the back of his neck. He kept up a cheerful banter, pointed out landmarks and got us safely to land without anyone else guessing we had been in trouble. He is that sort of a man. Now, however, he was flustered and flapping. I didn't know what to do. 'Do you think they were stolen from you in Lankawi? Could you have left them anywhere?' I asked, mostly for the benefit of the officers. I didn't want them to think we were totally disorganised and inept or—no, it was too silly to contemplate—surely they couldn't think we were smugglers or something? Still, we were behaving oddly. We were in deep trouble. I was so exhausted I could barely think but I grabbed onto the technique I use to track keys, spectacles and other regularly lost objects.

'Where did you go after going to the port office? Where did you put the papers then? Did you still have them when you came on board?'

'Yes, I'm certain I had them then. I remember climbing out of the dinghy and putting them on top of the hatch.' We kept going, building up a vivid picture of our last day in Langkawi, walking through it step by step. Under the finger-drumming impatient gaze of the navy officers, Allen was living through it: 'I went downstairs and I didn't want to put them on the shelf because I thought it might get rough during the crossing so I put them somewhere . . .'

I waited, not breathing.

'. . . safe.'

'Good, that's good.' I felt as if I were defusing a bomb. 'You wouldn't happen to know where?'

We all stared at him, me and the row of silent men. They gestured to the crew still aboard the cutter that they were ready to leave.

'Hang on a minute,' said Allen, diving down the hatch and reappearing triumphant a few seconds later. 'They were in that cupboard with the candles and champagne glasses.'

Even then the officials' sombre demeanour did not change, but we were allowed to enter the harbour.

It was an awkward mooring that required us to reverse into a narrow space while picking up two mooring buoys at the bow. Such manoeuvres are tricky in a powerboat or small yacht, but in a large yacht which, in reverse, blunders like a fat lush, and with only two crew aboard, they are impossible. A couple of yachties in a dinghy saw our dilemma and, as yachties typically do, came to our aid. A couple of days later, when we had completed formalities and recovered, we invited Richard and Paula from *Leviathan* over for a thank-you drink, but they were busy getting ready to leave the next day. We agreed to do it some other time but we never did. We never will.

Galle is Sri Lanka's oldest port. Unlike any other port we visited, there was strict security in the area where we were moored. We had been issued with passes which we had to show to the military guards when we passed in or out of the gates. As we had been warned, depth charges were fired underwater several times every night to deter Tamil underwater attacks. We became used to them, but the first night we woke up agitated each time the blasts vibrated through the hull.

The fortified old walled town of Galle is a world heritage site. Unlike so many other areas of historical interest, it is still vibrant. On our first day we went for a walk around the walls. A man approached us and asked where we were staying. I was immediately on guard—our

guidebook had warned us that the area was notorious for con artists
and touts—but, glancing at his watch, he explained that he had an
appointment in a few minutes. I relaxed. He was friendly and we chatted for a few minutes about where we were staying. I thought he might
be touting a hotel so I told him we were on board a boat. As he went,
I noticed him stop to speak briefly to a man who must have been standing nearby. Through the Singhalese I caught the word *harbour*. We
walked on, and a few minutes later the other man approached. 'Good
afternoon, captain! You are on a boat in the harbour. Do you remember me? I am the watchman, you walked past me at the gate.' He told
us that the port was quiet now but that there had been 31 yachts the
previous month. He explained that his job was to patrol the docks at
night after the curfew to ensure the yachts were safe. After that came
the moving spiel about a sick daughter who needed milk. Allen gave
him the money he requested, just a few dollars, and he went away
beaming. 'I think he was genuine, he knew all about us being on a boat
so he probably was telling the truth.' We looked back to see the man
we spoke to first waiting for the 'watchman'. They were a double act.
We found ourselves ruefully admiring.

Where there is a lot of poverty and people must struggle for ways
to survive they need to concoct a good strategy. Dealing with beggars,
with requests for money or help, is part of the everyday experience
when living in or visiting a poor country. We learnt early on that walking, especially in tourist areas, was a bad idea, but after almost two
weeks at sea we were desperate to use our legs. People think of sailing
as healthy and energetic but, though there is plenty of fresh air and
hauling sails keeps you busy, there is little legwork. This is why sailors
danced the hornpipe as a form of exercise. On *White Cloud* there was
little room for a jig and we just wanted to walk and walk. In Galle travelling by *tuktuk*, a cycle-rickshaw, was less stressful.

In the old town we had lunch at the New Oriental Hotel. The rambling old colonial hotel had a cool and whitewashed dining room with hangar-high ceilings, linen tablecloths, fresh flowers and orange-rimmed white hotel crockery that matched the orange-trimmed white uniforms of the waiters. We drank lime sodas and ate a feast of varied but unidentifiable curries and dhal with umpteen little bowls of pickles and chutney in a place where little, not even the prices, seemed to have changed for decades. It was grand and decaying, a nostalgia-machine that invoked sadness and regret for a time one has never known and a place one has never been. I wanted to stay there forever, to move into one of the rooms that lead out onto the shabby balcony overlooking the busy street, the walls of the fort and the sea beyond. I still yearn to return, to be right in the middle of the hubbub and noise and smells and heat and yet slightly removed, an observer, taking tiffin on the balcony of the New Oriental Hotel.

While we waited for a replacement bilge blower to arrive we went inland for a few days. We would normally have travelled by train but they were booked out by cricket fans so we hired a car and a driver. The driver abandoned us in Kandy when the owner of the guesthouse we'd booked into refused to pay him anything. Mrs Nanayakkara ticked him off soundly when he got out of the car to argue with her and then she helped us to organise another driver, reassuring us that drivers habitually intimidate guesthouse owners, threatening not to deliver customers to them if they do not offer them commissions. Mrs Nanayakkara and her husband were retired schoolteachers who both spoke excellent English. Staying with them gave us a taste of ordinary domestic life. We could walk from their house on a hillside overlooking the town down through the suburbs where boys played with sticks and hoops made from old wheels or gathered to play cricket in any bit of open space. Everyone was cricket-mad and assumed we were too.

'You have come from Galle, yes?'

'Yes.'

'You are English?'

'Yes.'

'You are here for the cricket.'

No, we were in search of the exotic, not the familiar. We dutifully visited the Temple of the Tooth, where one of Buddha's teeth is reputedly enshrined and the various museums are full of sparsely labelled collections of old grubby things. Even though Kandy is Sri Lanka's second-biggest town, there were not many places to linger when we were tired of trudging round antiquities. Stranded inland we were missing our travelling home.

After a couple of days in Kandy we travelled north to visit Sigiriya, a granite monolith on which an ancient fortress was built 1500 years ago. While I marvelled at the strange beauty of this place, the frescoes and the water gardens, and the vastness of the task of building it, complete with water tanks, on a rock 200 metres high, Allen ruminated about the logistics and concluded that it had been a daft place to build a fortress since it was intrinsically indefensible: all the enemy had to do was wait. As it happened, the invading army did not have to wait. Kasyapa, who built the fortress, went out by elephant to meet them, took a wrong turn, became bogged and committed suicide. Perhaps a fitting end for someone who had murdered his father and usurped his brother's throne. Tragedy, stupidity, beauty and folly, the story of Sigiriya is like stories of those mythical gods whose extravagant blunders continue to be re-enacted by human beings, generation after generation.

Polonnaruwa was another major tourist destination in Sri Lanka. It consists of acres of ruins in the jungle, including the Gal Vihara group of Buddha images carved from huge hunks of granite and a giant stone carving of an ola book. I had been reading *Anil's Ghost* by Michael

Ondaatje, in which this stone carving of a book is mentioned, though I still did not know what an ola book was. Nothing made sense, I could not grasp the significance of what I was seeing. It takes time to learn about the history, digest the stories and explore the contemporary significance of all these ancient sites. In the end, it is not visiting famous places that matters on a journey, but there was not enough time to wander, to stop and talk, and to find the way to what does.

The Dambulla Caves are the most famous of Sri Lanka's rock temples, some of which date back to the first century BC and which contain splendid Buddhist frescoes and statuary. But I was more enchanted by the rock monastery of Aluvihara, where the Indian scholar Buddhaghosa, Buddha-voice, was supposed to have spent some years and where the sutras, the words of the Buddha, were first written down in Pali. There monks still inscribe sutras on ola leaves, and at last I saw a real ola book. I asked the monk what he was writing and surprised him by joining in as he recited the *Tisarana*, the threefold refuge that, even in the Zen tradition, we still chant in Pali. He grinned and we conversed a while in smiles and little bows. It was reassuring, in the middle of this rapid journey around historic sites, to make a connection and touch upon the familiar.

It was around this time that the Taliban's destruction of Buddhist statues in Afghanistan was in the news. These 'treasures of all humanity' were not unlike those I had seen at Borobudur and Polonnaruwa, beautifully carved stones with an interesting history, but I found it disquieting that everyone seemed more concerned about the loss of the statues than about what the Taliban was doing to living people. News was seeping out about the extraordinary repression of women, who were forbidden to travel outside the house, to work, to help others and who were literally dying from anguish, but it was the destruction of statues that inspired the most widespread outrage.

Yet for me, it was making some connection with people, reaching across the barriers of language or culture or education or wealth to some common acknowledgement of shared humanity, that was precious on this journey. Of course it did not always happen that way. I ended many days feeling very disappointed with myself because I had refused so many requests for money or for more money than I had given. All over the world we dutifully move from white palm-fringed beach to resplendent or ancient cultural artifact but does it enhance cross-cultural understanding? Does it make poor people wealthier or the rich more compassionate or anyone happier? I feared that it might make me less so. Guilt exploded into irritation at mendicants always wanting more money than I could give, and left me wanting more peace of mind than I could have.

We were resigned to being hot all the time but we took the chance to escape by travelling into the high hill country where tea is grown and where the English used to retreat. We drove past countless tea plantations, acres of tidy bushes, still named Somerset and Argyle as if the British had never left, and for a couple of nights we booked into the Hill Club in Nuwara Eliya to see how life had been. It was very British, post-empire but pre- the chattering classes. It was the Britain of my childhood, and it smelt like boarding school. There were other similarities to an English boarding school: intercourse between the sexes was still frowned upon. The bedrooms were furnished like those I remembered in the comfortable homes of the middle classes in the 1950s. We asked for a room with a double bed. There was just one, and evidently it only had a double because it was too small for twin beds. As at school, hot water was rationed and baths could only be contemplated between set hours morning and evening, and there was a uniform: to be admitted to dine Allen would need to borrow a jacket and tie. The food was just like what we ate at school. It was both surreal and disturbingly familiar. So this was what the colonies had really been like for the colonists? Not the fantasy world of raffish exoticism invoked by the New Oriental Hotel, but exactly like boarding school. I had been on a scholarship and was part of a small clique who regarded ourselves as radical for our moderately left-wing political leanings, yet we had never given a thought to the workers around us and we barely noticed they were there at all. I had never thought about it until I stood on that polished staircase in Sri Lanka: what a wonderful training boarding schools had been for those destined to colonise an empire.

Once we returned to Galle we felt propelled in an uncharacteristic rush. We needed to get to Chagos before the change of monsoon but were waiting for customs to let us have the part we needed to fix the boat. In the meantime we were busy getting water, fuel and provisions. We did our provisioning at Mike's. I cannot write about Sri Lanka without a panegyric on Mike. He owned a shop which most yachties patronised, since it stocked essential items for the long-term cruiser such as tomato paste, vegemite and lime juice. I had first spotted him on the jetty, waving and shouting at us. He was wearing just a *lungi*—like a sarong—and with his long wild curls, bare tummy and apparent over-friendliness, he seemed the kind of person I should contrive not to notice. He proved, however, to be a living human treasure. As well as stocking provisions and being a source of practical information, he was our Internet access. His house was full of people who observed us with benign amusement as we traipsed through to the computer in a sparsely furnished bedroom that had walls and ceiling in a pink to die for, more shocking than shocking pink. Best of all, Mike would deliver provisions to the boats, which was extraordinarily helpful since we were not allowed to bring taxis or *tuktuks* inside the gate of the port, about a mile away from the yacht moorings. Mike explained that every

time there was a change of customs officer he had to get a friend, a government minister, to 'remind' the officer not to hassle him. The
difficulties we had with officialdom, the mounting payments necessary
to facilitate every transaction, were not specifically designed to frus-
trate foreigners. They just were. They frustrated everyone.

The port authorities would not relax the rules that forbade *tuktuk*
drivers entering the port area even to carry a passenger with severe disabilities to his boat. A couple of yachties were cruising with their adult
son, who had suffered a sporting accident that had not only caused
evident brain damage but meant he could walk only with difficulty and
very slowly using sticks. It was excruciating to watch his painful
progress for the half mile from the nearest jetty to the gate but, every
day, the guards on the gate did watch and never eased their rule.

The bilge blower finally arrived in the country but it was being kept
by a bond agent in Colombo. It could only be released to us personally.
In Colombo we filled in pages and pages of paperwork, and then found
they could not be processed until the next day, so we had to spend a
night there (which, together with the cost of the train fares and the
storage charges and the agent's fees and customs duties, made it the
most expensive bilge blower in maritime history). It was maddeningly
irritating, like so much of what happened in Sri Lanka.

My diary is awash with such frustrations and yet this is not what
I remember. Leaving Sri Lanka was like being torn away from someone
you have not known for very long, whom you had initially dismissed
as annoying and unfriendly, but of whom, despite everything, you are
becoming fond. Sri Lanka was difficult. It was very expensive as well as
time-consuming to do anything with a boat. The port was horrible,
dirty, dusty and full of commercial ships, and did not feel like somewhere I could walk around alone. Only the innocent cows, placidly
congregating to enjoy the shade provided by the warehouses, relieved

the desolation. The irritations were part of something much bigger and more complex that I never even began to explore. As well as being naturally beautiful, the country was dripping with spectacular art and architecture, secular and religious, evidence of centuries of sophisticated civilisation. I could not make sense of it. I had just zoomed round, glimpsing and gawping. I wanted to get to know better the people whose lives were embedded in these layers of history and art and gods. There is a long tradition of wisdom, vitality, elegance and intellect in Sri Lanka but I had not known how to access it. I wanted to make connections but the monsoons were soon to turn and our visas soon to expire. It was time to go to the Maldives. I vowed that one day I would go back to Serendib with enough time to lose my bearings and really find it. If I felt ambivalent, it was perhaps because I was in a land where ambivalence is so elegantly articulated. Whenever things were a little difficult in my negotiations with Sri Lankan people, they would waggle their heads, a sort of simultaneous nodding and shaking that seemed to imply the conflict of doing both together—doubt, ambivalence, paradox were all expressed as a kind of punctuation to the actual words being spoken. I felt as if I should learn to move my head like that too, to embody my feelings about this enchanting, infuriating isle.

ISLANDS
IN THE SUN

Sri Lanka to the Maldives to Chagos
March–May 2001

IT IS VERY UN-SAILOR LIKE TO THINK OF THE FUTURE.
— Charles Darwin

There is nothing that feels so much like freedom as setting off across the ocean on a boat. It opens up a vast space in life. When I was little there was a popular song about stopping the world, about wanting to get off. I knew exactly what it meant but I was amazed that grown-ups too understood that desire for an existential pause. Going on an extended sea voyage has the quality of a pause, just as a meditation retreat can. Such pauses are special, because when life resumes it is subtly different from before. During the pause we remain in the moment, not planning for the future or reminiscing about the past. In meditation this is a deliberate practice, called 'cutting off the mind road', but while sailing there is no choice about staying in the present moment. You would go crazy if you were waiting to arrive or worrying about bad weather coming. In sailing it is a state of alert awareness as survival strategy. And this is not the only similarity between an ocean voyage and a retreat. On this passage we had no regular radio contact, so interaction with the outside world was minimal and the constant low-level sleep deprivation resulted in a slight skewing of habitual reality. As well as the benefits of a retreat—a quietening-down of one's internal voices and a mindful alertness—sailing away offers additional measures of freedom. Not only do you feel as if you are in a different space at the end, you actually are in another part of the world. Slow travelling by boat creates a particular state of mind that enhances the experience. I love it. I love the feeling of being nowhere, being no one and, best of all, no shopping. Oh, I do it. I too can spend a Saturday afternoon trying on shoes or vacillating over paint colours, but at the end of the day I feel as if I have wasted some of my life. Sailing to a new country feels like a splendid achievement even if I have done nothing except be completely at sea.

Sailing itself had become much easier since leaving South-East Asia. There we had been mainly coastal-sailing, and the many fishing vessels could be hazardous, especially at night. If they lit their boats at all, they did it with oil lamps that rarely adhered to the conventions for navigation lights prescribed by international regulations. These are designed to make it easier to determine the direction in which a vessel is moving and its size. There are also special lights to indicate if a vessel is towing something or is engaged in fishing or trawling. Crossing the Bay of Bengal to Sri Lanka, and on subsequent Indian Ocean crossings, we rarely saw another vessel once we were more than a day's sail from land. This made night passages far less stressful but also more boring: there is nothing like the sight of lights appearing over the horizon to keep you awake. Since our over-intimate encounter with an Australian frigate when we were going to Rottnest at the start of my seafaring,

I was obsessive about ensuring we were not on a collision course with any vessel I could see. Allen would glance up and say, 'No, it's fine, it's going to pass behind us,' but I would check the angle at which it was approaching with binoculars and compass until I was satisfied, for if the angle does not change in relation to one's own boat, someone has to give way. Big ships have radar, but yachts do not always show up among the speckle and fuzz, especially if there is bad weather, so it is prudent to watch out for them.

Now, heading for the Maldives, there were few hazards, the weather was easy, and all we had to do was read books and sleep and eat, give the sails the occasional tweak, and scrape decomposing corpses from the floor each morning. In the fashion of other yachties, we had bought a bunch of bananas before leaving Sri Lanka. This was not a 'hand', as one normally buys, but a complete bunch, the entire produce of one tree, which we hung from the ceiling. We ate bananas copiously and constantly and Allen sliced and dried dozens of them, but still they ripened and fell, and at night we often trod on them. It was always a shock, the bursting skin, the oozing entrails squelching underfoot. We did not know then that bananas are regarded as unlucky on board, especially by fishing vessels. The origin of this lore is variously attributed: to the lurking tarantulas, to the volatile gases emitted by ripening bananas that have led to explosions that caused the loss of banana boats, and to the claim that bananas contain fish-repelling chemicals.

Arriving was not so easy. We reached Male, the capital of the Maldives where we had to check in, and just drifted in the dark and put away the sails, since there was no wind. At dawn the engine would not start, so we messed around for hours, pushing ourselves along with the dinghy and trying other solutions until eventually Allen managed to bypass the solenoid and start the engine. We anchored off Male and checked in.

The Maldives consists of a string of coral atolls, about nineteen in total. They are the ur-atolls. *Atoll* is probably the only word that English has stolen from Divehi, the language of the Maldives. Each atoll consists of numerous coral islands surrounding a deep lagoon. We anchored in a sub-lagoon next to a resort island. Most of the islands near to Male are resort islands; the whole nation resembles a tropical island paradise theme park. The sea was like sapphires, the shallow lagoons by the islands were in shades of turquoise and aquamarine, and the sand was dazzling white. The islands all have swaying palm trees and resorts with tropical huts boasting native ambience as well as exotic paradise essentials such as airconditioning and en suites, and bars where you can sit under a brass ceiling fan and sip cocktails.

It was not really paradise since, as everyone knows, bats live in the hell realms and every evening flocks of shadow pass overhead. Bats and flying foxes are often the only mammals living on remote islands. I do not know how they made their way across the vast reaches of the Indian and Pacific oceans, flying with such flapping effort compared with the gliding ease of big migratory birds. Perhaps they hitchhiked across the deeps, hanging upside down from the rigging of old sailing ships while those other great traveller mammals, rats, hid below.

Visitors to the Maldives arrive at the airport and are whisked off to their resort, where they will stay for two weeks before being popped back on the plane. In general they do not see any local people except those who work at the resort, and many of those employees are Sri Lankan, since Maldivians are Muslim and not allowed to serve alcohol. Very few women are employed in the resorts, just men who work there during the season and then return to their wives and families on distant atolls. Tourists are discouraged from mingling with locals, indeed prevented, since they are effectively stranded for the duration on the resorts. We decided to visit a resort to take a dekko. Male Maldivians, neat in white trousers and tropical shirts, politely pandered to the needs of bunches of pasty Poms who sat around swilling beer and gobbling chip butties in ugly flip-flops, shorts, T-shirts and baseball hats. Yachties are not really welcome, since they are less controllable than normal tourists and can sail to local islands by themselves. This is forbidden; one must get a permit and is then allowed only to visit resort islands. Resort islands generally do not want visiting boats and often send them away, because yachties do not like to spend money on cocktails and rooms with an ocean view. Yachties want somewhere to stock up on fuel, water and fresh provisions, and to experience something of local culture, even if they do often complain about it. All the Maldivians we met on Male wanted us to pay to go snorkelling and diving. 'We've been snorkelling and diving. We want land, people, music! We want to dance!' Essentially foreign visitors are a source of income. They are needed and tolerated but you wouldn't want them getting loose and running wild around the place, would you?

I wrote emails to Bee and Lucy:

'Sorry to go on about this kind of thing but the more I travel the more I see such gross inequality in the distribution of wealth, corruption, the maintenance of an uneducated workforce, the oppression of women and I feel more and more enraged at the way men grasp power and use religion to justify their hegemonic practices. I was looking at the distance education package that a young French boy on a yacht was doing and he, at age ten, was learning all about the Universal Declaration of Human Rights. Do they teach that in Australian primary schools? They certainly don't in the Maldives. Imagine if they did. People might discover that some people expect the right to freedom of belief, some women expect equality. No, keep the peasants ignorant. And this is not colonialism or even post-colonialism, this is people oppressing and exploiting their own people.'

'Sorry, this is called 'cabin fever' I believe ... the slowly going berserk of people too long at sea. I am starved of ordinary boring life. Of gossip. C'mon, girls, send me long juicy emails.'

This was before September 11, when everyone began to talk about Islam and discuss the relationship between Islamic beliefs and cultural practices. The Maldives nation proudly proclaims itself to be 100 per cent Muslim, and has been so since the twelfth century. I tangled myself in knots while I was there. I believe in tolerance, but I resisted tolerating intolerance, especially since it was directed towards me. I was one of the infidels who had to be kept at bay, but I worked at understanding. Later, when I found that the population was around 300 000 and there were almost half a million visitors to the country each year, the Maldivian apartheid began to make some sense. Imagine 30 million tourists arriving in Australia each year, smoking opium and eating dogs. How would we feel and what would we do? We expect visitors to adhere to the laws of our country. Under Maldivian law, the consumption of alcohol and pork are forbidden, but the Maldives needs the income from tourism. Western tourists will not go for a beach holiday to a place where they cannot indulge in alcohol, even if they can go without bacon or a pork pie for a week, and so tourists are allowed to indulge their illegal or offensive practices so long as they remain sequestered.

I was definitely in need of some gossip. Not anything special, just the ordinary gritty of daily life. News reached me well enough—I knew of births and deaths—but minor squabbles and fleeting affairs passed me by. In the absence of familiar trivia, I found the troubles of the world could occupy my mind or accidentally fill an email and become the story instead of what was all around: the golden cobwebs of sunlight that dazzled me as I snorkelled through the lagoon or the kindness of the security guard who helped fill our water bottles from a tap behind the resort.

After staying just long enough to fix the solenoid problem and do the usual tasks, we checked out, anchoring in the designated location as we had on arrival, a terrible deep anchorage in the entrance to the lagoon where the current runs fiercely. In the swirling and agitated waters, *White Cloud* swung around and the anchor chain became firmly entangled round a coral head. Allen had to dive to cut the chain and retrieve the anchor, which I had to haul up on the end of a rope while trying not to run over him, or rather, the line of breaking bubbles that was somewhere nearby. We vowed to avoid Male in future.

With relief we headed south down the island chain towards Chagos and by dawn were anchored inside a lagoon near Diffushi Island. It was uninhabited except for a few fishermen who approached us to sell us a netfin grouper that was swimming in the natural fish tank formed by the bilge of their small wooden boat. We snorkelled on a nearby reef but, as elsewhere in the Maldives, it was all bleached and bare, like swimming on the moon. The next day I vacuumed cheerfully while Allen tested the batteries and found they each had a faulty cell and needed replacing. We would have to return to Male. I felt a current of irritation pass through. Why hadn't he tested them before we left? Probably for the same reason I had not got around to vacuuming— exhaustion and the desire to keep moving to somewhere we felt more at home. Yet it seemed as if we were getting another chance, that since we had not done Male well the first time we were being given the rare opportunity for a re-run.

Despite optimism and good intentions, our return was as frustrating as the previous visit. Having had little wind heading south, we were battered by fierce headwinds travelling north again to arrive back in Male on April Fool's Day. Thus we had to go through all the check-in procedures, including paying the fees, for the second time in two weeks. The sea was so rough when the officials got alongside that they were too scared to come aboard and, instead, made Allen leap onto their boat while I drove around in circles, fearing to cut the engine in case it did not start again.

Back in the safety of the lagoon by Hululé, the airport island, Allen started to track down the problem. We knew the batteries needed replacing but had to find out why. I hovered while Allen tested every- thing with a voltmeter, his throat fluttering as if he had swallowed a small bird. It was a relief to hear eureka-grunts coming from the nar- row passageway we grandly called the engine room. The wire to the solenoid was broken. And fixed. But it still didn't work. Another 'Aha!', a disconnected wire to the alternator. Another test. I was hating it. It got worse. Removing the old batteries Allen did something that caused a loud explosion, sparks, smoke and the smell of fireworks and chemistry lessons to emit from the engine room.

After flipping off every switch, I called gingerly, 'What happened? Are you still alive?'

'I just shorted the battery and it blew up,' said a grimy, grinning face with a tone bordering on pride.

What is it with boys that makes them enjoy big bangs even if it nearly kills them?

We then had to spend a minor inheritance on replacing the bat- teries. My memory of the Maldives is of spending lots of money to be able to work very hard, getting tired, hot, grizzly and anxious, but there was a glimmer of redemption. Shahid, who was in charge of a safari boat, saw us trying to flag down passing *doanis*, local transport boats, and came over offering to help. We showed him around and gave him a drink, and then he and Ali, who worked on his boat, took us to Male in the morning on their big inflatable, helped us find boat parts and brought us, and our new batteries, back in the afternoon. Over the next days we visited each other on board, making clumsy conversation and exchanging small keepsakes.

Finally we left again for Diffushi. As usual I went to bed early but woke at around nine and peeped up into the cockpit. Allen wasn't there. I walked through the boat but I couldn't find him so I went back on deck and peered around. I couldn't see him anywhere. There are stories of people waking for their shift to find they are alone and I could feel my heart thumping as I stepped out of the cockpit to see more clearly.

'Allen!'

'What's the problem?'

'I've lost you!'

'No, you haven't.'

He was reclining on the foredeck in the dinghy, watching stars. I sat and watched too as we puttered through the windless night. A ring of fluffy clouds encircled us, reflected in the still black water where only our bow wave made ripples in the sea of silk.

Arriving early I climbed up the mast to guide us through the reef. Then we could relax. I cut Allen's hair, tendrils blowing away in the breeze, and then we snorkelled. Below, the sand glistened, reflecting the ripples in nets of gold. Further along, eagle rays winged their way over the pale damaged coral. There were smartly striped black and yellow sweetlips and even a Maori wrasse with its huge tattooed head. Hours passed. When Allen was hunting I never relaxed because it was me holding the bag, edgily watching for sharks, but that day we just flippered along lazily looking at the view. After snorkelling I looked up a field guide but it was hard to remember the colour around the eyes and whether there was a spot on the pectoral fin. Had I seen oriental or striped sweetlips? At least the wrasse was unmistakable.

By evening it was cool enough to sit on deck and watch the unicorn-fish. 'I wonder why they are swimming round with their horns out of the water,' mused Allen. 'There must be a reason.' We looked at each other and laughed, sharing the ongoing joke of how differently we see the world. He always looked for the reason while I preferred to embellish the mystery. We sat there, murmuring, till it grew quite dark. There was a full moon and we could see the reef below in the still night-water.

Allen was reading William Dampier's accounts of his voyages. He regularly captured ships but found they were loaded with quince marmalade instead of the pieces of eight he had hoped for. One fleet was entirely wrecked when the first ship went aground and fired warning shots. The rest, thinking they were under attack, put up all their sails and followed at full speed. The crew of one vessel had immediately set about getting drunk when they ran aground and hadn't noticed when they floated off out to sea in the damaged ship. All aboard were drowned. It all sounded more like Monty Python than swashbuckling adventure. It helped to read about people whose sailing life was a shambles too.

A few days later we arrived at Gan, the main town on Addu, the southernmost atoll in the Maldives, where we were allowed to enter for 72 hours. Unsure of the procedure and after waiting some time for the officials to arrive, we went ashore. We met them along the road, broken down, and push-started them so they could come to investigate us. We thought it was funny but they were encased in that air of official dignity that inhibits laughter.

A couple of other yachts shared our anchorage and, as was customary, we met for drinks and exchanged news and information. There had been two cyclones in Chagos during the preceding three weeks and another yacht had arrived in Gan, escaping from a cyclone, but had been unable to land because they had dogs aboard. The stories varied as to whether this was because of the Muslim dislike of dogs or the retention of British anti-rabies regulations.

JP was a Belgian economist with a mop of long, frizzy sand-coloured curls and a face of the type sported by older French film stars, like a battered cauliflower. His wife, Uschi, a former model, looked like a twenty-year-old blonde bombshell at a distance and a marginally older one close up, despite living on a yacht and claiming to be around fifty. They told us what they had gleaned about facilities in Gan, most vitally that we might be able to get hold of some potable water from a Sri Lankan factory that has a large desalinator. Water is a major issue in much of the Third World, and especially in the Maldives, except in the resorts, which all have their own desalinators. Local people got their supplies from the well at the mosque or from their own rainwater tanks.

Gan had been a British Air Force base from the mid fifties until the mid seventies, and this tropical coral island still had the air of regimented England with disciplined lawns and tidy flowerbeds. It also had Internet access, an unexpected miracle that enabled the plea to my daughters for gossip to be fulfilled.

Among my emails was one from a college friend of my brother whom I had met years ago when I was still at school. It was quite brief. He asked if I remembered him and said he had heard about my yacht trip from my brother. I did remember him. He had seemed gorgeous. I'd had a schoolgirl crush on him. I wrote back asking what he had been doing for the past thirty years. He responded: 'Mari, I am honoured that you remember me. I hope you are having a great time.' He told me he was married with two children and had a very senior job in a major American bank and that, though he'd had a triple heart bypass, he was now well. He told me about his wife, who also had an executive position, and told me in detail about his son, at university, who was 'handsome' and daughter who was 'absolutely gorgeous'. Then he listed his assets: 'Three cars—Ferrari 355, BMW 528 and a Jeep Grand Cherokee. Three-bedroom house in Knightsbridge worth a lot. I do not even bother trying to get it valued for the fear that I may

decide to sell it.' He also listed his overseas properties and ended: 'That's
my life. Let's hear about you and your fabulous life your brother tells
me about.'

I was not kind. When I eventually replied, months later, I wrote
about life in Kenya and briefly described Bee's and Lucy's endeavours,
though without any mention of their vital statistics. I could not resist
reciprocating by documenting my occupational status and material
assets: 'Allen and I are both unemployed, no cars, though I did have a
gorgeous 1969 Ford before I left Australia, no house and one fairly ramshackle but tough sailing boat.' Sometimes it just seems too hard to
explain, to reach across the gap. I never heard from him again.

After our 72 hours we headed off into winds and squalls on Friday
13, Good Friday. We had not known that bananas were unlucky but we
had noticed that we were one of the few yachts that ever set sail on a
Friday. We had spoken on the radio to JP and Uschi, who had left a couple of days earlier, and they'd told us that they'd had a few squalls
gusting up to about 40 knots. Our first couple of days we had epic sunrises when the towering thunderclouds glowed with all the majesty of
heaven. It was impossible to capture on film but was almost faith-
inducing in grandeur. I realised it was probably Easter, but I could not
be sure. I felt very far away from the world, yet right in it, experiencing
panoramas more beautiful and varied than anything I had imagined,
all created out of steam. But cloud forms that inspire awe come at a
price and each day, just at dusk, they moved into action.

On our third evening we saw squalls ahead and reefed as usual. The
first squall we rode through but the next one knocked us sideways.
I stood in the cockpit, my hands clenching the grab rail. I thought I was
being admirably stoical but I knew I was terrified when I realised that
I was humming and then noticed that, despite not having been to
church for decades, the tune was a hymn calling for divine help. We'd

seen a couple of big fishing boats nearby. They looked like ghost ships, vague white shapes against the spume and mist. We lost sight of them in the dusk and heavy rain; the sea was ugly, brown and frothy, the way I like coffee but not my whole world, and each gust seemed to tilt us over further. Where were the trawlers? We had too much sail up and needed to take some down. Before we could, the wind in the rigging began to howl even more urgently and then there was the noise. Something big had snapped.

'What is it?'

Allen was still turning the wheel but the boat was flailing. 'The steering's gone.' He had been hand steering because the autopilot had been struggling and groaning in the heavy weather. I had visions of drifting around for months.

'Put it back on auto.'

'What heading?'

'Just keep pointing us into the wind while we get down some sail.'

It felt better to be doing something. The chain that attaches the helm to the quadrant (which moves the rudder) had snapped, so we could not hand steer, but the autopilot, which is attached directly to the quadrant, still worked. So long as our electronics held and we did not need to do any intricate steering manoeuvres, we'd be fine, but it didn't feel good. We were still a hundred miles from Chagos and, although the squall had passed, we were obviously in the middle of a low.

'What's for dinner? I'm hungry now,' said Allen. That was another difference between us. In times of stress Allen wants to eat but my throat had closed up, every fibre in my body tight as wire. Still, going below and busying myself with cooking rice and dhal was an act of such banality it kept me just this side of sane.

'Go to bed, you need to sleep.' The adrenaline was still vibrating throughout my veins and I lay in the lurching berth, jumping at every sound, cringing when the wind shrieked in the rigging. I gave up trying to rest and went on watch so Allen could sleep, but I kept having to call him to help take sails up and down, trying to maximise speed but minimise problems. In light winds I could do it myself but not in stormy weather. There was lightning all around and I was scared of losing our electronics. Now we really needed them. I went to sleep at 5 am expecting it to be clear when I awoke. At 7 am I got up and wandered through to the main cabin.

'What's happening?'

Allen stuck his head down the hatch, 'You don't want to know. We're heading into another big storm. Go back to sleep.'

He was right. All around was bank on bank of grey cloud, rain squalls in every direction and rumbling thunder.

'Are you sure?'

I must have looked as wretched as I felt. He was sure.

I went back, not to sleep, but to reading *Miss Smilla's Feeling for Snow*, an allegory of colonisation masquerading as a thriller. 'We think there are limits to the dimensions of fear. Until we encounter the unknown. Then we can all feel boundless amounts of terror.' It may seem odd, but I found those words comforting as I rolled around on the berth while waves pounded and thunder crashed around me, hundreds of miles from anywhere and thousands from the possibility of rescue. I was calmed by the knowledge that someone else knew what it was like to feel very, very afraid and then discover that the fear can keep growing and growing, filling you up with hard stuff like granite till nothing soft or gentle remains.

The storm passed. I took over, and Allen went below to rest, but within minutes I had to call him to help me get in some more foresail. I could not face any more anxiety; I had overdosed on adrenaline and so the rest of the morning Allen stayed on watch with me. We radioed yachts at Salomon, one of the atolls in the Chagos group, when we were a few miles off, because we were apprehensive about entering a reef-strewn lagoon without proper steering. A yachtie met us at the entrance in his dinghy and guided us to an anchorage.

The feeling when terror ends can be described only as bliss. Is this why people climb mountains or jump out of planes? I cannot imagine any drug that could rival it. In this state, even cleaning the bathroom sink generates ecstatic wellbeing, and the feeling was long-lasting. These were days of grace.

Chagos truly is unlike anywhere else on earth. There are no officials, so none of the tedious, often stressful and invariably expensive procedures associated with arriving in a new country. It is part of the British Indian Ocean Territory and every few weeks the British arrived by ship from Diego Garcia, which is leased to the United States, to check on who was there and to collect some money. Salomon Atoll and Peros Banhos, the two atolls where yachts are permitted to anchor, are uninhabited. The only forms of terrestrial life are the huge coconut crabs, which are notoriously good to eat and easy to catch and are therefore protected, and the ship-borne rats. Apart from private yachts, there are no visitors. There are no airstrips, no charter boats. These atolls are several hundred miles from the southernmost tip of the Maldives archipelago and thousands of miles from any major landmass. There is nowhere else on earth that is so capable of supporting human life yet remains uninhabited. Prior to becoming part of the British Indian Ocean Territory, Chagos was a dependency of Mauritius. There were coconut plantations, for copra, but the transient population has now been relocated to Mauritius and the Seychelles.

We had never intended originally to go to Chagos—I had not been seduced by the castaway fantasies that seemed to lure yachts there.

Living in Arnhemland I had known solitude and wilderness and it did not beckon again. Most of the people we'd met who were going there from Australia travelled via Cocos and Christmas islands, other stepping stones on the fast route across the Indian Ocean, bypassing Asia. For me the point was not to sail to remote places with no one except fish and yachties for company, but to visit a variety of other cultures at a leisurely pace. However, it is not possible to sail to Africa from Malaysia without a stop in Chagos. People who left Malaysia weeks before us were still in Chagos when we arrived, waiting for the winds to change. To get to Africa it was necessary to head south, to cross the equator, which divides the earth's weather systems. Where the vast and independent systems of air meet and rub against each other used to be called the doldrums but has been renamed the Inter Tropical Convergence Zone, or ITCZ, which trips easily off American tongues, ayee tee see zee, but is clumsy for a zed-sayer. The doldrums were something of a misnomer, being so closely associated with dull inaction for, in reality, the ITCZ is a place of turbulent activity where pressure systems collide and let off steam. It was because we were travelling through the ITCZ from the Maldives to Chagos that we had encountered such majestic cloudscapes and such malevolent squalls.

Though many yachts stop at Chagos simply to wait for the change of monsoon after crossing the equator, others choose to stay for up to six months before heading off, either to Africa or Madagascar or back to Malaysia. Many of them return, year after year, and have contributed to a book of notes that circulates within the yachting community, with information about waypoints and anchorages and eulogising this uninhabited paradise full of fruit trees and fish, where people can live like castaways off the bounty of the sea.

For the first few days we remained at the anchorage we had initially been led to, just off Ile Fouquet, opposite the only entrance into the lagoon. Salomon Atoll is about 5 miles long and a couple of miles across, so from inside one can easily see the reefs and islands that encompass the entire atoll. Large and spacious, they still provide idyllic sheltered waters for mucking about in boats. There were a few yachts anchored nearby; others were scattered around the atoll, with most being off Boddam, the main island at the southern end. After repairing the steering chain, Allen, who, as usual, had a spare—in this case a spare missing link—went off to meet the neighbours while I lay around, reading and moozling in the very best of moods.

Just after we arrived Simon and Rachel came over by dinghy, yelling and waving, 'Hello, *White Cloud*.' When they had last seen us we had been planning to stay in Malaysia but we were able to tell them now that their words, 'You'd love Africa,' had burrowed in. A couple of days later I invited them over for muffins. It had become a habit in Indonesia to have morning tea with them and I'd saved my last packet of muffin mix in the hope that we would see their children, Emily and Oliver, again.

Chagos is almost shopping-free, though we bought someone's spare dinghy because our fairly new inflatable had become useless— the glue had disintegrated in the sea and sun and, despite repeated efforts to mend it, the whole dinghy just crumbled apart. The 20-year-old inflatable we bought, though faded and a little too small, remained stout and sturdy for the rest of our voyaging. There are no shops on Chagos and the nearest one is across several hundred miles of open ocean, so when you run out of chocolate, grog or cigarettes, you have to deal with it. Canny voyagers travel there oversupplied with those items of craving and addiction. Nor are there medical supplies or police or diplomatic agencies. Like many cruising yachties, we had no boat or medical insurance since the cost of either is, like the sea height in a cyclone, phenomenal. No television, no phone, no churches. There is radio, but there is radio across much of the ocean. So Chagos does not have any of the things many people need in order to feel secure but, of course, that is its allure. It is perhaps the last place on earth where you can pretend to be free of society and of law and where the people who visit create their own conventions.

Several of the neighbouring yachties told us they were bound for Madagascar for the rum that you could get by the jerry can for a couple of dollars. I was not tempted by cheap hangovers. Before I had left my friend Brigid had warned me, 'Yachties like their little drinkies.' Drinking too much is one of the dangers of yachting. It is a custom to have sundowners with other people, and yachting etiquette to take along one's own preferred tipple. In Chagos, since people stayed for months on end, there was a tradition of alcohol production. People brewed beer or made rice wine, and the exchange of recipes and the production of liquor was a serious pastime. Most of our time was occupied by fishing, food preparation, boat maintenance and walking around the islands, through the shallows where schools of cute little baby black-tipped reef sharks and eagle rays swam round our ankles in the pools left by the receding tide.

We washed our clothes and ourselves in a well on Takamaka Island, among the coconut palms that grew all over the islands. A fine white bird flew overhead with the kind of ostentatiously decorative tail usually associated with birds that cannot fly but only show off. The tropic bird flew over repeatedly as we did the washing, hauling the buckets of water from the well, washing a pile of clothes by hand, hauling up more buckets of water to rinse everything and then, in the heat, dripping with sweat, hauling up even more buckets of water to pour over ourselves. It took time and the days passed quickly. Increasingly the afternoons would have to be spent catching dinner. Most people headed off outside the reef in their big dinghies to catch the tuna that threw themselves at people there, but our dinghy was too small and slow to take into open ocean so we were restricted to fishing inside the lagoon. Allen would take his gidgee, a hand spear, and we would snorkel around the bommies, coral heads, where we usually found something edible. Our favourites were the squirrelfish, just the right size for a meal for two. Sometimes all we could get were parrotfish, which tend to be mushy when cooked but are good if simply marinated in lime then mixed with coconut milk and chilli. Even the shallow coral here was vividly alive, not bleached as in the Maldives, so that when we snorkelled to hunt for dinner we were meandering through rainbow gardens, pinks and mauves, yellows and greens.

Yet this was not an untouched Eden. When we first went ashore to find the well we were surprised to find a cleared path through the island. The path was swept and edged with a border of coconut shells. Further down the beach was a clearing where people had left beach chairs and set up a defined barbecue area. We later discovered, on other islands, more of these clearings to which people would return year after year. This was the process of colonisation, the beginnings of control; we human beings do not just live in the world but must immediately start to fashion it, to make paths and clearings, signposts and buildings. Of course it is prohibited to live ashore. We heard rumours that former inhabitants, now living in Mauritius, had put in a land claim for Chagos. We also heard that these inhabitants had no desire to live in such isolation but were being used as part of a commercially driven plan to obtain fishing rights in the surrounding waters. Whatever the truth of these stories, the British did not want to jeopardise negotiations and strictly forbade habitation. But there were many children on the French boats who were in their own kind of paradise and built playhouses from palms. These were rather elaborate; yacht-dwelling children are resourceful. They are like no other children.

One day we were visiting *Erias*, a French yacht we had first got to know in Darwin. On board were a couple with their two boys aged around eight and five. Allen stood on their boarding ladder and broke a rung but, before there was time to speak, the elder boy had dived into the water and retrieved it with the reflexes of a cormorant. It is not just that the children who grow up on boats are sea creatures rather than land creatures, but that they are like finely adapted wild animals, attuned to their environment, muscular and fast. I had known Aboriginal children like that in remote places, alert and quick, able to catch lizards as fast as cats can, and drive cars before they are tall enough to see out of the windscreen. Urban Western children often seem flabby and clumsy by comparison, their wildness constrained by a world where adventure playgrounds have plastic swings that do not swing high enough to make a stomach lurch, where paddling pools are fenced, and bicycles cannot be ridden without helmets. The world is a dangerous place, but I do not know how we expect to teach our children to face danger when they are always protected from it and never learn to turn adrenaline and bruises into speed and dexterity.

After a few days we moved down the lagoon a few miles to Boddam. Here the ruins of houses, entangled with vines and fern, work sheds, a church and a desolate graveyard marked the site of the main settlement when the atoll was a plantation. On the tilting, cracked tombstones buried under casuarina roots and thick moss, the few remaining inscriptions were in French, dating from 1880 to the early 1950s. It was dark and gloomy but, in the background, palms swayed in the sun, death mingling in a disturbing juxtaposition with the promise of hedonistic frolic. Boddam remains the de facto capital city. About 20 yachts were anchored there, and many were planning to stay for months. They were well organised. They had cleared areas and built fireplaces, installed tables and chairs and generally tried to make the place look 'civilised'. They also had rules. We were heartily rebuked by an efficient *Hausfrau* for burning our rubbish at the same time as the regular volleyball game instead of within the appointed hours and for not cleaning the fish-cleaning table properly. Each evening at 5 pm everyone at Boddam went ashore for drinks, so it was a chance to meet the other people.

Dave, one of the solo sailors, was travelling so slowly I felt as if I were speeding. A wiry little retired Aussie, he had initially expected to take seven years to circumnavigate but had already extended his estimate to nine. He had learnt some Thai and he was planning to study Malagasy in preparation for an extended visit to Madagascar. Sometimes his wife flew in to join him but most of the time he was on his own, managing the sailing with skill but still grappling with the bread-making. As we were all to discover at some time during our voyaging, yeast goes off and, when it does, no amount of kneading and waiting will result in anything other than a solid brick.

Rick and his wife Paula were travelling on a small yacht named *Leviathan*. It was Rick who had helped us to manoeuvre into the awkward mooring in Galle, but we had not spoken to Paula, a generously built Californian with vast breasts and pearlised-green fingernails, who talked at length about 'my baby', who I gradually inferred was a sea-going feline. Paula had the air of a drinker with her exuberant conversational style, but I think she was just Californian—her beverage was apparently pink Fanta.

'Have you been to Raro? Oh, I just loved Raro. We've put in our applications to live there. You aren't allowed to own land there but I have such good friends there and I want to build a house,' she said emphatically, 'a house. They're like family to me. They've more or less adopted me. I don't have any kids of my own so it doesn't matter. I'm just going to build a house there and when I die it can go—' she threw open her arms generously '——back to the people. They are wonderful, wonderful people. I don't want to sail any more, I just want to get back to Rarotonga and live there for the rest of my life.'

Rick, with his long blond hair and gold necklace, was a good-natured aging Californian adolescent. He was also a computer whiz-kid. Every yachtie with an electronic problem went to Rick, who was a busy man: every yachtie has an electronic problem. His skill was legendary. In Indonesia, it was rumoured, he had been called upon to rectify the computer system for their entire stock exchange.

The next evening Paula introduced me to another wizening beach boy whose reputation had preceded him. I had met his estranged wife, who had abandoned him mid voyage and was crewing on another yacht. She had told me stories that did not endear him to me, so I was bristling even as we met.

'What boat are you on?'

'*White Cloud.*'

'That's a ferro-cement Hartley, right?'

'Wrong, it's a Roberts and it's not ferro, it's . . .' The word 'fibreglass' had deserted me. 'It's made of that stuff, you know, that plastic stuff.' I went on to explain, defensively, that it had been home-built on a male mould, which was why the finish was a bit rough compared with production-built fibreglass boats.

'Yes, it does look rough, I didn't want to say anything because people get offended.'

They do. I did. No wonder it is a serious breach of yachting etiquette to criticise someone else's yacht; it's akin to telling someone they have ugly children and a boring spouse. I went off to join Allen, who was talking to a couple from Florida who were complaining that the customs officials at Gan had confiscated their gun. I could not muster the politeness to feign sympathy nor the energy to risk social disgrace by expressing my true opinions about firearms.

The third night we tried again. To be fair, Allen was doing fine. He is a gregarious pack animal who is happy to chat to anyone and expects that most people will have different opinions from him on most topics and is thus neither surprised nor irritated when his expectation is realised. He does not, as I do, feel some self-destructive urge to argue and contradict. When I found myself in the middle of a cosy grumble between a New Zealander and a South African about the natives in their respective countries, not to mention the dole-bludgers, I was ready to move on.

Yachties have left behind all kinds of lives but many are former small-businesspeople with the typical values of the petit bourgeoisie. It is not surprising, since yachties share many of the characteristics of successful businesspeople. Hard-working, risk-taking, resourceful and being quickly able to recover after setbacks are qualities essential to ocean cruising and, of course, people who had done well in business were the ones who had the financial resources to retire early, buy a comfortable boat and set off. Several of this kind were concentrated at Boddam. Even though many were around my age, their attitudes were so like those of my parent's generation when I was a teenager that I thought of them as much older. Perhaps social attitudes, like arteries, grow harder and more inflexible with the years, clogged up with the detritus that accumulates after hearing years of talkback radio or anxiously monitoring the meanderings of the share market. I was taken aback when I discovered that yachties, who symbolised freedom and adventure, could also be so socially and politically conservative, that they would so unconsciously impose order on one of the most remote corners of the earth.

We left Boddam and returned to the anchorages near Takamaka. Apart from a group of francophones, clustered on a sand patch where we stayed for some days, boats in this area were more spread out than at Boddam and social interaction more sporadic and haphazard. During the day we went snorkelling for pleasure but many afternoons we went on a hunting swim. Allen caught a dinner fish while I looked out for the sharks that were always waiting to snatch away our catch. I only ever saw black-tipped reef sharks but there were tiger sharks in the area. There was always something new, like the huge moray eel emerging from under a rock that revealed itself to be not an eel but one tentacle of an octopus, not the kind you find in a salad, but the kind that entangles the heroine in old Lloyd Bridges' films.

With nothing much to do ashore, preparing food became a major pastime and after a few weeks we were running out of supplies. Our fresh fruit was gone but we had some onions, carrots and three mouldering cabbages. Everything was rationed. I made bread about twice a week. We had eggs imported from India, the only ones available in the Maldives, with greyish, improperly formed yolks. Probably from greyish, improperly formed hens. They didn't seem to be rotten, but I used them only in baking, not fried or boiled. I worked hard at the cooking. One day we had a colourful sweetlips, marinated in soy and ginger, with rice and a pickled ginger and last-sliver-of-cucumber salad. The next day we had curried curd-cheese, an Indian recipe made with the yogurt packet mix that always curdled and had to be re-invented as panir. Sometimes I made pizza—all kinds of mysterious tinned things were edible when sandwiched between tinned tomato paste and tinned cheese.

Reading was another pastime but, like food, the reading matter was running out. Some afternoons we watched VCDs on the computer, silly blockbusters we had picked up in Malaysia and saved for a sunny day. There was even some good radio too, National Public Radio broadcast via American Forces Network from Diego Garcia. After a couple of weeks on Chagos I wrote emails I could not send: 'This is the most unbelievable place. Think of loneliness. Think of exile. I used not to

There is nothing that feels so much like freedom as setting off across the ocean on a boat. (Photo courtesy of a fellow slow traveller on Achates II*)*

We watched the little sooty terns coming to roost for the night.
An annoyed Genghis knew he could not pounce or he would fall overboard.

We anchored off a deserted small bay off some relaxed Thai island.
We slowed right down. This was different from being on holiday. This was cruising.

Top: Thaipusam festival at Penang where young males, their bodies pierced with hooks attached to ropes, are driven like beasts through the streets.

Bottom: Making a Sri Lankan flag—as a courtesy, the flag of the country one is visiting should be flown higher up than one's own national flag.

Top: Dolphins riding our bow wave, playing in the clear deep ultramarine—sometimes they were the only signs of life.

Bottom: Becalmed in the Indian Ocean—it was boring, waiting for something to change, to move, to happen, but it was also very peaceful.

Top: Chagos, an almost untouched paradise, had none of the things many people need in order to feel secure—but that was its allure.

Bottom: A Sunday afternoon concert in the Seychelles—it seemed to be what one did at the weekend in a place where shopping is neither pastime nor therapy.

*Top: Careening in Kilifi Creek—it was disturbing to see our home
lying on her side on the beach like a big sick animal.*

*Bottom: The Tanga Yacht Club—we became members so we could come and go
as we pleased since all along the African coast most land is privately owned.*

Back in Fremantle: it didn't matter that we would have to part with White Cloud,
travelling slowly was no longer just a manner of locomotion.
(Photo courtesy of Peter Boichel)

understand exile as a form of punishment. Why exile Napoleon to St Helena? Why not execute him? Oh exile is exquisite torture, especially when it is self-imposed.'

Yet by the time we left, we were almost reluctant, forced on by favourable winds and the need to replenish our food supplies. We had met some other people who admitted to suffering from attacks of tropical paradise fatigue too, fellow heretics, and we were enjoying our new anchorage off the fringing reef south of Takamaka. Manta rays played and fed around the boat almost constantly. When we snorkelled with them they would come close enough to touch. They were so graceful, flying through the water on ultra-tech wings, looping the loop right under us. It is very rare to get so close to manta rays, since usually they live in deep ocean, but they must breed in the lagoons and, like the baby sharks, live there until they are bigger and less vulnerable. The ones we saw had wingspans up to about 2.5 metres but they grow a lot bigger. Even so, I felt apprehensive as beings that resembled space-stations approached me with their head-flaps curled round, like open mouths big enough to swallow me whole, but they slid by.

We had started doing *zazen* again each morning. I had generally found myself following my breath during the long night watches, and during bad weather I would chant the sutra invoking the name of Kanzeon who, as well as being the bodhisattva of compassion, looks after seafarers. But there is something particularly tender and earthing about lighting incense and formally sitting in meditation with someone else.

Allen built a new bookshelf at the end of the bed to replace the one on which I kept banging my head. It rained and rained until one day it stopped and we had a bath in the dinghy that was full of fresh water. I fixed the sun covers, wrestling acres of canvas through the sewing machine. Allen changed the oil filters. Sometimes we took a day off and went walking round the island, blazing saturated lime and apple greens where the sunlight penetrated, deep jungly shades elsewhere, but always the clear, clean green of coconut forest. Sometimes, craving freshness, we cut a heart of palm. Coming home exhausted we talked over dinner about our families, especially our grown-up children making their own lives, their own triumphs and mistakes, and how only love helps. We all know our faults too well, it's our graces we need reminding of: I wrote long letters to post in the future.

This was life now. I was no longer fighting and wanting to be elsewhere. The memory of my former life was fading, and I could begin to imagine how people who live for years in remote places forget, in time, that it was ever else. It was in Chagos that our internal clocks changed: we hit frustration point so hard that time and distance lost their conventional meaning and we fell away, into another world where clock time stopped and life time began.

ISLANDS
IN A STORM

Chagos to the Seychelles to Kenya
May–June 2001

THERE IS AN OCEAN OF BRIGHT CLOUDS,
THERE IS AN OCEAN OF SOLEMN CLOUDS.
— Dogen Zenji

As the winds began to blow more regularly from the south-east, boats at Chagos began to set sail westwards, mostly to Madagascar and thence onwards to South Africa and the Cape, bypassing most of continental Africa. No one else on Chagos was planning to go straight west, via the Seychelles, to East Africa. It was over a thousand miles to the Seychelles and another thousand to Tanzania, a long way at a brisk walking pace, so we set off as soon as the winds seemed favourable.

The first few days at sea are always tiring, especially after several weeks at anchor, getting used to the constant motion and staying awake for half the night. After three days we were sailing well, making good speed, though it was blustery, the seas were choppy, and cooking was frustrating since nothing would keep still. Sleeping was bumpy.

The most comparable non-marine experience is trying to rest on a trampoline on which at least one other person is bouncing.

Each morning, along with other yachts in the south-eastern Indian Ocean, we would tune into *Kiore*'s sked to record our position and listen to a recent weather report. *Kiore* was the name of the yacht formerly owned by Tony, a radio ham living in Kilifi on the Kenyan coast, and he still used *Kiore* as his call sign. *White Cloud*, unlike our yacht's previous name, *Kaye Lorraine*, is short and easy to spell as well as easy to hear and understand over the radio, an important consideration when relying on marine telecommunication. Renaming a boat is not to be undertaken lightly and we followed all precautions. It is essential not to antagonise the current marine theocracy. The Titans, for example, were in office at the beginning of time but they were banished by Poseidon and other deities who remain in power to this day. *Titanic* was always a daring choice. A change of name must be accompanied by libations to the gods and so we had thrown a renaming party before moving onboard. I had woken in a panic the night before and, after hasty calculations, woke Allen to ask, 'Do you realise that fifty people is about three tons of flesh. Do you think we can carry that much extra cargo?' The three tons came aboard and participated in the ceremony. The old name was returned to the gods of wind and wave, copious libations were made, the new name was bestowed and *White Cloud* carried her additional load with ease. But the choice of name was not only determined by practical considerations, Taoist poets have traditionally celebrated the white cloud as a symbol of a liberated existence.

Although we had already heard the familiar breathless gasping that heralded the appearance of dolphins, and had seen a large pod of pygmy killer whales, I was unprepared when Allen called me on deck on the third morning to see hundreds of dolphins, leaping and spinning all around us. The ocean was teeming with dolphins in every direction: the world was dolphin all the way down. It was magnificent but dreadful, for I knew the old weather-rhyme: When the porpoise jumps, stand by at your pumps.

By the fourth day we were tired. Even walking required biceps-power. The wind was around 20 knots but it was sunny, the sky pale wedgewood and the sea darkly sparking, almost black, crumpled and restless. We were cantering along at a regular gait. Allen was tired, rough-faced and naked, reminding me of our much-missed cat Genghis on a sleepy morning, a brown animal. We wore as few clothes as possible because of the heat and limited water resources, and to save water Allen never shaved on passages and neither of us could wash our hair, which grew stiff and tangled. We were turning feral.

On the fifth day we each saw lights during the early morning watches. These were the only other vessels in our time on that vast ocean road. Later we reefed the sails as we watched a rainstorm approach. An agreement we made early in our sailing life was that if either of us wanted to reef, we reefed. It is easy to un-reef the sail if a storm fizzles, it was a task we could do single-handedly, but always a mistake to have too much sail up. The other understanding that developed was that during passages we would have a watch system day and night, and that whoever was off-watch was free to sleep or rest or do whatever they wanted and not feel bound to keep the other one company or do extra tasks unless they were essential. These were the nearest we got to having rules on board our small independent nation, and both were designed to ensure we were as rested and relaxed as possible on long passages.

Though Allen had mended the steering chain that had snapped in the storm on the way to Chagos, we knew the metal had started cracking and it needed replacing, which we could not do until we reached the Seychelles. Tony had told us that morning that we were on the fringe of a non-revolving low. 'Nothing to worry about,' he had said with therapeutic calm. I did though.

The day brought only mild squalls. The next day they were more persistent and the wind was changeable, so we gybed frequently. Tony told us that the low would be around for the next couple of days. I noted in my diary that 'mostly I think about having a shower' and that, although I managed to assemble beans on toast for lunch, the toast kept slipping off the plate before I could weigh it down with beans. The seas were spiky and peaky, grey-blue with a hard lumpy swell, and the clouds were sharp-edged and streaky or leaden masses. Nothing was rolling or curvy; the weather was all blades and daggers, and, although the sky had tatters of blue, it was not enough to make a pair of sailor's trousers.

Much of the time on watch is spent watching. 'What do you watch for?' asked a non-sailor. I had never thought of it as watching *for*, just as watching, because it is the unknown, signalled by the subtlest of changes, for which one watches. The changes in cloud patterns, from puffy lambkin clouds to mare's tails high in the stratosphere, may signal a change in the weather patterns before the wind rises or the barometer drops. When I first started sailing I had found channel markers, and other objects specifically designed to be seen, extremely difficult to spot at a distance. However, after years at sea my eyes, or perhaps it was my brain, had adjusted to the sky and sea and I would notice tiny birds sitting in the water or the changed texture of the ocean where two currents meet. The experienced yachtswoman who taught me in Darwin used to say, 'Look, you can see the wind coming over the water.' Where? What did she mean? See wind? But now I too could see the wind coming.

You notice changes in the boat as well, a shift in the sound of the engine or the movement through the water. On the seventh day, we observed an unwelcome change: the engine was overheating and no water was circulating. One possibility was that a plastic bag was blocking the intake, but jumping overboard to look was out of the question. Allen tightened the fanbelt, but that wasn't it, and he spent lunchtime silent and thoughtful, even reading the engine manual, a rare occurrence and a tactic of very last resort. Because we could not use the engine to recharge the batteries if they ran low, we did everything possible to conserve power, even turning off the fridge. The most likely explanation was that the impeller needed replacing, and that was indeed the case, but we couldn't fix that problem while underway in rough weather. The only option was to practise being sanguine. We used only torches at night. We didn't use the mizzen sail so that the solar panels were not shaded from the afternoon sun. We were puddling along with no immediate problems except the anxiety of knowing there was no backup in case of emergency.

It was at around this point in the journey that Allen asked, 'How do you feel about selling the boat in Africa?'

'I thought you liked fixing things.'

'It's all right as a hobby; now it's my whole life. If I'd wanted to do this I could've been a motor mechanic.'

'Well, everyone says that cruising is about fixing boats in exotic places. We were warned beforehand.'

'It's meant to be a joke. I didn't know it was all I'd ever do.'

I was glad we were heading due west and not going with the crowd further south to Madagascar. We were having a better time than Dave, the solo sailor who had set off there from Chagos a few days earlier and had experienced foul weather which had smashed his hatches and severely damaged his rudder bearing, so that he was having difficulty keeping course. He had sounded so despondent on the radio that morning when Tony had apologetically told him that the weather forecast was for continuing strong winds. As the day continued the winds lessened but the seas were high so that, like a merry-go-round pony, we were travelling a long way up and down but making little forward progress. I spent all my time trimming sails, which was a blessed distraction through the long night that followed.

Next morning Tony explained enthusiastically how to approach Kilifi when we finally reached the African mainland.

'We were actually intending to head straight to Tanga,' said Allen.

'Well, that's no problem at all. But you can get to Tanga in three days from here. That's easy. People do it all the time. Still, that's perfectly all right if you want to go to Tanga and miss Kenya,' he added in the particular snipped tone of voice my mother used when saying, 'nothing's the matter,' in order to convey that there was a matter of monumental proportions on her mind and if you didn't realise and put it right, then, as she would have said, 'Woe betide you.'

I was delighted by this emotional pressure and the reassurances that, despite the strong currents up the coast, we would be able to go south from Kilifi even during the south monsoon. One of the main pleasures of cruising is having plans regularly sabotaged by weather or whim. For no reason I could articulate, since I then knew little about the different African countries, I wanted to visit Kenya.

Eleven days after leaving Chagos, the sunrise clouds were so spectacular I spent the early morning taking photographs instead of waking Allen to take over the watch. By mid morning, the clouds that had been towering displays of pink and gold were looming walls of storm. We were only 30 miles from Port Victoria in the Seychelles but we were hit by squall after squall that sometimes carried us at 8 knots towards our destination, even with heavily reefed sails, and at other times blew us equally fast in the opposite direction. The winds were predominantly blowing us north, and we were worried that we might be blown north of the islands and, without a motor, be unable to sail back into the wind, so we tacked day and night through the howling winds and blinding rain, finally dropping anchor in the bay outside Port Victoria an hour or two after midnight.

Normally we would have hung off until daylight and not attempted to enter an unknown anchorage at night, especially one that was so surrounded by reef and whose topography seemed to bear little relation to the chart. But as we approached, the authorities who took our radio call at Port Victoria were very helpful and gave us a waypoint position where we could anchor. It is not easy to anchor 13 tons of boat with only two people aboard in 50-knot winds, in the middle of a reef-infested waterway in the dark, but we did it without very much more shouting than usual.

The next morning, in kitten-soft breezes, we looked at how close to the reef we were anchored, grateful at our luck in avoiding the obstacles that had strewn our dark path. The islands of the Mahé group that had been obscured by the driving rain, emerging only as looming grey rock, were pretty green hills quite unlike the low coral atolls of the Maldives and Chagos. Though they look volcanic, they are bits that broke off from India eons ago. We also understood our nocturnal confusion: there had been substantial land-reclamation that was not marked on the charts.

When the officials arrived Allen was on deck but I stayed below and was surprised when the immigration officer came down and suggested I fill in some of the forms to save time. He spoke to me. He thought I was capable of filling in a form. It was only then that I realised how accustomed I had become to being invisible. After spending a year in places where, as a woman, I had no status, I was becoming invisible even to myself. I was so happy to exist again, to be spoken to, and I asked the officials about the language they were speaking. It was Seselwa, the French-based creole that is the lingua franca on these islands. The islands had been uninhabited when they were claimed by France in the seventeenth century and, though the British took over between the Napoleonic Wars and independence, French influence remained strong.

After moving to the inner harbour we went ashore. Wandering down the main street of Port Victoria we heard wild yelling from an upstairs balcony where JP and Uschi—the pair we'd met in the Maldives—were having coffee. 'Come up here and join us!' They had been intending to stay only a week in the Seychelles before heading to Mayotte but were enjoying it so much they hadn't left, despite the expense. It was crazy and lovely to be in a coffee shop among this hodgepodge of peoples originating from Africa, Europe and India, to let go and relax, wearing clothes that felt normal. Most of all it was good to talk and not feel conspicuous, too loud and too big, as I had done ever since leaving Australia.

Back at the yacht club, Kim, one of the single-handers we'd met briefly at Chagos, came and joined us. Then, as we were sitting there I saw a familiar face at another table. It was Kevin who worked at one of the chandleries in Fremantle where we had spent too much money when we had been fixing up *White Cloud*. He and his wife, Judy, who had spent several years yacht-chartering in the Seychelles, had come back for a holiday. Then Uschi and JP arrived, so it ended up being more like a dinner party with old friends than arrival in an unknown place.

Port Victoria seemed terribly familiar even though the language was strange and the relaxed Euro-African ambience was different from anywhere I had ever been. It was vibrantly polychromatic. The markets were piled with fruit and vegetables, red bundles of chillies, coriander, eggplants, broccoli, beans, courgettes: a blaze of primary colour. It had been too long since I had tasted fresh vegetables. The Seychelles are not renowned for their shopping opportunities, but after weeks at sea, this was a feast for eyes and palate. The people too were colourful. They wore bright clothes and looked confident and at ease in their bodies. The men swaggered, swinging their shoulders. The women swayed their hips. They looked like beings who knew their right to walk the earth. I could stop scurrying around in the long-sleeved loose tops and calf-length trousers I had worn elsewhere on my travels to avoid offending local sensibilities. It was a relief to see women's legs for the first time in over a year, for wherever women are obliged to cover their bodies it is often a sign they are constrained in more significant ways too. It felt wonderful. There is a tendency to project one's mood onto the universe, but I felt sure people here really were friendly and relaxed.

Kevin and Judy suggested that we go with them to Chez Gaby on Round Island for Sunday lunch. Usually the restaurant caters to tourist groups but on Sunday the Creole cuisine is for locals and their friends. On the way back to the main island, Judy reminisced about her time in the Seychelles: 'My friends have so much and we have nothing because we spent so much time, eight years when we were young, sailing. But I have my memories.' Would all this be a memory for me one day? Would I speak about it with that look in my eyes, that yearning?

That afternoon we saw crowds perambulating in the park adjacent to the yacht club. It seemed to be what one did at the weekend in a place where shopping is neither pastime nor therapy, and we strolled too until, following the sound of singing, we found a concert. Unlike at lunch, where most people had been of French descent, the concert-goers looked African. They say the devil has the best tunes, but at this Christian gospel concert in the park God competed strongly. There was a band from South Africa, a lead singer in the sharpest suit you ever saw and a male chorus-line in brown pyjamas with gold spots who pranced and sang till the crowd howled and clapped. I was yelling out HALLELUJAHS before I'd even noticed. I took photos of people because it didn't seem awkward. Everyone smiled: grannies in their straw hats and fluoro pink and green blouses with yellow handbags bags and scarlet patent-leather shoes, a guy taking photographs wearing a T-shirt that said 'Women Lead Africa', and a seven-year-old boy and girl paddling palms on the grass.

Back at the crowded yacht club where we had managed to squeeze *White Cloud*, we met Kim again. He was a surveyor for an oil company and had managed to organise his life so he spent a year working and then a year sailing. Over dinner he asked, 'What do you miss most about life ashore?' I was shocked. Yachties rarely ask questions like that and it seemed almost heretical to suggest that land life might have any appeal.

I took a while. 'An independent life doing something I'm competent at.'

'Family and friends,' said Allen. 'How about you?'

'Intellectual stimulation.'

That was what I had meant but I had circumvented saying so because there was another taboo against implying that a life of cruising did not provide it.

Kim had found a way to do the sailing life, but it's rare to find a well-paid job you can pick up and put down as he did, and most yachties had to choose between land life and cruising. Family and friends were what most people missed, or admitted to missing, and if there was any one reason, apart from being forced by lack of money or ill health, that pulled people back to land, it was relationships. Yachties are mostly quite sociable people and there is a strong sense of community, yet it is always transitory, people move on, and on. We were missing real friendships, the kind where you have arguments and misunderstand-ings but you work through them and don't just sail away.

The Seychelles government controls imports and foreign exchange, which leads to chaotic shortages. The whole island ran out of toilet paper the week before we arrived because the factory that manufac-tures it did not have enough foreign exchange to buy the necessary raw materials. People learnt to stock up when items were available at the state-run supermarket, but despite the grumbles of expatriates, people looked healthy and well fed and clothed. Indeed the United Nations development reports show that the Seychelles ranked higher on an index measuring health, life expectancy, knowledge and standard of living than any place we visited except for Singapore. The low infant mortality rates, birth rates and longer female life expectancy might be because, though you may not have been able to buy toilet paper, there were diaphragms aplenty, piles of them, in display cases in the Chinese general store—or perhaps they were some strange kind of mushroom.

Allen installed the spare impeller, thus fixing the overheating prob-lem in our engine, and even found motorbike chain so he was able to repair the steering properly. We were ready to sail—except that we were unable to provision. We had plenty of toilet paper, but needed other items that were unavailable. We went shopping each day, buying what we needed as we saw it, before supplies ran out again.

Once, in the queue, a man asked, 'Where are you from?'

'Australia.'

'Thought so,' and, seeing we were about to have lunch, asked, 'Mind if I join you?'

Michael told us about a regular monthly meeting of Australian expatriates on the beach at Beau Vallon and invited us to join him and his family there the next day. He was a psychologist employed to advise local social workers about children's issues, as the Seychelles had recently become a signatory to the UN Convention on the Rights of the Child. He was frustrated by courts that would order a woman who sought a restraining order to go home to a violent husband. There was no concept of fostering, so abused children were sent to one of the two over-full orphanages. He told us that generational beating had led to a lack of attachment formation; adults beaten as children became parents who beat or abandoned their children. The legal system, in which judges were appointed for only five years at a time, resulted in little challenge to the status quo in which violence towards children was ubiquitous. 'What do you do? I saw a woman the other day and she was typical, she had no idea how to parent without violence. "My mum beat me and it didn't do me any harm." Yet she never visited her daughter in the orphanage where she had been taken for her own protection.' This was a different view from the sunny, cheerful island I saw. People working in child welfare always see the underbelly of a culture, the families whose dysfunction is kept hidden from view.

Wandering round the art galley we met Stephen, an American painter, scruffy in jeans, hanging his exhibition of portraits. He invited us to the opening, which he hosted impeccably in a white linen suit, talking to everyone as if they were the most interesting person on earth for between two and five minutes. One of the paintings was of Kanti, reputedly the most famous Seychellois, a vegan octogenarian regarded as an expert on almost everything to do with the Indian Ocean, named on a UN Global 500 Roll of Honour and a Fellow of the Royal Geographical Society as well as being an artist, writer and skilled cook. Renowned for his ability to charm young women while confiding that he been celibate for over half a century, ascetic in his tastes while claiming friendship with the rich and famous, he energetically embodied paradox. 'What do you think of my portrait?' he asked with glee. It caught his impishness but, at the time, I did not know him well enough to tell him so.

A few days later I visited Kanti in his shop in the middle of town, where he sold all kinds of odds and ends, fabric and thread, postcards, whatever the ship had brought in.

'I hope this is not an inconvenient time to call.'

'Not at all, I always have time for an intelligent woman,' replied Kanti gallantly, leading me through to a back room lined with books, hundreds of books about the Seychelles and the Indian Ocean, including a vast collection of rare illustrated books on natural history. 'Without books I'd go mad. Show me your hand. You're not a Libra, you're Scorpio.' My birthday is on the cusp, but I have identified myself as Libra for the bulk of my life, insofar as one does identify, for social purposes, with something in which one has no belief at all. It is bizarre, isn't it, that intelligent people read their horoscopes yet sigh over the superstitions of people from other cultures? Still, having my palm read was seductive: who can resist being told sweet nothings dressed up as mumbo jumbo? Perspicacious mumbo jumbo. Kanti told me I was wasting energy on endless circular arguments about what I was doing—energy that could be used more creatively.

Then he took me upstairs to see his living quarters. It was a typical Port Victoria building, timber with a steeply pitched tin roof and dormer windows—French provincial in the tropics—abundant chaos, books and more books, stone and wood Buddhas, Chinese ceramics and a fabulous shell collection, a serious one, in a cabinet full of ultra-shallow drawers. It was like the storehouse for a museum, room after room, leading eventually to a simple kitchen fragrant with roasted spices. The house itself was ramshackle: the boards were all higgledy-piggledy colours, some greens, some blues and some ancient bare timbers, the staircases steep and narrow as ladders. There was a healing room, through which a gentle cooling breeze blew even at equatorial noon, where Kanti practised Ayurvedic medicine. He showed me photographs and press cuttings of himself with celebrities and film stars, from the days before he had lost his villa to the socialist state and his multimillion-dollar antique collection to thieves. Rascal, healer, scholar, merchant, cook, artist, millionaire, ascetic, imp—Kanti at 80 was still living each moment with an intensity which, like that of a Zen master, forced lively response. I still don't know if he was more ego-maniac or saint but I loved his eccentricity, his vigorous generosity and the lingering poison of his parting shot: 'Don't waste your energy. Use it to help people.'

One Sunday there was a rally to celebrate the reign of the president of the Seychelles, France-Albert René, who took power in a socialist coup over 30 years ago. The whole of the Seychellois army was out in the streets parading. Everyone was wearing T-shirts that read '*Lekur dan Lekur*', which translates as 'heart in heart'. I hadn't seen soldiers march-ing for years, and when you do see soldiers in the West these days they are usually solemn and impersonal. These soldiers were laughing and waving to their friends in the crowd, and it was hard to imagine them fighting, which made it a bit easier to deal with the fact that I was there watching the parade at all—we had to do something while we waited for wheat flour and rice to reappear in the shops. And we both had haircuts for the first time in months. Just because you are out in a boat for months on end doesn't mean you want to look like a faded old scarecrow; it is just what happens.

One day when I went shopping there was almost a profusion: there was whole-nut peanut butter, maple syrup, wholemeal strong flour, good eggs and toilet paper in the shops, even if most of the shelves remained bare. A ship had come in. I stocked up with dry provisions, meat and groceries. Still I was reluctant to go from a place I felt so com-fortable. Perhaps it was because when I spoke French there people answered instead of looking at me with that peculiar Gallic disdain the metropolitan French reserve for anglophones who mangle their language.

As well as waiting for provisions, we had been waiting for a spell of no wind so we could re-install the furling foresail we had taken down to repair. Finally it came and we had no more excuses to linger. The last day, I sewed the sail and made two big loaves using freshly bought Canadian wholemeal flour while Allen did the usual engine maintenance. In the evening we went to a concert of local music and dance. There were steel drums, an ancient Belgian button-accordionist, classical Indian dance, dances like boot-scooting crossed with hip-waggling sambas, and an extraordinary dance in which betwigged people, looking like bundles of grass or trees, shuffled around the stage until one of them fell over apparently and gave birth to a baby twiggy bundle, whereupon another woman came and kicked her. I never discovered what it was all about because the next morning we set sail for Africa.

We had hoped to stop briefly, and unofficially, at Praslin, an island about 20 miles north of Mahé, but the wind was blowing at around 30 knots and it was more comfortable to sail west, straight to Kenya. Soon, however, I was berating myself for not expecting the worst. I had imagined I would prepare some meals for the voyage at anchor off Praslin, but now we were underway in very blustery conditions and it was impossible to cook. Every time I moved around the boat I bruised another bit of my body. Meanwhile Allen was abed, being horribly seasick. The weather was marvellous really, blue skies and a stiff wind in the right direction, but I was almost jealous of the characters in a novel I was reading who were on a cruise on the *QE 2*. Theoretically we were enjoying perfect sailing conditions, the kind racing crews relish, but I preferred to go more slowly and be able to eat and sleep in comfort. By the next day the regular strong wind had built up the waves and, though we were making good speed, *White Cloud* felt like one of those fun-park rides you wish would end. By nightfall it had been raining for hours and the solar panels had not had enough sun, so I started the engine to recharge the batteries for an hour or so and went to bed.

It must rank as one of life's least pleasant experiences, to go below in a boat and find oneself ankle-deep in water. It evokes that sinking feeling. Within seconds of my yelling out, 'It's very wet down here,' Allen and I were both frantically ripping out carpets and cushions and boards in search of the hole. At times like this we were glad we had removed the fixed cupboards that previous owners had installed. Many sailing boats are prettily fitted out with fancy timberwork with no regard for the need to be able to access all parts of the hull at any-time. You don't need to be arguing about whether or not to sacrifice the expensive teak panelling when searching for a leak. We were baf-fled, since we had not felt or heard any impact, but it was not the time for pondering. We were nearly 200 miles from the Seychelles and 800 miles from the coast of Africa, in a storm, at night, with water fill-ing the boat. There was no sign of a hole in the exposed hull of the aft cabin. The water was coming through a drainage hole from further back, the lazarette, but because the drainage hole from the cabin to the bilge further forward was blocked, the water was building up, rising towards our shins.

Allen poked some wire through the hole and the water drained away, but it was still coming in. The bilge pump was not going to keep up with the flow.

'Grab a torch and have a look in the lazarette,' said Allen.

I rushed off, but before I got there I heard a roar, 'Cut the engine!' I hurtled into the cockpit and slammed the fuel line shut and stuck my head down the hatch to see what was going on.

Allen looked up triumphantly. Though he was still sloshing around in the cabin, the water was slowly draining away. He explained that, as he suspected, the engine water outlet hose had come loose so water was pumping into the boat instead of out through the hull.

But how had he known this?

'The water's warm, didn't you notice?'

I hadn't. That's one of the differences between us, and it's why there is no one I'd rather be with in a life-threatening emergency. I was thinking, 'So this is how it ends. I wonder if Bee and Lucy will ever find out what happened or whether they will one day tell their children, "Your grandmother set sail for Africa but she never arrived."' Allen was thinking, 'This water is warm, that means it is not coming directly from the ocean but from the engine-cooling system.'

We put on harnesses to go on deck and empty the contents of the lazarette into the cockpit. Waves washed over us as we lurched and clung. As Allen had guessed, the violent movement had dislodged items stored in the lazarette and they had knocked the hose off the outlet pipe at the back of the boat. He reattached the hose and we got everything back, spare anchors, lines, fenders and jerry cans. Crisis over, Allen reverted to vomiting and I went back to bed to try to get a couple of hours sleep before my watch. But relief couldn't override the adrenaline and I lay listening to the storm and thinking these islands were like the hidden treasure in a fairytale, encircled by a magical barrier of violent weather.

The next morning I tuned into *Kiore*'s sked and told Tony about our night. 'There are some very funny weather patterns down south, there's a high that seems to have doubled back leaving a ridge over Madagascar and Mozambique.' Everyone who had left Chagos was facing storms, and Paula and Rick on *Leviathan* had not kept their radio sked with the other yachts bound for Madagascar for three days. 'Keep an ear out for them will you?'

I was doing the skeds and navigation, anything that involved going being below, since Allen was still coping with seasickness and could do little other than sleep or sit up on watch. He was often queasy for a day or so, but this time it continued and I was worried that he would get weak if he did not eat soon. By the fourth day he said he had the worst headache he had ever known. I gave him a Panadol and sent him back to bed.

'I wish there was something I could do to make it better.'

'Shoot me and throw me overboard. Put me out of my misery.'

'It's not that bad, is it?'

He gave that look and I tiptoed away.

Two days later I wrote in my diary, 'He's better! He's human!' Seasickness is awful, it reduces people to miserable wretches. I am amazed again and again that so many cruising yachties admit to suffering from it. I had gone for a rest after a lunch Allen had felt too ill to eat. When I returned on deck a couple of hours later there was a cheerful man tucking into the saved lunch. He was transformed: the lines had eased, he looked pink and healthy instead of shrivelled and green, and already the amnesia that also affects sufferers, wiping away the memory of anything except halcyon days, had set in.

We read and watched birds try to land—'touch and go' it's called in a plane—and had a silly giggly conversation about what to call the bits of spectacles that latch over the ears. Wings? Ear hooks? Our vocabulary seemed to be disappearing overboard. I was reading *Lempriere's Dictionary*. I had left the Seychelles with several books I'd bartered for. This novel by Lawrence Norfolk was full of nautical words I shamefully did not understand, like 'pinnace' and 'carrack', and I took to reading dictionaries again. It reminded me of how I used to collect words as a child. I was so happy when I was standing behind a leopard at the zoo in Colwyn Bay when it pissed on me because then I was able to say I had not known leopards were retromingent. I'd been saving that word for a long time.

After the fear and seasickness stage, followed by the silly stage, came the musing phase of the voyage. I made a list of what I valued most:

Safety

Warmth

Food

Sleep

Health

Company

That was the order the words hit the page at dusk, rushing to write before it got too dark to see. They were simple desires. By safety, I didn't mean those soul-destroying attempts to protect oneself from the normal risks of being alive by increasing the use of surveillance and regulation, or staying at home and watching television. I was just acknowledging that being so often in the middle of life-threatening situations could get trying. Rereading months later I was surprised to see warmth made the list but, although we were on the equator, it was cold at night and, for the first time since travelling up the coast of Western Australia, we were closing the clear plastic cockpit covers at night on the windward side and wrapping ourselves in sarongs to keep warm.

After only seven days at sea we were just 36 miles from Africa but, having made extraordinarily good time, we suddenly seemed to be getting no closer to land. We spoke to Tony on the radio and he advised us to head as far south as possible because of the strong north-setting current that was pulling us up the coast. 'Aim for Mombasa.' There was no sign of the vast continent, not even a fishing boat, and the current was terribly strong. Even motor-sailing and heading as close to the wind as we could, we only just managed to reach the marker-leads on the cliffs just south of Kilifi Creek that led us through the break in the reef as the sun was halfway down the sky. We headed straight for the cliffs and then, as soon as we were through the reef, veered to starboard to follow the marker-leads into the creek itself.

Creek was not the word I'd have used for the wide, gentle waterway that opened up before us to become a huge lagoon surrounded by majestic green trees, baobabs, palms and exuberant flowering things— all so big, so splendidly and greenly thriving. Nestled amid the lush verdure along the cliffs were gracious whitewashed buildings with thatched roofs or crenellated walls, surrounded by park-like lawns and gardens. We took down the sail and edged cautiously upriver towards the powerlines and road bridge that spanned the creek, preventing yachts with tall masts from going any further upstream.

'Are we clear, are we going to get under it, do you think?' asked Allen as we approached.

'I can't tell from this angle. I'd have to climb the mast. It looks as if it's going to hit the bridge,' I said nervously.

'Well, is it or isn't it?'

'I don't know, there's no way to tell just by looking from here.'

Allen was exasperated.

'Yes, yes, we're fine, the mast will make it easily. No worries. Is that better?' I asked, ensuring that if we were about to be electrocuted we would die squabbling.

We swanned easily under the bridge and the powerlines, past the boatyard and the sunken ferry, to where six yachts rested at anchor under a cliff. At the top of this cliff perched Tony's house. Upstream in the far distance the receding layers of blue hills were darkening against the dusky pink sky. Nothing I had ever heard about Africa prepared me for this first encounter. No one had told me it was so heartbreakingly beautiful. I fell in love, as you do, and even as I fell I knew it was an impossible love, both irresistible and unrequited. There was no defence, nothing to do but sit on deck sipping a gin and tonic.

INTO AFRICA

Kenya

June – August 2001

THE BOAT SANK.

GET OVER IT.

Message on the T-shirt of a

passenger on a bus in Mombasa

'*Kiore, Kiore, Kiore.* This is *White Cloud, White Cloud.*'

'*White Cloud, Kiore,* how are you this morning?'

'Fine thanks, Tony. And you?'

Since leaving Chagos I had spoken each morning to Tony and I was looking forward to meeting the man whose voice had helped me through some bad days. In the morning we went ashore. We climbed the crazy-paved stairway that wound through a bougainvillea forest to the house at the top of the cliff. I'd been charmed by Tony's placid urbanity over the radio, by his professional, calm, modulated radio manner, imagining an old-style BBC newsreader type, suave but gentlemanly. I was dumbfounded to meet a scruffy little man with a few horrible teeth, and hair and moustache like a mangy terrier.

'You're exactly the same in real life as you are on the radio—breathless,' he said accusingly.

It was just as well that I was breathless because it rescued me from responding, 'Well, you aren't a bit how you sounded—well groomed and handsome.'

Tony's wife, Daphne, wore frocks and her hair in a bun and was motherly in a briskly English way, though she herself is South African. She took all newly arrived yachties under her wing, driving them to the customs office, introducing them to the local shopkeepers and being a reliable source of everything else one would generally need, from refills for gas bottles to information. She and Tony painlessly inducted arriving yachties into the ways of this new continent, saving us time and easing frustration. There were two dogs too: a gruff little terrier (like Tony) and a gigantic but soppy ridgeback called Lulu, who was optimistically referred to as a guard dog.

Inside the house for tea and muffins, Tony told us the story on his mind. Days earlier, when we were in the midst of stormy weather, he had mentioned that *Leviathan* had lost radio contact for three days but he had only now discovered that Rick and Paula had set off their EPIRB (emergency position indicating radio beacon) several days ago, at the same time as they first lost radio contact. A 406 EPIRB is carried by most offshore vessels, as well as aeroplanes, and sends a message to a satellite that gives the identity and position, to within a mile, of the vessel in distress. Each part of the world's oceans is under the jurisdiction of a country that is responsible for coordinating rescue efforts. In this case, *Leviathan* set off the EPIRB in the Indian Ocean not far north of Madagascar. The message was picked up in Réunion. Nothing was done. After six hours the EPIRB stopped transmitting and the officials in Réunion assumed it had been turned off. No yachtie sets off an EPIRB unless the yacht is sinking. It is an action of last resort because if

you set off a distress signal that will trigger a rescue effort, you know
you will have to abandon your boat. No one in Réunion did anything
at all. 'I've been phoning everywhere, South Africa, Réunion, it's a
shambles but at last I got the South Africans to agree to notify Miami,
where it was registered, and see what they want to do about it.'

'Why didn't anyone in Réunion do anything?'

'The boat was not their responsibility. It was an American-
registered yacht and it was in trouble in an area under the jurisdiction
of Delhi, thousands of miles away, and India doesn't have the resources
to go looking for a couple of tourists.'

'But couldn't the people in Réunion have at least alerted shipping
that there was a yacht in trouble? After all, there were other yachts
around. If they'd known *Leviathan* was in trouble they'd have gone to
look.'

'Yes, but I think the problem was that no one knew what to do.
There's no coordination or communication. The people in Réunion
didn't know I ran a marine net here in Kenya or that Alistair runs one
from South Africa. They do now, but it's too late to help *Leviathan* I fear.'

When, due to Tony's persistence, the US authorities were informed,
they sent a search plane, but two weeks had passed since the original
distress call was sent out and *Leviathan* has never been seen again. Paula
and Rick never reached their new home in Rarotonga. Their cry for
help, beeping through space and alerting the world to their distress,
went unanswered. Each of us was subdued over morning tea, alone
and quietly lost in the deep wild dark of the ocean.

Kilifi, we quickly discovered, was where wealthy white Kenyans traditionally have their waterfront retreats or retirement homes, which
explained the extraordinarily beautiful, thatched, whitewashed mega-
cottages we had seen as we sailed in: home counties rustic idyll crossed

with exotic tropical splendour. All of them had swarms of servants, though nobody uses the word. Wealthier Africans invariably had servants too but there were very few of them in Kilifi. In the advertisements for the Kenya Commercial Bank gold cards, 'for those who appreciate the finer things in life', there was a photomontage of a man in a suit, at his desk in a high-rise office, playing golf, relaxing with a skimpily dressed woman by the side of a pool sipping cocktails, and beside a new suburban mansion. Each one a Westernised consumer capitalist fantasy. The advertised benefits included lower than normal bank rates for those with a bank balance over 20000 Kenyan shillings, about $A450. Nothing, except the skin colour of the people themselves, suggested Africa, let alone Kenya, as if everyone's highest aspiration were to become part of a homogeneous global urbanity. Few Kilifi Africans could dream of a bank balance, let alone that kind of bank balance. They tended to live in humble thatched mud houses, with gardens where they grew food crops such as maize and cashew nuts. Elsewhere, on the urban fringes, the huts were often very rough shacks of timber, tin or even cardboard.

As soon as we arrived Daphne offered the services of her 'chaps' who would do maintenance tasks on boats or look after them at night for a ridiculously modest fee while their owners were travelling abroad or up-country. It is difficult to find secure anchorages where one can safely leave a yacht, and we had already been persuaded that we must go on safari, so we were glad of a chap to sleep on board at night. We never really planned to go on safari. We could not possibly afford those advertised in travel agents' glossy brochures where great white hunter manqués in designer khaki and lugging obscenely long lenses were served with cocktails in a treetop lodge while watching the leopards come to baited hides. It wasn't just the money either; this was not the sort of thing I thought I did. It reeked of colonialism and decadence.

'Of course you'll be going on safari. Look, take these with you to look at,' said Daphne, handing me timetables and pamphlets galore. 'All the yachties go on these camping trips, it's not expensive. You can take a bus to Nairobi and book one there. Ask Glen and Dave about it, they've just come back.' We did and, faced with the opportunity to actually go and camp on the Masai Mara among lions and elephants, giraffe and zebra, and even though a cheap safari cost more than we could really afford, any ideological misgivings disappeared. I wanted to go on safari more than anything else in the world. With the pathetic excuse that the weather was preventing us from going south, we went.

Colonialism and decadence were on my mind. There had been an article in the *Daily Nation* saying that Kenyans did not understand why tourist operators were calling for a cut in the cost of visas. At US$50, the cost was making Kenya less attractive as a tourist destination, but tourists were seen as big spenders who are rich enough to waste money on 'travel for its own sake'. In a country where half the population does not know the source of their next meal, driving around to look at animals for fun looks pretty decadent. We had been for lunch with some yachties who were house-sitting in Kilifi. We started with drinks on the patio overlooking the creek, followed by an Indian smorgasbord served in the dining room with silver service, damask tablecloths and napkins. We were served by women in blue and white gingham uniforms with glistening white cloths tied around their heads, in the style of that worn by Little Black Sambo's mother. After lunch we walked back down the cliff to the dinghy and motored back to the boat. All the houses on the river had waterfrontage, so that the few remaining local fisherfolk had no access. While we were in Kilifi, the last empty block, from where they had been able to launch their boats, was sold. It was a world I imagined had ended with independence. It was horrible. It was seductive. It seemed wrong but it felt nice. The rich, including all Westerners—even those of relatively modest means—had servants and large guard dogs. They kept their valuables securely locked up all the time and made sure all the doors and windows were heavily barred and bolted at night—some people even had an inner set of iron bars surrounding their bedroom—and took a chap to guard the car in town when they were shopping. It was a life of luxury. It came at a price and I was complicit in it. I appeared rich in a country where most people lived in poverty, and it seemed to be my fault. I was uncomfortable. I had never been on the wrong side like this before.

We left Kilifi for Nairobi early in the morning, having been given strict instructions not to wear anything valuable and to hold on tight to our luggage. The bus ride was long and tiring. I knew there would only be one short break for lunch and, as usual, it was necessary to try to balance the fine line between overstretching the bladder and getting seriously dehydrated. Later, when I met a Finnish aid worker who had lived and worked in Africa for years, she told me she was still baffled by her colleagues' apparent lack of any need to pee, eat, or even drink anything all day, even on field trips. 'I tell them I get headaches if I don't eat so I always take sandwiches and some water, but I feel so greedy. Sometimes they buy bananas on the road. It's better when I go with Mwanaidi. She's always hungry and thirsty and has to go to the toilet quite often. Tanzanians have a nice expression for "I need to use the bathroom". They say, "I would like to look for some medicinal herbs in the bush." I was told that I should use this expression if I needed to pee when travelling by a bus.' I too had been told that it was acceptable to request a toilet stop but I think it just meant the bus would stop at the side of the road. You still have the problem of how to effect the collection of herbs with dignity.

We arrived in Nairobi in mid afternoon. We thought we were prepared. Knowing the bus station was on the wrong side of town, we had carefully studied our maps so we knew exactly where to go, but we became temporarily disoriented because the sign for Accra Avenue was pointing down Tom Mboya Street. Our purposeful stride became a hesitant meander for a few seconds as we read the sign and decided it was bent, but that was long enough: a man grabbed at Allen's wrist, tore off his watch and ran away. Around us people stared and walked on. There must have been 20 witnesses to the robbery but no one said or did anything. Like us, they just watched the thief go.

'Why did you wear your watch? Everyone told us not to.'

'I didn't think anyone would bother to steal a plastic one like that. It wasn't very expensive.'

'It's not the point. It was waterproof and reliable, and now you don't have a watch and everyone warned us. Mine's in my pocket. Why didn't you listen?' Worry had reduced me to nagging.

'I told you, it wasn't that important. I can get another watch. It doesn't matter.'

'Yes, it does. It does matter.'

It mattered because if someone could come up to a big man in broad daylight on a busy street in the centre of the city and rip a watch from off his wrist—then what was safe? Was it because we were white that no one helped? Would it have been different if the thief had been more violent? I was scared and vulnerable. I felt that anything could happen. I wanted to get off the streets as fast as I could.

When we arrived at the hotel, the noticeboard was full of warnings: not to have sex, not to carry more than we could afford to lose and to hand over all our valuables and money if confronted. We needed to go out to organise our safari but I was too tired to face the jungle of Nairobi streets straightaway. Instead I sat in the dingy hotel room and read in the paper that, according to Transparency International, Kenya was the fourth most corrupt country in the world. Most people in Kenya are poor. Teachers are paid A$30–100 per month and government doctors about A$300, yet a young student doing voluntary work for the UN told me the monthly rent for an average two-bedroom apartment she shared in Nairobi was A$900 per month. Her middle-class Parisian parents were paying. Allen was right. Almost everyone in Kenya needed his watch more than he did. We went for an early dinner in the misnamed Taverna Garden Hotel next door. It was devoid of both alcohol and any form of plant life, but we had little choice about where to eat, since no one walked around Nairobi after dark.

After breakfast we headed for the safari company that been recommended to us and then spent the next couple of days in the middle of the up-market hotel district where tourists could safely wander round art galleries, museums and bookshops. I felt so ignorant. In Kilifi, walking along the dirt road into town, we passed mud houses the colour of persimmons, and children ran out calling, 'Jambo, jambo, give me bonbons.' Their mothers, with their bright cotton kangas, the cloths they wrapped around their heads or hips or used as a baby sling, looked feminine and elegant. They smiled and greeted us. Yet I knew nothing of their lives. I searched out books by local authors, Grace Ogot and Ngugi wa Thiong'o, to help me make sense of what I could not understand. I do not know if it helped. I was confused by Ogot's stance regarding women, especially wives: I never knew whether she was being ironic or whether our worlds were just oceans apart.

'What do Kenyan women read?' I asked Nazin, who ran the bookshop. 'Self-help books by Afro-American preachers are very popular,' she told me, 'especially if they've been on Oprah. Joyce Meyer's *Eat and Stay Thin: Simple, Spiritual, Satisfying Weight Control* sells well.'

'Nothing by African women?'

'I've spoken with some American professors here who've worked with women here but they say they are too ashamed to write down their feelings.'

I wondered if that was the real issue or whether fiction had no place in Kenya, whether it is an art form that is peculiarly suited to cultures that valorise the individual and totally irrelevant to the lives of people with different cultural values. Or is it just economics? Only the very rich could afford spiritual weight loss. The rest mostly needed food.

Our safari company gave its clients free accommodation in its Nairobi offices in Moi Avenue, so we moved into a tent on the verandah of the ninth floor and listened to the traffic crashing and squealing all night. Throughout Nairobi, the public water supplies were available only at night, so the lavatories filled up and stank all day. The prospect of fire was alarming, since all the windows were barred, access to the fire escape was blocked and the lift only worked some of the time. Yet the people who worked in the office were friendly, cheerful, helpful and happy to let us practise our Swahili on them, though they were all first-language Kikuyu-speakers. Allen caused a sensation by going into the kitchen to make me a cup of tea. Where did I find him? No African man would make himself a cup of tea, let alone make one for his wife and, though it was undoubtedly nice, it was not quite manly—would I still respect him in the morning?

In our minibus, as well as the driver, Tom, who also acted as guide, were five other people. There were a couple of Scottish criminal lawyers.

'Why criminal law?'

'Family lawyers deal all day with people who are probably quite reasonable, nice people who happen to be temporarily behaving crazily: mad with grief, rage or jealousy. Our clients are unreasonable, behave offensively and are generally anti-social, but happen to be temporarily on their best behaviour. Moreover, they're grateful if you get them a lighter sentence than they expected. People fighting over custody or divorce settlements hate their lawyers whatever the outcome.'

The other three were medical students, one of whom had been doing voluntary work in a Ugandan hospital for children with neuro-logical problems, and at the campsite we joined several others doing voluntary work or environmental research. There was even someone who shared my interest in counteracting linguistic imperialism. People who start off as hopeless romantics and idealists and crazy optimists often become crusty with age, as if the world had disappointed them, when mostly they have disappointed themselves. It was enjoyable to be around young people who had not yet stopped believing they could do something to make the world better, even though many had already seen enough of the world to test their faith.

The drive to the Masai Mara took several hours. We talked and talked until we started to see animals along the roadside as we drove through the Rift Valley: zebra and buffalo and Thompson's gazelle, as well as the mixed herds of donkeys and sheep and cattle. Sometimes the zebras joined the domesticated herds. The boundaries of herd animals are fluid. After all, anything that does not eat you might be protection from being eaten, so everyone is welcome. I had felt stirrings of excitement when I saw the first zebra but once inside the reserve I felt like a three-year-old at Christmas. We arrived late in the afternoon but within minutes we saw giraffes and wildebeest, elephants and vultures, several kinds of deer, impala, topi and the little dik-dik, as well as a couple of lions. I had almost forgotten the feeling of being completely delighted and surprised by the magic of the world just as it is. I had seen all these animals in zoos and on film, but to see them in the wild in their own habitat was shockingly different, mainly because they were all together, all part of a whole.

We have become so unused to interacting with difference. Urban dwellers have so little experience with other species, except for things that were pets before I started travelling and had become *companion animals* when I got back (somehow highlighting the extent to which all

relationships are bound up in the politics of correct terminology).
I loved the mixedness of lives, the danger, the safety, the chaos and the
organisation, the complexity of a world in which there are many different beings. They are so large and there, living their lives out in the open.
Things bigger and stronger than people, things that eat us, things that
could put us in our place serve to remind us that we are not the only
creatures that share this little planet. It is like that underwater too, the
profusion of life around the reefs, fish and mammals and other forms of
life, all carrying on, interacting or not, as predators, as parasites, or in
symbiosis—all the different ways of being together. It makes the mono-
speciesness of our cities, and the way we stick not only around people,
but around people like us, seem terrifying. This was the manifestation
of god. Not the imaginary god-with-beard so beloved of men, but the
stripey god and the carrion-eating god, the big, fast pussy god playing
with her cubs and the god who waddles across the road in his shell. I
know, theoretically, that most life comes in the form of bacteria and
fungi and that even plants are a minority group in the scheme of things,
but it was when I saw so many different animals in one place that I was
able to feel comfortably small and unimportant, the way you do when
exceedingly happy.

In the soft light of morning, herds were grazing as we set off to do
more gawping. We drove all day, stopping only to eat a picnic lunch
under a thorn tree on a gentle hill in the middle of a plain from where
we could view any approaching wildlife. But the only life we encountered there was another minibus full of tourists. At times, there would
be a circle of minibuses almost surrounding a pair of lions or a line of
them facing a cheetah with her cubs in the distance. People get very
snobby about this, as if the experience of seeing an animal is diminished
if others share it too. I wanted to share it. I wanted my children to
come to Africa. I wanted everyone to do this just once and know how
marvellous and various are the lives on earth, especially at this place

where so many of the big mammals first evolved. And anyway, weren't we just being human, travelling in hordes for protection and company, as we have always done?

The numbers of human beings, even with all their steel-armouring paraphernalia, seemed insignificant alongside the hundreds of thousands of herd animals, especially the zebra and wildebeest. Seeing a few zebras standing around in a zoo is dull. They are dull. In the wild, *punda milia* (literally translating as 'striped-donkey' in Swahili) are alert, compactly squeezed into skins that seem always a size too small, and fun to watch. They do not want to be alone and move as part of a huge group, hundreds at a time. If by chance they lose their herd they will join up with some wildebeest rather than travel alone, easy prey. Wildebeest are gnu. So gnu were not figments of my childhood imagination, it's just that everyone calls them by the Dutch 'wildebeest' these days, which is a pity since the indigenous Khoi term 'gnu' is gnicer. We saw almost everything I had imagined I would, and far more than I had expected I might possibly see on safari: the ones I knew well, such as big cats, elephants, hippos and flamingoes, and others I had never seen before, such as hyrax, small furry cousins to the elephant, and dik-dik, gazelle the size of cocker spaniels. Walking by Lake Elementaitia, we heard the thousands of flamingoes, an infinity of pink, all buzzing, like trumpets or trombones but with no voice, just a low vibration. Further on at Nakuru we saw a white rhino and her baby, as well as baboons and warthogs, impala and leopards in the distance. Not everyone was so satisfied. A woman in another minibus was most disgruntled, having come all the way from the United States especially to see a tiger.

I began thinking I should learn more, not just sound as if I was collecting animals like a trainspotter, and be able to make informed observations about animal behaviour, about global eco-systems, poaching, about the competition between man and other species for the world's diminishing resources. There are so many arguments and issues. Is poaching caused by the inexhaustible desire of Asian medicine for rhinoceros horn or by corruption in Kenya? Does the tourist industry encourage the protection of animals at the cost of the livelihood of the fast-growing local population? But these were issues to debate another time. On safari it was more than enough to recapture, albeit briefly, childish wonder, and to find that, although Santa Claus and happily-ever-after proved to be fizzers, sometimes dreams really do come true.

Our plan, after arriving in East Africa, was to travel slowly down the Tanzanian coast until winter was past and then continue down via Mozambique to South Africa. The bottom of the boat needed anti-fouling, since it was growing forests of weed, becoming a mobile reef, so we arranged to get *White Cloud* hauled out at the boatyard where we could paint her. The new boatyard owner was fixing up the boat-lifter, and another yacht, used for charters, was booked in to make some repairs. We would have to wait. We puddled around doing the endless maintenance tasks that boat-dwellers do, sanding and varnishing, fixing and patching. Every Saturday there was a lunch at the boatyard. Any yachties in Kilifi generally went along, as did many of Kilifi's wealthier residents. We met several of the local regulars at the boatyard lunches. We were not at all their usual kind of people but we side-stepped talking about politics and thus stumbled past muster. We were stuck and bored and, though we were dying to get involved somehow in a different kind of life, it was interesting in the meantime to glimpse into the world of the leftover whites in Kenya. Their children generally live elsewhere, in England or Australia or South Africa, but they have called it home for so long they cannot leave, even though it is hopeless and they know it.

In Kenya I remembered how it was to be English. At the boatyard we met a man who said, 'Come for drinks at twelve.'

We went.

'It'll be lunch won't it?' Allen asked me.

'No, he said drinks. That means he'll give us drinks and then we go home again.'

'Whoever heard of asking someone for drinks at twelve and then not offering them lunch. That's lunchtime.'

'Well, that's how it was done in England,' I explained. 'Drinks means drinks.'

'I don't believe it, I bet he'll give us lunch.'

'Bet he won't. I know.' When I went back to England years before, I told him, three of us went to a party, and I persuaded the other two we didn't need to eat. No one had actually stipulated dinner, but who'd have a party that started at 7.30 pm and not feed you? The hosts had pots of money and it was at a swish hotel, yet all they had to eat were mingy nibbles. Plenty of champagne, but we were starving and everyone was cross with me. 'Believe me,' I repeated, 'it will be drinks.'

Our host offered us a beer and, at ten past twelve, when a grave African man started laying the table for one, it was plain that we were not invited for lunch. Our host had left England in the fifties—'It was awful you know, after the war'—to find the place England had been When We Were Very Young. The Never-Never Land where Christopher Robin still went down with Alice, the clock had stopped at ten to three and there was honey still for tea. This parody of England in the dying days of empire lingers on in Kenya even now, with its chaps who still say 'crikey' and 'orf'—as in 'orf the planet'. John boasted about his wealthy banker son while he sat in clothes that looked as if they had come from an op shop. He was waited on as he ate his Sunday lunch alone while his wife—'that was the old bat on the phone'—visited

family back home. He reminded me of the dormouse sleeping amid
the chrysanthemums yellow and white, dreaming he was still in a bed
of delphiniums blue and geraniums red.

A couple of weeks passed and we were still waiting to haul the boat
out, so we took a bus to Lamu. The bus trip took nine hours. There was
a danger that Somali *shiftas*—the Swahili word for bandit, perfectly
evoking both motion and untrustworthiness—would attack the
buses, so they travelled in convoy with guards armed with semi-auto-
matics. The buses were the only transport in the northern area of the
Kenya coast because it was unsafe for *matatus*, the mini-buses usually
used for short bus trips. We stopped to pick up and set down passengers
every few miles, so the long trip was even longer. The bus was stuffed
full of people and other creatures. I had a baby perched on my shoulder, someone's bags and white patent high-heeled shoes on my lap, and
a chicken in the overhead rack. We stopped for refreshments in a
remote village about an hour from the ferry to Lamu and, since no one
spoke English, we could order in Swahili. We even got what we
expected. Lamu is a charming old Swahili island on which there are no
motor vehicles, only donkeys. It was for a long time a haunt of only the
most intrepid travellers, but nowadays people fly in rather than make
the long bus and dhow trip. I felt a bit cheated—like when you climb
a mountain and find everyone else has taken the train, yet their souls
are quite healthy despite the lack of blisters and suffering.

Celebrities such as Princess Caroline still sequestered themselves in
the high-walled villas south of the main town of Lamu. It had once
been popular with backpackers too, but we saw few tourists in the
town. The people we met at our hotel turned out to be Stella and
Kenneth, an American missionary couple who had been in Kenya for
30 years, two Swedish medical students who had just been in Uganda
negotiating exchange programs with students there, and an American

archaeology student who was hoping to examine the DNA of skeletons on Lamu. Every evening we sat on the verandah at the front of the old hotel and looked out over the wide esplanade that ran alongside the wharf as people emerged to promenade: old men in their hats and robes engaged in earnest conversation, women in *bui-bui*, long black hooded coats, young men with dreadlocks and blonde holiday-romance girlfriends in tow, and little boys having donkey races.

One evening there was a huge commotion. It seemed as if every person on Lamu was on the waterfront and the air was humming with expectancy. We asked the hotel owner what was happening, was it a political meeting, had something happened?

'Oh, there is an important man arriving on a boat. They are waiting for him.'

'Must be very important, everyone seems very excited.'

'I wonder who the important person was,' I said to Kenneth later, 'the one they were all waiting for.'

He laughed. 'They were waiting for their *miraa*; the shipment was due in today.' Miraa leaf is chewed for its stimulant and aphrodisiac effects.

Kenneth told us that he and Stella had just been to dinner with the local imam to discuss joint strategies for dealing with AIDS. The imam had said that prostitution was rampant on the island. The women we saw were all shrouded in the black *bui-bui* worn by devout Muslim women along the coast, especially the offshore islands of Lamu and Zanzibar, which had long been the strongholds for Arab traders. He said it was a long-standing local joke that men should be sure to recognise their wives' feet or they might end up paying for what they could get free at home.

I was encouraged that religious leaders ate and joked together, even if it took the acknowledgement of the common enemy of AIDS to unite them. Trying to combat AIDS in Africa is difficult because of cultural attitudes. Stella told me she knew a man with an important position in the education department who had been dying. 'His wife asked me if I would drive him to the hospital. He looked terrible, very thin, you know the way people do when they have AIDS, and I asked the doctor about his prognosis but he said, "You know I can't tell you that." I said, "But what about Pauline and the children, they need to know," and so he wrote it on a piece of paper, "HIV positive". He died a few days later but everyone was angry with me for suggesting he'd had AIDS, his wife and his colleagues. They are all educated people but they said, "How can you say such a terrible thing?" Of course his brother inherited his wife, according to Luo custom, and he and his other wives all died too.'

Stella asked me about Australia, and wanted to know, as everyone did, whether it was as racist as everyone claimed. The only person she knew who had ever been there was a Kenyan friend in Nairobi, a lawyer and human rights activist who had spent some time doing land rights work in Australia when he was still a member of the Seventh Day Adventist church. He had gone along to services until he was approached by the pastor and told, 'The Aboriginal church is over there.'

'I'm not Aboriginal.'

'Well, the church for people like you is over there.'

He has never been inside a church since.

'There are some parts of Australia that are still very parochial and redneck,' I explained. 'Do you know where in Australia it happened?'

'Melbourne.'

'Oh, I hate stories like that. Everyone seems to have a racist story about Australia but it's not really that bad. I don't think it's worse than the UK, where I grew up. Most Australians aren't racist.' I did not know then that, before the end of the year, an event would occur that would firmly and embarrassingly establish Australia's reputation as racist in the eyes of the rest of world.

Back in Kilifi the boat that was being repaired before ours was still in the cradle, so we waited some more. We were tired of being tourists, voyeurs of other people's lives, and Kilifi was driving Allen to make remarks like 'I'd rather live in Mount Druitt', a sure sign of batty despair from someone who has spent his life escaping from a childhood in Sydney's western suburbs. Yet we wanted to stay in East Africa, to find out more about what lay beyond the stultifying comfort of Kilifi. Initially I was seduced by the pervasive beauty, the pink softness of the air, which is like wearing rose-tinted spectacles and turns everything into the romantic Africa of big animals, exotic people and impossible dreams. But that wasn't what made me want to stay. I had already sailed to more beautiful exotic places than I had ever dreamed of. It was something more, a fascination with a place that seemed to exemplify, more than anywhere I have ever been, the complex, crazy muddle of human life. The consequences of greed, hatred and ignorance, the human traits that arise ceaselessly and are the cause of all suffering, seemed more raw here, the interconnectedness of life more real. It was impossible to fool myself that other people's suffering wasn't my problem, that the poverty, hunger and disease and unrest in the Third World was unconnected to me. If I turned away and ignored it, I would be cutting off a part of myself. If I had an impossible dream it was to do something that would allow us to stay and become involved and perhaps even be mildly useful. Allen felt the same and we decided to look for opportunities to do some work.

Down at the boatyard the repairs on the charter boat were eventually finished after six weeks, and the boat-lifter would be ours, but it was neap tides and the other boat would have to wait another week, till the next spring tide, to relaunch. We had watched the slow progress and realised that many of the problems were because the boatyard was so rundown and everything was held together with string and prayer. The new owner was planning improvements, but at that time the main improvement had been the extensions to the bar and the introduction of chic gingham cloth napkins at the Saturday lunches. The eagerly awaited new boat-lifter was not yet in operation. After all this time watching the palaver fixing the other yacht, we became reluctant to put *White Cloud* on the rickety, rusting cradle on the crumbling slipway. Yet the antifouling was urgent, so we did what we swore we would never do. We careened her.

Tony was delighted. He had been urging us to do this from the beginning—'Just run it up onto the beach, our chaps know exactly what to do'—and had seemed rather miffed that we had even considered using the boatyard. But it was not his boat, and driving your boat onto a beach has the same degree of instinctive appeal as driving your car over the edge of a cliff. At high tide, just before dawn, we headed for the lights on the shore, the torches held by Tony's chaps who had placed sandbags on the beach the previous day and, like wreckers who lure boats aground to be looted, guided our boat to run aground in the shadowy dark. *White Cloud* was stuck. As the light came up, the waters went down and we tied a halyard from the main mast to a sturdy mangrove tree and hauled ourselves over sideways as the tide went out, so that the boat would not tip over suddenly. By this stage we were literally climbing up the walls. The chaps scrubbed and painted the hull as the tide receded and were finished almost before the tide had turned. We sat on the beach anxiously waiting for another six painful hours to see if she would ever float again. Our home lay on her side on the beach like a big sick animal. It was a beautiful moment when we felt the earth move and the depth sounder recorded water beneath the keel again. The worst part was knowing we would have to go through it all again the next day to do the other side, but we had been invited to a party that night and it provided a remedial dosage of distraction.

We had dinghied across the creek to the boatyard on Sunday for lunch as usual and found that there were many more people than had been there previously. June and July are when white Kenyans go 'home' to England but by August they were drifting back. A woman wove over to us, her fourth gin and tonic in one hand, a cigarette-in-holder in the other. 'You sailed here, I heard. Tell me, did you see whales—the animals, not that ghaaastly little country?' She had a point. It is only through the soft focus of nostalgia that my homeland has become more charming. When I left I had thought it was ghastly too, but my hackles were bristling. It's like family. One may grumble freely about one's own, but if one is critical of someone else's then their reptile-mind will reassert itself. Watch the clenched fist, the throbbing vein, the twitch. The oblivious woman was rescued by the arrival of a bulky man with streetwise eyes. 'Hello, Serena, coming to my party on Monday? I don't know who you two are but come as well. I live there,' he said, waving vaguely towards a whitewashed palace on the cliff on the opposite shore. 'Just park your dinghy at the hotel. I own the jetty, so they can't complain, there's a path up from there.' I wonder if I told him it was frightfully nice of him to ask. It was like that. Words like *frightfully* and *gosh* were popping out of my mouth but, though my vowels had shifted back to the days of boarding school elocution lessons, I hadn't quite mastered the tone of exasperated boredom nor the predilection for conversations about 'these people' as in 'these people have no sense of time / haven't a clue about how to run a business / were much better off under the British, they'll tell you that themselves'.

So on Monday night we scrambled up the cliffs in the dark, not quite finding the path, following the buzz that led over the rolling lawns towards the conversation and lights on the ballroom-sized verandah. It was a *damned fine bash*, plenty of food and good wine and everyone got rather *squiffy*. It became easy to understand why people stayed, even though many of them said they were bored, passing the time building boats or playing bridge. Apart from us, everyone knew each other, and it was still possible to afford to live in a comfortable pseudo-colonial world of big houses and servants and acres of well-tended lawns. But there was a price too. Health care and security were a constant worry. This was the country where many of them had been born, or spent most of their adulthood and, although there were tensions and layers of social distinction that would have taken a decade or two to unravel and interpret, it was a community; people knew each other and minded each other's business. After being transient for so long, making friends and then saying goodbye, I envied people the knotty rough ties of community. Although it was not a community I wanted to belong to, it was plain that for those Europeans who had remained in Kenya after independence it was the perfect retirement home.

On Wednesday I went to a meeting of the East Africa Women's League. Daphne took me and another Australian yachtie who was house-minding in Kilifi. I was glad that she too was not wearing a smart frock. You get out of the habit of high heels and pressed skirts when you have to clamber into a damp dinghy and then wade ashore for every event. The League had been established 80 years before when a young Englishwoman, the wife of a junior colonial officer, committed suicide because she was so isolated, since one was allowed to mix socially only with those of equal rank or one below. After that the women decided to get together to provide a support network for all the expatriate women so that no one again died of loneliness.

The meeting was just like the Women's Institute meetings I had occasionally gone to with my mother as a child in the fifties and sixties, full of well-meaning women with permed hair and a penchant for competitive baking. The meeting started with business, a discussion of the forthcoming fundraiser—a goat derby—followed by a talk by the wife of one of the Kenya Medical Research Institute (KEMRI) doctors about a library she had established for local primary schoolchildren. She was soliciting help from other *wazungu* to raise funds to get a proper building and expand the service. Six hundred children used the library, flocking from all over the town and outlying areas. The children would queue for up to an hour after school to be able to get a book to read.

Although after the Women's League meeting I did get to know some of the KEMRI crowd, they did not mix socially with the majority of other white Kilifi residents whom they called 'colonialists'. The colonialists called them 'do-gooders' and said, 'They take themselves too seriously.' One of the issues of contention was that, although the 'do-gooders' too had African servants, they paid them more than the going rate, 8000 shillings a month plus overtime, as well as providing maize and school fees for their children. At the boatyard for the Sunday afternoon races the do-gooders and the colonialists sat separately on opposing sides of the bar and we fluttered between them like Aesop's bat.

Once the boat was deforested and the wind had started to ease, there was no excuse not to keep heading south. After our awful crossing from the Seychelles to Kenya, the thought of leaving this safe haven to go out to sea and face southerly winds and opposing current was not tempting. Yet, as Tony had predicted, we reached Mtwapa quite painlessly, and after a couple of weeks there, we sailed south across the border to Tanzania.

IT TAKES TWO
TO TANGA

Tanzania
August 2001–February 2002

IN THE SLOW DANCE OF MORNING IN THE STRANGE DEPTHS OF NIGHT
IN THE BLESSING OF FLEETS IN THE MAKING OF ARRANGEMENTS
IN THE LETTING GO AND THE TAKING HOLD OF
IN RED WOOLLEN SOCKS
ZEN MEETS MY LIFE.
– Brigid Lowry

Even now, when I remember Tanga, it twangs at my heart strings.
I used to think that was a metaphor but there really are cords that run
from your heart up your neck to the back of your eyes. When you try
not to cry you can feel them tighten on either side of the throat; if you
leave them open, tears fall. Sometimes we know we have it all. In
Tanga I knew. I wrote at the time: 'Right now, we are anchored off the
yacht club in the sheltered waters of Tanga in Northern Tanzania.
Going ashore to walk to market or to collect some milk, still warm

from the cow, I often pass some vervets on the wall of the club. These monkeys, who often hang around hotels and campsites, stealing from unwary travellers, are famous for their light fingers and stunning turquoise testicles. Dhows still ply their trade between Tanga and neighbouring islands and we are free of the invasive engine sound of commercial ships elsewhere as these stately sailing ships carry their cargoes of cloves past in graceful silence. Each night people come from all over town to sit on our beach and watch another spectacular, soft pink sunset over the Usambara Mountains at the far end of the bay. I cannot imagine anywhere I would rather be.'

Kenya had glamoured me, but I was afraid that it was not simply the land lazing under the soft pink sky that had lured me, but some repressed desire to inhabit the romances of Isak Dinesen, Beryl Markham and Elspeth Huxley. Tanzania would put my ardour to the test. It was never colonised like Kenya, and though it had been under German and then British administration, settlement had not been encouraged. After independence in 1961, a socialist government had nationalised most industries, and so it was not a place that had latterly attracted European fortune hunters. Kilifi whites had warned me off— 'Oh, Tanzania's an awful place, boring, and the natives there are just dreadfully stupid, not like our Kikuyu. It's much more backward than Kenya.' This seemed promising.

Tanga was a large working port and we followed protocol and announced our arrival by radio before proceeding to immigration and customs. It was all a muddle. We paid hundreds of dollars but after protracted negotiations we were still given only a two-week visa, though we knew it was usual for yachties to be able to stay for three months. Our protests were dismissed: 'We do not have stamps for three months here.'

After anchoring off the yacht club we rowed ashore, where a woman as bouncing and cheerful as her masses of red curls approached us. 'Karibu Tanga. Welcome to Tanga. Have you just arrived on a yacht? How fabulous! Where did you sail from? Wow, all that way! Let me get you a drink. Tell me all about yourselves. I'm Debra, I'm Canadian and I teach at the International School here. The principal is Australian, you must meet her. How long are you here for? Oh, you'll love it here, you should stay. It's so nice to have new people in town.'

We told her about our visa problems.

'Did you speak to Charles? No? Charles is in charge of immigration and he's a member of the yacht club, he might even be here later on. Don't worry, Charles will sort it out, just go and see him tomorrow.'

The next day, simply mentioning Charles' name produced face-saving explanations about misunderstandings and yes of course we could have a three-month visa.

It was not just sorting out the visa that was a relief but also to be in a place where Africans were not only in charge of immigration but were members of the yacht club. Not that everyone's attitudes were necessarily different in Tanzania. We had already encountered again the cries of 'Africans never learn!' and 'Africa will just sink back into the mire!' as a yachtie and expatriate farmer exchanged the usual unpleasantries, but there was hope.

The advantage of the yacht club was that we were no longer beholden to anyone. All along the coast of Africa most land is privately owned, so one cannot just anchor near a beach and go ashore. In Kilifi we had been able to anchor because Tony and Daphne let us trail back and forth across their property, and also let us use their water supply. In Mtwapa, where we stayed for a couple of weeks, the resort managers were former yachties and allowed us to moor our dinghies at their jetty, use their showers and have access to the street. Without such people, secure anchorages where boats and dinghies can remain in comparative safety would be hard to find. At Tanga Yacht Club we could come and go as we pleased, no longer dependent on someone's generosity and goodwill.

From the club we could walk along the cliff-top road, keeping to the shade of the flamboya trees that lined the route to the town. The spacious wide streets could be imagined as gracious boulevards, though they had ended up dusty and lined with charmless concrete buildings. Many of them were empty—car showrooms with no cars, banks with no money. There was a pharmacy though, where it was possible to buy generic versions of almost any drug, from aspirin to Zoloft, over the counter, as well as a covered marketplace, known as the *wazungu* market, with produce stalls and a small shop, known as the supermarket, that sold exotic luxuries such as toilet paper, Nivea cream, ghee, chocolate and peanut butter. There was a dairy down a back road where they sold fresh milk, yoghurt and *mtindi*, a mild sort of yoghurt, translated unenticingly as 'coagulated milk'. A newsagency sold the local paper, poor quality exercise books and a few aged postcards, none of them of Tanga.

On the other side of the railway tracks spread the acres of small concrete houses and shops of Mganiani where the local Africans lived and did their shopping. We went shopping there sometimes, but you had to know exactly where to go. The coffee shop, where we could buy Tanzanian coffee by the kilogram for a fraction of the cost of the small imported vacuum packets in the supermarket, was just a small house, undistinguished by any signs, where an old man sat in the doorway in his white hat and long robe watching the world. One day the shop was apparently gone but some women led me to another anonymous house in a nearby lane. Later, when I learnt how business people, typically Indian or Arab, were regularly hassled for bribes euphemistically called tea or chai, I realised there might be a reason for the lack of signs and the peripatetic nature of businesses. There were several small streets of shops. One had nothing but bicycle repairers, another the bicycles themselves, the simple, black Chinese or Indian bicycles like the ones that old spinsters used to ride around in my home town in North Wales in the fifties ('sit-up-and-beg bicycles' my mother called them). Others specialised in *kangas*, or were lined with secondhand clothes stalls or small hardware shops with nuts and bolts and a limited range of tools. These were not places to browse for long; there was little to see or buy. We could not even get money. There were no ATMs and the banks were not computerised so we could not get cash advances on our credit card, which was how we had got money everywhere else in the world: Kalimantan, Sri Lanka, Kenya and the Maldives. Nothing to buy and no money to buy it with: like the noise of traffic, the tension created by consumer society is only apparent when it stops. With no advertising and no shop windows full of temptations, it felt like the rural Wales of my childhood, before supermarkets, television and weekend trading. Most of us who live in the cities of the Western world can barely remember, or even imagine, what that feels like any more.

Although there were few shops, there were several places where we could send email. Our regular one was painted scarlet inside and out and, like many other Internet places in Tanga, it had several little booths inside—these ones made from woven palm leaves—so that you could play online in private, presumably an important aspect of the service in a place where the most prominent desktop icons were Lust and Desire.

The anchorage was perfect. We could anchor so close to shore that it was only a short, leisurely swim for our friends to visit, and we started to make friends as soon as we arrived. We just had to sit on the beach, watching the pied crows with their shaggy wings like flying border collies, and wait, or chat to Abdullah, the barman at the yacht club. He was a long-suffering recipient of our mangled Swahili and he loved to tease and joke. When we asked him about taking a bus to Arusha, he told us with delight about the bus that had been stopped by bandits who told everyone to strip and took everything, leaving a naked driver to continue with his busload of naked passengers.

For the first few days I was tired and often rested on board while Allen went to reconnoitre ashore. He would come back to report. He had been talking to a local man at the club when his Somalian girl-friend arrived. 'I asked her if she was Muslim and she said she was, so I asked her if she had to wear a *bui-bui*. She showed me, it was in her backpack. She wore it to leave the house where she lived with her parents and then took it off before coming into the yacht club dressed in sexy Western gear, and looking really cool and confident, to meet her boyfriend. Illicitly, of course. I suppose it's one of the few places you can go that's private.' Over time, we observed that it was indeed a place where local men often met their mistresses, and I suppose it must have afforded some privacy to them, though for the expats it was the opposite, the place where everyone learnt everyone else's business.

Adele had been in Tanzania for twenty years. For the first ten years she had been an aid worker but later she established an eco-tourist resort island near Zanzibar which has won many international awards. Adele still acted as a consultant to aid projects but said she thought it would be best if aid stopped completely. She was one of many aid workers who had grown dubious about the value of their work over the years. It was never quite clear if this was a symptom of burn-out and cynicism, or whether it was a realistic assessment.

She warned us against staying in Tanzania and told us she wanted to leave, to go to Australia. '*Wazungu* are expected to have money; if you are here without money no one will help you, you're white trash. It is not a place to be old.' She was not the first person to warn us off. We met others who had their hopes of making a fortune frustrated by corruption or dreams of philanthropy frustrated by everything from bureaucracy to black magic.

Adele said that Africa does not want white people and she was full of awful stories to prove it. 'The doctors and nurses are only after money. Once, at a teacher's camp, I took a man to hospital who was very sick but he said he wanted to go home. I left him there but after four days I went back to visit and found he was dying. He had no money so no one had treated him. The doctor said it was meningitis though no tests had been done. I made them do some and of course they showed he had malaria, so I paid for a drip, because by now he was very dehydrated, but the nurse I paid to watch him fell asleep and didn't change the drip, so he died anyway.' Most health workers had similar tales, though unless they had given up hope and were ready to leave, they usually refrained from regaling newcomers with them.

I was grappling with all the stories as I met new people. I was told that the Cuban doctors who came to Tanga as an act of solidarity to help the nascent socialist regime ended up doing all the work, and I was told that the schoolteachers were irresponsible: 'They had no professional ethics, they used to take time off school to go and queue for sugar.'

'What did *you* do?' I asked the aid worker telling the story.

'Well, I could afford black market prices so I didn't have to queue.'

'So you could afford professional ethics?'

'Yes, yes, I suppose I could.' She paused, nodding. 'I never thought of it like that.'

Later, when my daughter Lucy joined us for a holiday she asked, 'Are all conversations like this?' They were. Discussion of money too, or more particularly its distribution, was never far away in Tanga,

partly because so many of the people there were trying to help solve
the problems, or at least deal with the consequences, of the unequal
distribution of wealth in the world, which is so evident in Africa. One
of the effects is that people fight over access to scarce resources. There
are wars, and where there are wars, there are refugees. I had just heard
a vague rumour about a refugee ship being turned away from
Australia.

'Is it true? What is it about Australians? Why do they dislike other
people so much?'

'I don't know. I don't know.'

I had kept trying to explain that Australians weren't all racists, that
Pauline Hanson, the most well-known Australian politician abroad,
represented a small, uninformed minority, but my arguments were
wearing thin.

Lucy had been saving hard all year and planned to join us for a couple of months towards the end of the year. She sent emails: 'Where
shall I fly to, Mum?' All along I had been telling her we would probably meet her in Durban but I was resisting going to South Africa. I kept
meeting South Africans who, after talking to me for five minutes
would say, 'Oh, you must go to South Africa, you'll love it.'

'Why do they say it?' I asked Kerstin, a Swedish aid worker and vet-
eran of the student uprisings of the sixties, who had worked in Soweto.
'How do they know what I would love?'

'They mean the swimming pools and big houses.'

'I feared that's what they meant. What do you think? Do you think
I would love it?'

'No, South Africa is so divided, everyone is asking what side you are
on. This is better.'

I emailed Lucy: 'Fly to Dar not Durban.'

She emailed back: 'Where's Dar?' The travel agent and I figured out you must mean Dar es Salaam but can you let me know so I can finalise my booking?'

So we were committed. We would still be in Tanzania in November, and by then it would be the cyclone season and too late to travel south. We would have to wait until the following September to travel either south, to the cape, or east, back to Malaysia.

Birgit and Luuk were a couple of Dutch vets who had been in Africa for years, working on various cattle-related projects. They and their two young children lived in a government-owned house near the yacht club on the cliff overlooking the water. They kept a couple of cows, some goats, ducks, chickens, rabbits and various odd and often invisible things in aquaria. It was like a child's picture-book farmyard. Luuk had given Birgit her first cow more than ten years before. It was the custom in Zambia, where they had worked, for a man to give his wife a cow to bring the fire back into their marriage. In the morning Allen or I would walk over to collect some milk. We could have got milk at the dairy, but, these days, how often do you get the chance to talk to and learn the names, Mulito and Zawadi, of the cows who nourish you?

Birgit told me she had always wanted to be a farmer or a vet but, 'in the Netherlands you have to have to be a millionaire or be the child of a farmer to be able to have a farm. Being a vet in Europe is horrible: all the decisions about farm animals are based on profit, "Is it economic to save this animal?" It's all decided like that. You don't go out delivering lambs or anything. It's a business. Of course you can work with pets, but that's all about plastic hip implants for poodles. That's why I want to stay here.' She had her farm and she was a vet working with real issues and real animals, tsetse fly prevention and a project to help small dairy farmers to get started with a first cow.

Jan was the school principal and had been in Tanzania for eighteen years. She and Holger, a Danish farmer, had met and married in Tanzania where they both started as aid volunteers. 'When we got married we had to fill in a form and tick one of three boxes: monogamous, potentially polygamous or polygamous.' Jan is one of those archetypal Australian women, tough, hard-working, drily witty, with a heart of gold and fully functioning bullshit detectors. I didn't need to ask which box. She is also the person everyone is thinking of when they say, 'If you want to get something done, ask a busy person.'

The International School was along the road from the yacht club, past Birgit and Luuk's farmyard, in the house where the Cuban doctors had once lived. We were invited for morning tea in the garden, *nylon*, deep-fried sweet potato served with coconut chutney and cassava with chilli, *pilipili*. In Kenya, the only people we met socially were *wazungu*, but here Africans and Asians are members of the yacht club, and the International School has children and staff from a variety of ethnic groups. Of course there is economic segregation—most Africans can neither afford to join the yacht club nor send their children to the school, even at the special rates for residents—but at least the economic lines were not entirely parallel with ethnic ones.

Around the classroom were displays of the children's work. They had completed sentences that began, 'I feel grumpy when . . . I get irritated when . . . I want to cry when . . .'

'Interesting, isn't it? It's a program I got from Australia. So many of these children, especially the Muslim ones, the boys, can't talk about feelings, they had no language for talking about feelings, and it's taken me all term to get them doing this. How can you express your feelings if you don't know the words, if you don't know you *can* talk about them? It must all be bottled up inside them, all muddled up, poor things.' While we were having tea, the father of one of these boys arrived to joyfully announce that his son had gained admission, through competitive examination, into a school in Oman, and there was an email from the boy himself to Jan: 'This is the first email I have sent and it is for you because you first opened my eyes.'

After committing to staying in Tanga, symbolised by applying for full membership of the yacht club, Allen started to get busy. Through Birgit he was helping a local dairy farming co-op put together a grant proposal to start a UHT milk processing plant, and sometimes he travelled to inland villages with a local vet who worked on animal husbandry. He also helped set up a database for Humana People to People, an organisation that made money by importing secondhand clothes from Europe, sorting them and selling them to stallholders who retailed them at the market. Their aim was to model ethical business practice and use the profits to fund community welfare projects. Kerstin, who had been working for over twenty years in Africa, was just starting Humana's operations in Tanzania, alongside Hadji, a Tanzanian man who has worked for the organisation in Zimbabwe for ten years.

One evening after dinner, feeling the need for company, we went ashore to the club. None of the people we had started to make friends with were there, just the people we'd tagged the old colonial crowd, as well as an abundant, middle-aged Goan woman, who with with glossy, full red lips, masses of black hair and a penchant for leopard-skin-patterned hotpants always met her gloomy lover there. Among other regulars were some long-time residents, farmers and businessmen, who tended to congregate together and to spend their days huntin', shootin' and fishin'. Mostly fishin' these days. And drinkin'. They were friendly enough but more out of necessity than choice. One particularly patrician couple would bestow a few words of gracious chit-chat as though granting a favour. I was told they had retired from up-country and had initially intended to mix only with people from

their own social stratum, the plantation owners, ex-colonial adminis-
trators and so on. 'But,' said my informant, not without pleasure, 'they
found that there were so few who weren't alcoholic or senile that they
had to lower their standards and mix with hoi-polloi like us!'

The yacht club was, in effect, the beach for expats, and even those
who were not club members could pay to use the facilities on a daily
basis, as Kerstin did until, months later, we heard she had been banned
for head-hunting Abdullah, the yacht club barman, to act as office
manager for Humana in Tanga—a position he retains to this day.

There were three beaches in Tanga: the African beach, the Indian
beach and the yacht club. All charged admission and provided tables
and chairs and refreshments in separate coves along the foreshore, but
the yacht club was where people went to swim in real undress, in
swimming costumes—Africans, Arabs, Sikhs and Muslims as well as
wazungu. It had not always been like that. Evan, a Greek national,
though he had never visited the country, had been refused admission
in colonial times when the very Aryan club had felt a Greek was too
Asian. Now Evan presides at the club, everyone addresses him as
'bwana', and he holds court, distributing his largesse.

'Come on, Mari, sit down, have a drink.'

'No thanks, I'm just going back to the boat, I'm tired.'

'Sit down, have a drink. Abdullah, a double whisky over here!'

A few hours later I'd be glad that home was just a short row away.
This was a dangerous place. 'Don't stay at the yacht club too long,'
warned Evan. 'You'll become an alcoholic. Abdullah! The same again
all round!'

On September 11, I noted in my journal, 'Really bizarre stuff'. I had
just met Karl, a Lutheran missionary who was visiting Tanga with his
young wife and sons. Karl looked more like a distinguished banker
than a missionary and, indeed, it turned out he had once been a banker.

His delicate young wife was dowdy and pale, with her straight hair parted at the side like a schoolgirl. They had been working with the Maasai people, the nomadic cattle-herders of Tanzania and Kenya.

'The Maasai are intelligent people, but cursed. They drink blood.'

'Cursed, why?'

'Because it is forbidden to drink blood.'

'Christianity doesn't forbid it. I never heard that. Isn't it just Mosaic law? Surely it's not Christianity. Where does Jesus forbid it?'

Karl was a bit vague. Acts, or perhaps James.

'Well, I've never heard that. What about all those blood sausages people eat in France?'

'In Germany also, I'm afraid,' he said, shaking his head sadly.

That someone should be telling the Maasai, famous for their dignified resistance to outside influences and admired for the integrity of their social system, that their way of life is cursed because of their eating habits was mind-boggling. There are terrible problems in Africa, millions of people are dying from AIDS, and some traditional practices such as female circumcision, performed with the same tools for everyone, or wife-sharing among members of the same age-set, exacerbate the problem, so there is an argument for telling people about the health consequences of such cultural practices and discouraging them. But this: what was he doing? Evidently the Maasai are not fooled by Karl, who admitted he had made no converts, though there are Christian Maasai. Tales circulated about an illiterate old man who had demanded his family read aloud to him till he had memorised the entire New Testament. He would have known what Jesus thought about blood.

That day on the beach Allen was supposed to be meeting Karl and his family to help him set up an email account, but first he was meeting one of the African vets, and Allen didn't want Karl to interrupt

their discussion, so I was delegated to look out for him. When I saw
Karl he was on the beach, his shortwave radio clutched to his ear.
'America has been attacked by terrorists, they hijacked some planes.
I can't hear very well but I think they flew them into the Pentagon and
somewhere in New York.' I felt a shiver of fear but also a strange excitement, like when someone finally challenges the school bully in the
playground and everyone stops breathing, waiting to see how he is
going to react. I went back to the boat and tuned into BBC Africa.
Later, while Allen was reading an article about Gandhi, Zen and deep
ecology, I was just sitting in bed listening to the world: something
chirruping, the dinghy slapping and voices in the distance, totally at
peace in this bay in Tanzania where it was said a third of the population
was Christian, a third Muslim and a third Animist, a world away from
New York. People were talking about the attack, but life for us was
more calm and settled than it had been for a long time. I felt secure in
a place where Muslims were not mysterious aliens but the man from
whom you bought bananas, insisting you learn to do it in Swahili
under his patient instruction, and the woman who waxed your legs at
the beauty parlour where, under their veils, women are skilled in the
arts of preening.

We had settled down to a regular sort of a life. Allen went ashore
most days to work with cows and computers. The first day he went
to discuss the cattle project he noticed that all the Africans he was
working with were smartly dressed in pressed trousers and shirts and
ties, so he struggled to scrub up. Without an iron and having to wade
ashore from the dinghy, it was hard to maintain a neat businesslike
look and, as we discovered everywhere we went, no one thinks, 'This
person is crumpled because they live on a boat.' They just see a disre-
spectful scruffiness. It seems trivial but, living on a boat at anchor and
trying to have a working life, small things gather into a cumulus of

awkwardnesses. A less trivial problem was that most jobs were in major cities, not the quiet coastal towns where one can easily live on a boat. It was beginning to become an issue because the time when we were going to run out of money was no longer out of sight beyond the horizon. Many yachties we met had reached retirement age and were living on their superannuation, but many of the rest of us had to work. I had optimistically imagined that we would find employment anywhere if we were flexible and expecting only a modest income, but we were becoming increasingly aware that we were not very useful. It was sobering. I seriously began to regret I had not trained as a doctor, water engineer or agronomist, for it is in dealing with those most basic of human needs that there was much to do in Africa. It was not just the money, we wanted to get involved with the community on land again, work and relationship, gritty though they are.

Sometimes when I was alone on board I would hear a voice calling my name. Kerstin had swum over. I'd put down the ladder so she could climb on board. We talked about her work and about god and the universe, as you do. She was not a member of the yacht club, did not have a car and lived as simply as is practicable. Originally, she explained, her organisation encouraged people to live exactly as local people did, but they were in danger of dying exactly as local people did, of malaria or dysentery, preventable diseases that still kill millions. She was one of the few Europeans we knew in Tanga who did not have a car. I told her, 'Allen asked those American missionaries, you know, the ones with the big house on the water and the Landcruiser, if they did community work or health work or anything, and they said they didn't have enough money to do anything except build churches.'

Kerstin laughed, 'When Jesus said, "Go out and build my church," I don't think he expected to be taken so literally.' She never seemed discouraged by the enormity of her task, though she was scathing at the

way so much development work had become a career. 'It's like the old
colonial civil service, everyone has a grade and they only mix with people in the same level.' Although she was essentially in charge of
operations in Tanzania, she was committed to the idea of equality and
she was responsible, along with everyone else, for cleaning the office
and the toilets, though some of the men who worked with her would
order the women workers to do it if she were not around.

Every Wednesday afternoon, after the children had finished dinghy
racing, a few of us would gather to learn to sail. I had never been in a
sailing dinghy before. I felt really silly, grappling with what seemed to
be a toy boat after sailing all that way. It required so much conscious
effort, like learning to drive. You had to be quick too. The difference
was like riding a skittish pony instead of a well-trained old cart horse.

Afterwards we had to put the boats away because the workers
had already gone home, but Pam, a former Peace Corps worker, and
I ended up carrying most of them. So many people who live there forget that floors do not clean themselves, food does not cook itself and
dinghies do not hop up the beach. Even aid workers become accustomed to a life with servants. Jan said, 'The most common excuse the
kids at my school have for not handing in their homework is "the
housemaid forgot to put it in my bag".'

Debra and I often went for a walk in the early evening, before the
sudden dark of the tropics threw its curfew over the town. After sun-
down people only went out if they had cars. I had thought this was just
wazungu paranoia but Johnson, one of the Africans I knew, said he too
was scared of riding his bicycle home after dark: 'There are bad men
hiding under the bridge over the railway.' Debra and I talked of how
the extraordinary became ordinary, the dirt roads, the monkeys, the
lack of street addresses, the regular power failures, all the things you
noticed at first. Some things never seemed ordinary though. There was
a sense of being more intimate with the deeply unknowable.

'Yesterday when I was reading to the children, *Charlotte's Web*—do you know it?—I was reading the part where all the animals can understand human speech and I got this really weird feeling and I looked down the row and there at the end there was a huge old male monkey.'

'One of the vervets?'

'Yes, and you know I got up and shooed him away, but he seemed to really know his way around and he was so relaxed and I realised he's been there before, listening, but, you know, I just didn't notice, he just blended in with the group.'

A month or so after we arrived some friends asked us to house-sit for them while they were away for a few weeks. They lived in a company-owned house near the yacht club and from the roof we could see *White Cloud*. We had, I confess, been looking forward to it: clean clothes, hot showers, even airconditioning. I could easily live without them, but it would be a treat not to be grubby and sweaty for a little while. In the event it was oddly uncomfortable, a kind of luxurious prison. There were locks on all the doors and security guards who let us in and out through the big iron gates. There was a gardener, a housekeeper and a woman who came to iron.

I would scoot upstairs after breakfast to work on the computer while Johnson cleaned the house. I felt I had to look busy but I wanted to sample cable television, so I sneaked down when he was at lunch and turned on the fashion channel. There were dead-faced women striding and spinning down catwalks in fabulously expensive drab grey rags, torn or frayed and exposing breasts or buttocks so they looked like zombie-whores. Our changed sensibility to women's bodies creeps up slowly. It was shocking to see these fashion models in the way it would be shocking to see a plucked chicken walking around. It is hard these days to relate to Victorian attitudes to ankles, but after living in mostly Islamic countries for over a year it jolted me to see women's bodies so exposed in public. Watching cable television I could understand why the Islamic world looked in horror at the West. Even a medical aid worker in Tanga, who had a reputation for being a rascal, had returned to Tanga after a visit home to London reeling, 'Bleeding 'ell, all the women in Oxford Street looked like whores, tits everywhere, skirts up 'ere, they looked like they was in their underwear.'

Flipping to a news channel there were dead-faced war refugees trudging in drab grey rags, and then the footage of Afghani women, clad from head to toe in their burkas, being publicly executed. Watching cable television, I could no longer understand anything.

'I think having servants is bad for my soul.'

'No,' said Allen, 'it's good for your soul to experience it.'

I talked to Birgit about the servant issue. At first they didn't have any. 'Now we have seven. Two could do the work but we pay the children's school fees and doctor's bills.' People like her who treated their staff well were always besieged by other members of the family eager to join the payroll too. She threw up her hands—what to do? In the absence of the infrastructure and labour-saving devices we take for granted, it was impossible for her to fulfil her work commitments without people to clean and cook and wash clothes. It provided employment and *wazungu* who did not employ anyone were seen as tight, not sharing their wealth around by providing highly sought work. It was also a way for people whose lives are so far apart to make contact, to start to understand each other. But all this did not really convince me.

'You're right, it is good to experience this,' I told Allen. I had forgotten that inequality damages the rich as well as the poor. You have to ignore the knowledge that we are all equally human and shut something down to be able to employ servants at wages that we ourselves could not imagine being able to survive on and be able to live comfortably with the gap between; you see them as different, less sensitive to pain or insult. One of the things I had liked when I first went to

Australia was that, at the time, compared with England, it seemed so egalitarian, a place where people escaping from anything—the English class system, the aftermath of war in Vietnam, or the coup in Chile— could have the opportunity to make a new life. Together we mourned the loss of the dream, of young and free.

One day at the house the power went off yet again. Johnson, as usual, rang for a *fundi*, a workman, to fix it. After a few hours of using my computer on battery power, it began to fail, so I went down to investigate. In the garage, by the fuse box, was a big handle with a knob on it.

'Johnson, what's that for?'

'I don't know, mama.'

'I think it's probably a circuit breaker. I think if I pull it down, the electricity might come back.'

'Ho! Mama!' said Johnson, shaking his head and backing away.

'It's okay, I'll do it.'

It was, and it did. After years on a boat with Allen, I was learning that if there is a switch or a knob or a handle, you flick it or push it or pull it. Sometimes it helps.

Around this time I had an email from a friend in Australia who told me, 'Eat and appreciate your strawberry while you can.' She reminded me about the Zen story of the man running from a tiger to the edge of a cliff only to discover another tiger waiting for him below. He sees a vine growing from the cliff and it has a ripe strawberry on it. While he hangs from the vine, two mice, one black, one white, are starting to nibble at it. He reaches out with one hand and eats the berry. 'How delicious it is.' My friend added that she was having some health problems at the moment and concluded with a haiku:

after eating the strawberry
it is time to feed
the tiger . . .

A few days later I heard she had unsuccessfully tried to kill herself after learning she had terminal cancer. She had been deadly serious about feeding the tiger.

I talked to Johnson about it. He told me, 'Ladies take overdoses, if they are pregnant sometimes. Gentlemen use rope. White men use guns.' He said he was a Christian. 'God says I should not kill. Many people do it if they have the HIV but not me. But if I had an accident and my backbone was broken or if I could not go to the toilet and had tubes inside me, I would kill myself. I think God would not be cross about that.'

I had just picked some flowers and was putting them in vases.

'White people put flowers inside but . . .'

'You think they're crazy.' He laughed. 'You know, where I come from, men give flowers to a woman if they love her.'

'We give money.'

Money was on my mind. We had none. Our credit card had been forged and the bank had cancelled it after someone in Hong Kong ran our account over the limit. We had no other way of getting money because, when travelling, we just kept our credit account topped up and used cash advances from ATMs to access our money. Anywhere else, we would have become frantic, but Tanga was the kind of place where people rallied to help, where there were still people trusting enough to lend substantial amounts of money to a couple of yachties who could sail away overnight. Thus, on borrowed money, we threw a party to celebrate our fiftieth birthdays which were just ten days apart. The house we were minding had a rooftop that was perfect for dancing, eating and watching the ocean.

Around that time, I won some money for a short piece I'd written during my days at anchor off Africa. That too eased the financial pressure and we sailed briefly back to Kenya to collect the prize. The weather was warmer than when we had been there before and now, each evening, Tony and Daphne and their visiting yachties would gather around the swimming pool in their garden. Over the weeks we had spent in Kilifi before, I had developed a great respect and fondness for Tony and Daphne—the unstinting way they looked after the constant stream of visiting yachties passing along the coast, and maintained a healthily ironic gaze on their situation.

'Oh, this place is cloud-cuckoo land, I know that,' Daphne told me one day, amused at how I fretted. Yet something was wrong. We all knew Tony could be prickly. 'You've already said that,' he would snap when Allen meandered back over the same narrative territory. Now, by the pool, he had taken to sitting with his back to us, though judging by his tart, but always apposite, interjections, he was evidently listening to everything. On our last day we went to say goodbye.

'So you really are leaving?' Tony asked, forlorn. 'I'm sad about that.'

I was astounded. He had been such a grouch. Why had he not shown any sign he was glad to see us before? Now it was too late. We had to keep heading south to meet Lucy.

During all of our voyaging, despite regularly throwing out a line, we had failed to catch a fish while underway. There had been the tern early on, and after that nothing. People were amazed that anyone could be so very bad at fishing. Once, at Tony and Daphne's, we had confessed our piscatory incompetence to Bobby, a professional fisherman. 'You've got to think like a fish. Cut the bait up into pieces half an inch long and throw those in.' I do not think like a fish. I would think, 'Uh-uh, somebody's been cutting these sardines into neat little bite-sized portions; I'd better watch out.' In my estimation, 'This is good. I want it. I want as much as possible and I want it now,' does not even count as thought. Probably I, rather than any banana, had jinxed the fishing.

Soon after leaving Mtwapa, the second day of the three it would take to reach Tanga, I noticed something in the water.

'Oh, it's probably just a bit of rubbish, seaweed or something,' said Allen, resignedly winding in the hand line. 'It's a bit heavy, hope it's not another bird.'

Spanish mackerel is splendid. I took the man-with-big-fish photo, and that night, wallowing around in the exposed anchorage at Wasin Island on the Kenyan border, we feasted on tender fish steaks with an okra curry.

'Welcome back. *Karibuni*,' said everyone in Tanga. It was good to return to the hubbub of our life but after a few days it was time to head off for an overnight sail to Dar es Salaam. On the way, Allen caught another Spanish mackerel and a skipjack tuna. We anchored off the yacht club where, as members of Tanga Yacht Club, we now had reciprocal membership. It was very hot and a long walk to anywhere. It is easy to forget that most of the time we were very hot. I was not feeling terribly well, troubled by those shadowy ailments my mother's friends used to talk about as 'women's problems' but which my mother had raised me to believe were 'no problem at all in this day and age'. I was no longer in this day and age. Tampons, or even disposable sanitary towels, are scarce commodities in Africa. One of the major reasons why girls did not continue their education in Kenya was because schools were not equipped with lavatories, or not ones accommodating to menstruating girls and, in any case, most girls could not afford sanitary protection. I think it was Germaine Greer who wrote that it was not the pill but tampons that had liberated women. Living, and especially travelling by public transport, in a place where tampons are unavailable and toilets, if you can find one at all, are not equipped for the disposal of sanitary protection of any kind, you suspect she is right. You know you are living in a man's world. I went in search of a chemical hormonal solution. I couldn't change the world.

We arrived in Dar while ocean yacht races were being held, and many of the Kilifi crowd were still there when Lucy arrived. She was shocked. I suppose that I had become a little immune to the civilised snobbery and the macho gallantry. I played the game: 'mwa, mwa' on each cheek, and casually mentioned being at boarding school and Cambridge. I passed as white.

'Mum, what are you doing? These people are just awful!'

I laughed it off, but actually I was shocked too. I had fallen into the habit of keeping quiet, playing along, not saying what I thought.

I had been rather nervous about Lucy's visit. In the close confines of a small boat, the best of relationships can fray in days, and she had arrived for two months. What was Lucy going to make of the odd assortment of Tanga people, most of them much closer in age to me than to her?

Anxious to escape the clashing world of Lucy and the colonial remnants, we soon sailed to Zanzibar, the island whose name conjured up images of spice and pleasure. I once heard that it was named from *zingiber*, Latin for ginger, though as the main centre of the Arab slave trade, the romance was unevenly spread. We sailed past the old stone town with its clutter of domes and minarets to stop in the bay near a resort where, we'd heard on the yachtie grapevine, we could safely anchor and buy drinks and food outside the strict hours decreed by Ramadan. Most tourists bypass the old town and go straight to the resorts on the other side of the island where they can laze on the picture-postcard beaches a whole Weltanschauung away, untouched by the Islamic sensibility that characterises Zanzibar town.

It took a whole day of wandering around Stone Town to check in with customs, immigration and police. Zanzibar does not consider itself quite part of Tanzania, and insists on repeating the formalities. We trailed around the streets, which seemed to come to an end and then, at the last moment, reveal an alleyway. This might open up to disclose

a perfect view—crimson bougainvillea blazing up a whitewashed
wall—or might end in an evilly narrow place of foetid water and rubbish, a sticky or dead end. By evening my head ached. I needed water.
Across the road from the bus depot by the markets were some stalls
selling refreshments, but the vendor would not sell me a drink. 'It is
Ramadan. I cannot sell you water, everyone will be angry.' Being hot,
bothered and dehydrated I was a bit grizzly myself, but it was probably
the only occasion in years of travelling when Islamic regulations
impinged on me.

We did a spice tour. We had resisted in Sri Lanka but it was nice having Lucy as an excuse to do touristy things. Silly really, needing an
excuse. One of the best days of my life was when Allen and I played
truant from work once and went to the zoo without any children or
grandchildren to justify doing it. Allen kept getting phone calls from
students asking, 'What's that funny noise in the background?' as things
squawked and roared around us. There in Zanzibar we saw pepper-
corns on vines and cardamom plants like lilies, cloves, nutmegs
wrapped in their webs of crimson mace, and we discovered the hours
of work that go into processing vanilla. Vanilla comes from the bean-
like pods of a climbing orchid which are green and odourless. Only
after months of careful curing does the sweet fragrance of vanillin
emerge. On the way, we stopped at the ruins of what I misheard as
some passion baths built by the first Sultan for his wife. I could become
fond of a man who built me passion baths.

Heading back to Tanga we meandered from bay to bay along
Zanzibar and Panza, but had bad luck with wind and current. Our
anchorage was relentlessly rolly in the north wind, and after a miserable night we fought wind and current all the next day to get to Pemba
just before dark. There was supposed to be an interesting wreck, so we
took the dinghy and went for a stressful snorkel in strong currents,

searching for it. After we got back and put the dinghy and motor away, an awkward, difficult job in strong winds with lots of waves, Lucy asked, 'Is that it? There, look, right out of the water.' But none of us could face the bother of going through the whole launching process to get back in again.

Early next morning we set sail, looking for a calm place to anchor. Lucy went down and hid while we negotiated the narrow passage between the reefs. I had stopped noticing that we always yelled at each other getting in and out of difficult anchorages. Mostly it's because you have to yell to be heard. Allen would be up the front operating the anchor winch and I'd be steering. He'd be bawling out which direction to go in, as well as gesturing, and I'd be bellowing out the depths, 'We've got point one of a metre under us!' or 'How the hell am I supposed to know that when you flap your hand like that it means slow down? I thought you were pointing at that rock!' Somehow over the years I had become immune to the shouting, though I must confess that for the first year or so I often secretly cried a bit and contemplated divorce for at least fifteen minutes after each time we anchored or set sail. After several months I learnt from other couples that this was standard procedure on most yachts.

We reached a small island that seemed to be a possible anchorage but it was difficult to get a hold and it was over coral, never a place we like to stop. Since the rudder was responding a bit oddly we paused so we could investigate but some men approached in a boat, telling us we were in a marine park and demanding a hefty fee. We were not sure if it was really a park, but decided to move since it was a dicey anchorage anyway, too close to reef and strong current for comfort. By this time Lucy was getting the hang of cruising: that it was stressful, hot and consisted of a perpetual search for a comfortable, safe anchorage and then, when you found one, spending the day hauling water. Finally we

stopped for a couple of days at Funzi. It wasn't exciting but it was isolated, and we could swim, read, do the usual maintenance chores such
as cleaning the hull, or just do nothing. After all the hassles and anxiety, Lucy could understand why being safely anchored in a sheltered
bay was ecstasy. In the end, just being safe and alive is all you want.

When Lucy first arrived in Tanga she would ask where Allen was. 'If
I was home I'd be able to SMS him. Doesn't it bother you, not knowing
where he is? I always know where my friends are but he didn't come
home for lunch.'

'Look, you can't get lost here. Somebody'll know where he is.'

Somebody always did. When we got back from visiting Debra that
afternoon, Allen was waiting for us at the yacht club.

'Been visiting Debra?' he asked.

'How did you know?'

'Emil was here having a drink a minute ago, saw you on the road
and said you were probably there.'

Friends were people you saw every day, not just when you arranged
a dinner party. Most days we took the jug to get milk and would often
stop for coffee and a chat if Birgit or Luuk was home. When I cycled
into town to go to the market or check my email, I would stop at the
Food Palace for a cup of tea and usually there was someone there I
knew, or I might call into the Humana office and see Kerstin. On
Tuesdays the International School students went swimming, getting
into practice for their annual race to the island about a mile away
across the bay, and on Wednesday they learnt to sail. Both days parents
came to watch, then stayed on to swim and meet others who arrived
later, for a drink before dinner. A couple of times a week Debra and I
and some other women went walking, and sometimes we would get
together to meditate or for an informal yoga session on the lawn,
much to the amazement of the crowd of giggling local women who

gathered to watch. There was Rotary—where we were both invited to give talks and which was a good way to meet members of the local community, African and Indian as well as some *wazungu*—volleyball, dinghy-racing, fundraisers, festivals, exhibitions and parties. There was always something happening and it was impossible to go to any event in Tanga and not know several people there. It was a community. Like the muddled-up animals, people congregated in mixed herds so that, as with family, there were people you liked and others you coped with but, I was repeatedly assured, 'in times of trouble everyone mucks in to help'.

I had lived abroad before, in Japan, and knew that it was easy to slip into becoming part of an expat scene. With youthful arrogance we used to sneer at expats there, the diplomats and businesspeople who lived in Westernised ghettoes. I had lived in the same way locals did and counted them among my friends. Later, working with Aboriginal people in remote parts of Australia, I'd avoided being the kind of whitefella who only mixed with other whitefellas, and in some communities I mixed only with local Aboriginal people. Pushing at the edges of comfort, it wasn't always easy, but it was possible.

Yet in Africa I had little contact with local African people except for a few women who were married to Westerners, and people's servants. Allen had invited one of the African vets he worked with to meet us for a drink. Though he had lived in the USSR and Germany for years, he did not seem at ease. Maybe he just wasn't interested. Even Kerstin, who more than anyone else I knew there, avoided being part of the expat scene, struggled to have a social relationship with her co-organiser, Hadji, outside work. He was often there when we were invited to dinner at her house and he came to the boat with her sometimes, but he always seemed happy to escape as soon as he decently could. One evening Allen came home from a Rotary meeting and repeated the

story told by one of the young African men there. 'A man saw a butterfly coming out of its cocoon, struggling out through a tiny, tiny
hole. He picked it up and, with a pair of nail scissors, carefully cut along
the cocoon, being very gentle so as not to damage the butterfly. Then
he put it down but the butterfly never emerged. You see, it was the
struggle, the squeezing through the tiny hole that pushed fluid into
the wings. Without a struggle, the butterfly cannot fly.' How oppres-
sive it must be when all the foreigners you encounter have come to
help you, to change you, to educate you, to make you more like them.

One former aid worker described a project she had worked on to
educate people out of the belief that *tauni*, plague, which is still preva-
lent in areas of Tanzania, was caused by witchcraft and to encourage
them to seek medical help.'The death rate dropped from about 400 to
30 a year, but the project lapsed. People forgot. The health department
did not want to support any more education programs. They denied
that anyone believed in witchcraft. They thought the education programs were evidence that *wazungu* regarded the people as backward and
stupid.'

Of course the *wazungu* claim they do not think this but are just
educating people about basic germ theory, though at some level many
of them do scorn the belief in curses. Yet in the West too we have
our myths. The metaphors of illness frequently frame disease as the
punishment for some misdeed: eating bad food, having sex with the
wrong people, being too angry or not angry enough. We spend billions
on alternative therapies, many of which have no scientific explanation.
Allopathic medicine seems to underestimate the role of fear, love and
spirit in the welfare of the physical body. People often talked of the
African belief in witchcraft and the supernatural as if the West were
free from irrational superstition.

So many Westerner's stories referred to the supposedly vast gap

between Africans and us, as if to demonstrate that there is no chance
of making real contact. Other people wanted to reconstruct Africa in
the image of the West, to colonise it with ideas, if not with bodies.
Ironically, those who complained most were often people who were,
or had been, aid workers, health workers or missionaries. They were
the ones who were always trying to change people and make them
behave more like us. And their lack of success was understandably
frustrating for them. For example, regular hand-washing does help
prevent infection, but village medical workers would often just stitch
and slice, apparently unconcerned about cross-infection or contact
with blood. Yet often the complaints seemed more a failure of imagination. Many people find it intolerable that there are ways of seeing the
world that they can't comprehend but, for me, it is a comfort that
there are ways of being that stretch out beyond my grasp.

Being in Tanga had convinced us that we wanted to be involved
again in the muddle of life, of family, friends and work, part of a community. Contrary to advice we had been given earlier, a couple of
Fremantle yachties who had just arrived in Tanga and who were familiar with the weather patterns around Indonesia told us that if we left in
February it was possible to sail back to Australia south instead of north
of the equator, thus bypassing the Melaka Straits and heading to the
Sunda Straits. After diligently scrutinising the pilot charts, we concluded
that leaving in February was likely to make the journey quicker, easier
and safer than going in September. In matters of voyage-planning we
always tried to choose the best odds.

I was loath to leave Tanga and we did not mention to anyone that
we were thinking of leaving. It was here, in the slow old port town on
the edge of the continent that spawned us all and continues to intrigue
and perplex us, that I had found my paradise. Kerstin, Debra, Allen,
Lucy and I attended a small Eid lunch party that Tusha, a local Hindu,

held on his verandah in the main street of Tanga. Eid is the two-day holiday that marks the end of Ramadan. It was reassuring, so soon after September 11, to be celebrating Eid with a Hindu, as well as Christmas and New Year with all kinds of people.

We spent Christmas Eve with a recently arrived aid worker and his family. There was another couple there too, from East Germany. The woman had come to work in a hospital but had been so horrified by the living conditions that they were heading home before she even started work. They were drippy with gloom. I felt tetchy. I had long ceased to expect the comforts of European cities and I was used to people, yachties and expats in Africa alike, who didn't grumble. I was probably jealous too; if either of us could find regular work we would be able to stay. It was only later, when I heard the full story of their complicated and unhappy relationship, that it made sense. Going to a difficult place is not a prop for a dysfunctional relationship, though it may be a cure—like everything else in a pared-back life, you either fix things or let them go.

Christmas itself was a feast at Jan and Holger's house. They had invited friends of assorted cultures and faiths to join them, particularly anyone who lived alone. Jan once told me that one of the worst days of her life had been a solitary Christmas Day when she first arrived as a young volunteer. 'I sat in a cafe eating chicken curry and cried.' She wanted to ensure no one else ever spent Christmas watching tears drip onto the plate, though when we arrived, she was a little nervous about the neighbours. They were also preparing for a big party, and the last time they had done so they had followed the typical local custom of slaughtering one of their cows for the feast. Most of the lawns around the big houses inhabited by Africans were used to support cattle and goats. Only the *wazungu* persisted with flowerbeds. It was a good idea and ensured the meat was fresh, but the sound and sight of the murdering of a large noisy mammal just over the fence can put the more delicate guests off their dinner. All was well. It seemed they had bought their barbeque pre-slaughtered that day.

After New Year we drove with Debra into the Usambaras, where African violets grow wild, to stay in one of the many guesthouses Europeans traditionally go to for the cool air and the make-believe world of herbaceous borders and vegetable gardens straight out of Peter Rabbit. On dusty ochre tracks, we meandered around the edges of hills where houses moulded from the same red earth seemed to have just grown. Looking to the distance it was possible to make out hamlets, camouflaged amid the trees and corn. In the lush valleys men tended long rows of cabbages and cauliflowers, while downstream women sang like busy angels as they washed their clothes, spreading them out to dry on the grass. We walked quietly and unannounced, listening to their song. Even the cattle looked contented. When I went back to Tanga, Birgit disputed my descriptions of bucolic bliss. I contended that perhaps the best thing for us all to do is go home, mind our own business and leave the people of Africa to get on with life as they have always done. 'Oh, it looks very charming and pretty, sure, but ask the women about their children dying of dysentery or malaria. And the market gardens, the cabbages and cauliflowers, are all for export; the farmers get almost nothing.' I had been swayed by the singing, but who can tell how to measure the happiness of another life?

I had promised Lucy that if she got herself to Africa, I would treat her to a safari, so we went to Arusha to organise the trip. At the hotel, which served the ubiquitous something very meaty with *chipsi*—it's not hard to guess what that Swahili means—while we sat around discussing whether we could tolerate another high dose of cholesterol, Chris introduced himself. He'd overheard our conversation and asked if we'd like to join him and his wife Sophie for dinner at a good Italian

restaurant he knew. Chris was a Romanian who had been sent to
Rwanda with the UN peacekeeping forces but left when he was posted
to Bosnia. 'I couldn't fight my neighbours so I got out and came back to
Africa.' His time in the army had given him engineering skills, and he
ran several businesses in Nairobi, including one that imported medical
equipment. Sophie, a doctor's daughter, was a costume designer. With
her mop of mini dreadlocks and funky clothes, she didn't look like the
mother of four children under eight (who should, in all fairness to the
rest of us, look like an exhausted wreck). She was a bundle of energetic
attitude. 'Kenyans are different from Tanzanians, we ask for what we
want. Does a baby get fed if it doesn't cry? The way I dress, the way I
walk, the way I do my hair, people here know I'm from Kenya, but even
in Nairobi the street kids don't give me any trouble.' She translated the
words of the songs the band were singing. Most of them were moral
tales, like proverbs, she said, but one was a love song: 'I won't go to
prostitutes any more now I have found you, the one I love.'

The band started playing a samba and to Lucy's undisguised dismay
Allen and I got up to dance. Once we started, others joined in, including three magnificent women from the next table who, we discovered,
worked for the UN and came from Togo. They were each about six-
and-a-half feet tall and big eaters. One wore an elegant brown caftan;
another wore a traditional long cotton outfit with a matching cloth
swathed around her head, and the third had several kilos of elaborate
plaited hair extensions and wore a kind of Mother Hubbard dress in red
satin trimmed with masses of crocheted cream lace. 'Very expensive,'
Sophie whispered, as if she knew I was having trouble reading the
implications of this fashion statement. They danced gracefully, shim-
mying their enormous hips quite independently of their bodies,
defying the world to say that big isn't beautiful. 'You practise by tying
a scarf round your hips and then trying to move it while keeping your

shoulders still. You need to do it in front of a mirror,' explained Sophie. Eventually everyone was dancing, even Lucy.

No, not everyone danced: not the Indian couple on a nearby table who were staging a little play of their own. The woman was clutching a bouquet of red roses, and during the meal other gifts were brought to the table, a frilly cake followed by a present which he insisted she unwrap. It was a silvery jewel box. Inside was a gold chain which he pressured her to put on. For whom was this display? The woman was obviously uncomfortable. Was she his wife who slaved all year but was being presented to the world as spoilt? Was she a girlfriend, not happy to accept his advances? Sophie followed my gaze but was less absorbed in their personal drama: 'Indians are all grab, grab, grab. They take what they can from Africa but they never give anything back.'

We had told her we were in Arusha to go on safari. She had been on one, but that was unusual for a Kenyan. 'We want to go to cities, to New York or London when we go on holiday. We could never understand white people coming to Africa to go to look at animals but I went once, so that I'd understand, and I realised why people did it. Before I just thought they were silly. Most Africans think it's silly but African people don't know anything about the animals any more.'

In a jeep with a driver and cook, just the five of us set off and stopped at different campsites each night, including one in the Serengeti. Lucy still manages to dine out on her story of her night in there, an unfenced site in the middle of the reserve where she was kept awake all night by the sound of lions roaring and padding back and forth through the camp. 'And you went for a pee! I was so petrified. I just knew it was you.'

'Well, what was I supposed to do?'

'Go before you went to bed. Or hold on. Mum, why did you do it? It was crazy. There were lions everywhere.'

'Well, I didn't hear a thing. I just woke up and went outside and straight back to sleep. I didn't feel scared.' After the boat, nothing felt very scary any more, though I didn't know until later that lions tend to pounce when they see animals stop to relieve themselves.

Having our own driver we could stop as long as we liked, just watching. The first time we went on safari most people were trying to tick off as many animals as possible. We were happy to stare for ever at a leopard, casually slung in a far-off tree, but people who had joined our bus later were anxious to see something more than a hint of spots and the promise of pouncing. This time we could notice more detail. The gnu, with their long beards and oddly stiff gait, were like old men trying to frolic; giraffes appeared to move in slow motion; the bundles of rock hyraxes flopped on the rock like little fat seals. The zebras and gazelles, the herd animals, are all so sleek and young and fit because if they do not keep their bodies trim and terrific they do not just get laughed at for being fat, they die. That was why the zebras liked to find a friend, resting in pairs, their heads on each other's shoulders so that they could keep a lookout all around. I sympathised with the nervous prey animals; after being on a boat I knew what it was like to never quite relax and to always sleep with one ear open for trouble. Buffaloes are less vulnerable. We saw one with a swollen leg that looked like the parasitical disease elephantiasis. And the birds, hundreds of them, from the francolin, guinea fowl and secretary birds to little sunshine-yellow weavers and splendid starlings. Initially it is the big mammals, the ones that inhabit the E for elephant, L for lion world of every schoolchild, that attract attention. Later it is the density and variety of the animal world in all its forms.

One evening, while standing on a hill overlooking the plains of the Serengeti, we saw a lone elephant, which we had overtaken earlier on the road, still strolling in the distance. It reminded me of the opening words of the Shodoka, an old Zen poem: 'There is the leisurely one, walking the Tao, beyond philosophy. Not avoiding fantasy, not seeking truth.' There in the valley from where the first humans are thought to have evolved and walked out over the entire earth, we become again just one of the menagerie, no longer the odd one, the one that is so often searching for something, for answers, for more, and far from leisurely. Briefly, I was there. Then I was leaving, disentangling myself from the vast chaos that is Africa, a place where it is still possible to be free of the illusion that everything is under control. There in the fecund shambles of the Serengeti it was possible to rejoice in the diversity of life forms and feel relief that we are not really as special as we think we are but just another animal species trying to survive.

Travelling back to Tanga on the bus, we were carrying large amounts of cash. Arusha was one of the two places in Tanzania where it is possible to get money from overseas bank accounts and we had stocked up with dollars ready for our voyage. This was not like the kind of long-distance bus you might take from Sydney to Brisbane or London to Rome; it was an ancient rattling thing with a ceiling carpeted in the purple swirls and flowers of a sixties pub. The walls were blue laminex and the windows had grimy red curtains tied in knots to keep them out of the way. There was a television that didn't work and several signs such as, 'If God be for us who can be against us?' The only stop in the day-long trip was at Moshi, in the middle of a hectic bus station, where two separate attempts were made to separate us from our money. I felt the unbuttoning of my trouser pocket by someone masquerading as a devout Muslim in his white prayer hat and robe, and Allen was hit on by a gang of adolescents, whose complicated scam, which involved pretending they had mislaid something under his seat, was foiled by Lucy, who was observing from a seat further back. Once the bus set off again we could almost relax—none of the unsuccessful thieves had been passengers. Arriving at Tanga bus depot we had to escape the offers of bogus taxis and help with our bags, which bedevil every arrival. 'I just swing my bag and hit everyone,' Kerstin told me later. I must have looked shocked because she laughed. 'Well, you have to, you know, otherwise they just walk off with everything.' After a lifetime of aid work she is realistic. She doesn't expect the poor to be grateful. She expects them to do what they have to in order to survive, and she does the same, even if it means that a white woman of a certain age has to use her computer bag as a weapon to escape from the bus depot. All this makes Africa sound like a dangerous place, but when I checked my email, Bee had written to say she had been mugged at knife-point at a suburban Sydney station on her way home from work. She was unharmed, but had lost her mobile phone, despite being in a place where surveillance cameras monitor the public space. In Australia we lived in an illusion of safety, surrounded by cameras, dutifully wearing our bike helmets, standing behind the yellow line on the platform, paying our taxes and insurance premiums. Nothing can shield us entirely from acts of desperation.

Apart from occasional news reports about remote Aboriginal communities, poverty was something that hadn't registered on the screen of our reality in Australia. Poverty was something that happened somewhere else. Here in Africa poverty was the masses of people thronging around at the bus depot, all hoping to sell a twisted paper full of peanuts, a plastic bag of cordial or an orange trilby hat. It was in the grubby old bus and the rough, dusty road. It was in the post office where the ancient, faded postcards were kept safely in a locked glass cabinet. It was in the generic drugs you bought, imported from India, that might or might not work. It meant things seemed cheap, such as the black bicycle like something out of an old French film, which Allen bought for A$50, brand new, but which had wheels that were not quite round. The roundness of wheels is something one takes for granted, and not-quite-roundness turns out to be more of problem to fix than one might imagine. Poverty was not hidden, though tourists did not want to see it. That is why most of them were carefully put on private buses from airport to resort to safari park, bypassing any uncomfortable brush with suffering that can so take the pleasure out of a luxury holiday.

Yet it was why I loved Africa. It was chaotic, it felt closer to the realities of life and death and the consequences of your own actions, especially less sensible ones. I don't think I had set off across the ocean in search of anything in particular; here I realised I had found it in that strange world of exiles-in-Africa. Not that we exactly fitted, but then, who did? It was a self-selected community of misfits, an asylum for people who find the normal world insane. That this club was in Africa helped; the big soft sky, the unlikely trees, almost the whole contents of the Ark and few rules. Though it was a bit risky, that was part of the pleasure. Like living on a boat, it was a world that bypassed the regulations of real life.

Back on board we started to disentangle, to say goodbye and make plans for the long voyage back to Australia. Lucy, who had also grown to love the life in Tanga, flew home to Sydney. The winds were ready for us and as soon as we had provisioned and plotted our course, we headed out to sea.

GOING HOME

Tanzania to Australia
February — July 2002

IT IS A STRANGE THING THAT IN SEA VOYAGES,
WHERE THERE IS NOTHING TO BE SEEN BUT SKY AND SEA,
MEN SHOULD MAKE DIARIES.
— Francis Bacon

I was scared of the long journey across the Indian Ocean. It did
not help that we had just heard that an Australian couple we knew
who were preparing to head home across the southern Indian Ocean,
had hit a wreck and sunk entering port in South Africa. It wasn't just
the 4000 miles of sailing that was looming, it was home itself. Leaping
off is easy, helped by the gravitational force of romance and adventure.
Clambering back was going to require different skills. But the voyage
would give us time to hone those, especially patience and the ability to
bend with the weather. The day we left, the winds were brisk and by
mid morning we could no longer see Africa. Until we set sail I felt
nothing but sadness at leaving. I was in love with the place and until
the last moment I was waiting for a sign that I could interpret as 'Stay!'

But as we headed out to sea, I was surprised to find myself humming bits of a Beatles song about coming home yeah, yeah, and noticed I was happy.

Before leaving, Allen had complained of horrible headaches and went for a blood test, which confirmed he had malaria. I had a test too, a normal precaution for yachties about to leave a malaria area on an extended voyage, which showed that I also had asymptomatic beginnings of the disease. We both took the drugs we had on board and bought extra supplies for the trip. Everyone we knew in Tanga had malaria regularly. They just casually took medication each time, but many local people could not afford any treatment. The demented ones who hung around the streets begging usually had untreated malaria, which eventually attacked the brain. It was hard not to despair of how Africa is going to deal with AIDS since so many people there cannot afford or get access to even the relatively cheap and simple medication for malaria and dysentry. I wanted to remember that: the difficulty and frustration, as well as the inexplicable mad passion I felt for East Africa. It is an implacable, vast, stoic land, full of such poverty and richness and so frustrating to every European who asks, 'Why is Africa in such a mess?' As if we are not all in such a mess.

We are connected. People are like they are in Africa, in Asia, in Aboriginal communities, because of what we are like. Centuries of European interference, altruism as well as greed, has shaped our entangled histories. Africa did not need me there trying to fix things, rather, I needed to go home and fix things at that end. If we cannot talk to our next-door neighbours (because they scream at their kids, vote for Howard, smoke dope or have a poodle—whatever it is that presses our buttons), how can we expect to reach out across bigger divides? But I was scared that I would get back and be sucked into a world that skilfully erased my memory of the possibility of difference, a world where consumerism wraps us in a cocoon of almost-satisfied till we can no longer remember what it is that we really need and love.

Though we were making good time, averaging around 5 knots, we were not happy little sailors. We were heeled over more than usual and the water was bumpy. It was tiring and bruising, and a strong south-setting current was pulling us off course. The hose from the starboard watertank was leaking and we spent hours mucking around with buckets in the middle of the night. Allen looked like a depressed teddy bear. Each morning we tuned into *Kiore*'s regular schedule, but an American yachtie anchored at Kilifi was standing in for Tony, who had malaria. I was disappointed. Tony, though he could be prickly face to face, was balm at sea, and I had been looking forward to having him soothe the passage home. Years of being an airline pilot had trained him to maintain a reassuring radio manner and wry humour when all hell was loose in the elements. (The last words of pilots most usually recorded on black boxes retrieved from the wreckage of plane crashes, and the first that betray anything approaching anxiety, are 'Oh shit!')

After a couple of days, we crossed a line where dark ocean-blue changed to a shifting, choppy river of mottled turquoises that looked like shallow water but was 4 miles deep. Immediately our angle of sail improved; we had joined the equatorial counter-current. We could pass the days reading as usual. At the time it was a book by Abdulrazak Gurnah, in which the unnamed narrator returns to Zanzibar to visit his family. It describes Zanzibar from the viewpoint of a lapsed Muslim who had finally unravelled the mysteries of how to navigate the life of a left-wing intellectual in England. As well as providing an Islamic per-spective on fundamentalism, the narrator complains about how impossible he finds it to explain the life of petty hardships experienced by everyone in the Third World to anyone who has not experienced it. Lavatories are not a big issue for people who just let their fingers do the

walking when they need a plumber, people who have never had to deal
with the shit themselves. Reading fiction by local writers—especially
since they are often people who travel and live in the world of cultural
misunderstanding—helps explain so much more than is possible to
comprehend from the outside. I used to feel guilty for reading, especially fiction, as if I were wasting time reading instead of living, but what
is the point of wandering round baffled? Books help, fiction especially;
that's what stories are for, after all, to help us make sense of the whole
show.

Moods as usual coincided with the weather, sun and moon. Funny
how it seems a conceit, pathetic fallacy, when mood in art matches that
in nature, but at sea it was so clear that the elements were, well, elementary. As the night dissolved enough to let the colours seep back
into the world I would start to feel more at ease, and when the sun rose
I would find myself humming 'Morning has broken', which we sang in
school assemblies before it became better known as a pop song.
Mornings should indeed be praised with elation. For a few days, singing
sunrises were followed by gentle sailing, the sort that lead to conversations of the 'maybe after a few years we could get a catamaran' kind.
Other days, I watched the sky anxiously for signs.

One day, the sky was like a sample chart for the clouds. Simultaneously
we could see little fluffy lambs, mackerel, towering thunderheads, elsewhere dull grey walls of approaching rain, flat greys, flat whites, silver
wisps high, high up and creamy lumps, cumuli. The wind had freshened
and we were averaging 6 knots, squalls blew through and a noddy tern
landed on deck, turned up his little webbed toes, tipped over onto his
back with his wings spread and neck twisted, and died. When Allen
came on deck he scooped him up, carefully folded his wings and held
him in his hands saying, 'You came from the sea and now you are going
back to the sea,' as he tossed him into the waves. I don't know if it was

sentimentality or superstition but, out there, it seemed like the right thing to do.

The weather became more squally and uncomfortable but we were moving fast, and after nine days arrived back in the Seychelles at Port Victoria. It was only when we went for a stroll around the town after dinner that we realised how long it had been since we had walked in the dark, how accustomed we had become to the curfew that nightfall had imposed on pedestrians and cyclists in Africa. Despite endless rain, the place was still bursting with colour, men carried bright patterned umbrellas and the shops were brimming with temptation, even Tim-Tams, for heaven's sake! In a week we were ready to head off to Chagos, another 1000 miles east.

When we had left Fremantle we had enough food for a small flotilla, kilos of every dried bean known to womankind, as well as dehydrated vegetables and tofu, most of which we had thrown away as the use-by dates passed, since we had been able to find fresh local produce everywhere. Leaving the Seychelles I felt slightly understocked for the first time. I had left the provisioning till Saturday morning and then gone to see the first Harry Potter film. We were the only unaccompanied adults there, but it was the only show in town, as well as the first time in nearly two years we had seen anything on a big screen, so we did not care. When we got out all the shops had closed, but we had already checked out, sewn sails, baked bread, refuelled and filled the water tanks. We were ready to go, and I thought that we would manage on the rations till we reached Indonesia in a month or so. Sailing across the Seychelles Bank, the area of shallow water that surrounds the islands, we caught a couple of tuna, which would feed us for a week. The sun shone, we were doing 6 knots over a flat sea, and by night it was perfect, the stars close and luminous in the moonless sky.

A couple of days later, the wind kept dropping until we were lolling about on a calm sea, sails flopping and banging. It was boring—we were going nowhere at all. I stared into the glassy black for hours as though hypnotised, waiting for something to change, to move, to happen. We switched on the radio and were shocked to discover that Tony had died. His malaria had caused both his diabetes and heart condition to worsen. Though we had known he was in hospital in Mombasa, there had been no hint that his condition was so bad. Ridiculously, I felt cross because I had not said goodbye—a manifestation of inappropriate anger that sometimes afflicts the bereaved before grief descends. I mourned not just the early death of a friend but the loss of an institution. In a world of user-pays, the traditions of altruism that have supported seafarers throughout the ages are in decline. Tony's dependable radio net, every day of the year, was one of those little delights of the universe. Later we received an email that was being circulated around the yachting community giving news of his sudden death and commenting: 'Tony was as odd as two left shoes but the welcome he and Daphne extended to us yachties was remarkable.' Eccentric but Good seems an enviable epitaph, worth aspiring to.

Every day, we spoke to other yachts in the Seychelles and at Chagos. No one was heading out to sea until the unusual conditions that were affecting the entire Indian Ocean changed. After about a week, everyone on the radio referred to us as *Poor White Cloud* as we reported our unchanged position. But being becalmed was not all bad. We gave up bothering with night watches and both went to sleep; by morning we would have barely moved. In the quiet flat, the only danger was other vessels but we saw nothing and heard no traffic on the radio. Day after day the sea had become ever more glazed. We could not fish, as to catch pelagic fish it is necessary to be moving, trolling at the speed of escaping prey. I was carefully rationing our diminishing food supplies, eating half what I normally did, feeling always a little hungry and thinking about people for whom the question 'Can I feed myself and my family today?' is a relentless, gnawing worry.

Maintenance chores did not stop entirely. The float switch for the bilge pump stopped working, so Allen changed it, hanging upside-down in the engine room grunting, and we cleaned out the bilges, a hot, messy job. With no wind the heat was intense but we could not shower often on our limited water supplies. Each afternoon, just before the sun slid into the sea, we bathed in salt water using a canvas bucket. This cooled us and prevented us from becoming rancid, but we were starting to develop sores and I felt like a human pickle, so we showered in fresh water once a week. Another day, just before sun-down, we noticed a big tear in the foresail. In light winds it had flogged against the rigging. We took it down and sat on deck in the darkening, sewing together by the light of a head torch. Allen wore a palm to push the big needle through the canvas and I used pliers to pull the needle from the other side, stitch by stitch, side by side, working our way across the ocean.

We read and I made bread and did other time-consuming cookery, but much of the time we just stared at the big, still pond. Sometimes an area of almost-ripples would shift across the stillness, igniting hope before dying. Some days I was becalmed too, but other times I cried. My hormones were doing their half-century thing and my body was in chaos, bleeding ceaselessly whenever I stopped taking the precious sup-ply of pills I had got in the Seychelles, the doctor's entire stock. I was used to ignoring my body. Kept fed and clean it generally worked, and I was alarmed and frightened by these first signs that age was going to affect me. I didn't want to hang onto youth but I thought I had made a kind of bargain: if I didn't try to cheat by injecting botox or dressing like a lamb, then time would be kind. It was not working, and I felt scared that perhaps this was not simply time's reward but something more serious. In the end I burst into tears and told Allen what was worrying me. He made tea and spent precious sunlight-energy on some music— we were never sure how many amps the CD player used so were cautious about playing music at sea. 'Don't look at me as if I'm trying to cheer you up and you're determined to resist. We had far worse days than this when we teaching at uni, and it's certainly a heap better than working on the Burma Railway.' He knew how to make me laugh.

After a few days we were becoming known as a dosshouse for boobies. At dusk they would appear, first one or two, but as time went by they came by the dozen. Dumb clodhopping birds, they would even land on the windvane and sit there having daft merry-go-rounds. Allen spent an afternoon fashioning a slingshot in order to try to scare them away, since they are big birds and windvanes are delicate but essential equipment. All that happened when he occasionally hit them was that they looked around in a puzzled way and completely ignored him. Eventually we found that booby-shouting, a kind of dance accompanied by loud, unmelodious sounds, was more effective. Every afternoon as dusk approached we stood on deck and, as a booby arrived with landing gear out—webbed feet spread, tail- and wing-feathers fanned out—we would both roar and shout, bounce and wave our arms. They would try landing again and again until it grew too dark and they flew away into the night.

There we stayed, wandering around between 5 and 6 degrees south, 60 and 65 degrees east, with nothing to do but eat, sleep and dance. Our legs were atrophying so we jiggled to Van Morrison as best we could in the confines of the rolling cockpit. Fish frolicked around, teasing 'Can't catch me!', and we wallowed in the deep, long, rolling swell that unhinges the brain, wave after wave of silent silver. When the music stopped, the only sound was the creaking of timber and wire and the voice in my head wondering whether I had accidentally done some damage to an albatross.

After being becalmed for fourteen days we decided to motor to Gan, 300 miles north of track on the southernmost atoll of the Maldives, instead of going the 170 miles to Chagos as planned. There we would be able to provision and take on the extra fuel we feared we might need to reach our next landfall, 2000 miles away, in Indonesia. We had expected to sail from the Seychelles to Java, using the motor only as a backup and for manoeuvring into harbour, but in Gan we took on enough extra fuel to allow us to chug along for almost a thousand miles if necessary.

I was sorry we were not going to Chagos. I knew it could be my last chance to revisit this unique place inhabited only by cruising yachties. I was going to miss them. Social capital was not a term I knew before setting sail but it was the one I would need when I came back. It describes precisely the allure of slow travel, the accumulation of a wealth of connections made with fellow slow travellers. Of course I had family and friends at home but what distinguished the connections I made travelling was that these were people I would not have met in the course of everyday life. It is very easy to find oneself spending time only with people with shared values and interests, the same level of education or income, not out of any deliberate choice but just because it's the way things happen. We live in cities where we do not know our neighbours' first names, call professionals when we need help fixing anything, from leaking roofs to breaking hearts, and remember with nostalgia the days when it was safe to hitchhike.

We motored for almost three days all the way to Gan. There was no wind. We put out lines in the night but caught nothing except strange fish with external skeletons that, like artichokes, were fiddly and took hours to eat. After spending four out of the five past weeks at sea our

legs were getting soft and wobbly. I had never really believed in organised exercise—a healthy body for a healthy mind always seemed like
moralistic propaganda designed by sadistic school games teachers—but
I was beginning to believe it now. I fantasised about walks and yoga.
I craved them in a way I had never imagined possible before. I wanted
a walk the way I had once wanted a cigarette.

In Gan we found Justin and Caroline, the Fremantle yachties we
had recently seen in Tanga. Like us, they were heading back across the
Indian Ocean. They had left East Africa a month before us and had
reached Chagos before the winds had stopped, but Caroline's mother
was gravely ill. She planned to fly home to Perth while Justin sailed to
Indonesia single-handedly. We ran around, competing with all the
other yachties to find strong 10-litre cooking oil containers. We washed
them out, filled them with fuel and tied them to the deck. It was
becoming apparent that the strange weather patterns, the lack of
wind, or wind from entirely atypical directions, signalled the start of an
El Niño, so everyone was taking on extra fuel as insurance against the
unpredictable weather. The mood of Gan had shifted since our previous visit. I noticed brand new motorbikes, though we had hardly seen
any the year before. Everyone seemed just a little more friendly. The
local coastguard on the military boat in the harbour even gave us
40 litres of desalinated water and some bananas.

By the time we left we had full tanks and an extra 250 litres of fuel
on deck, so we had a motoring range of about a thousand miles, half
the distance to our next possible landfall on the west coast of Sumatra.
There was no wind and it was grim and overcast. During the night it
was like being inside a black hole. I saw only one blurry star all night
and lightning in the distance. We motored for the first two days, but on
the third, fierce squalls gave us good wind and rampaging adrenaline
hits for hours. 'Let's not forget nights like this when we get nostalgic

about sailing,' said Allen. It was a world of blackness and rain, no moon, no stars and the squalls striking out of nowhere—you could not see them coming in this deep darkness.

Every day as evening approached, even in the tropical heat of mid ocean, the grey dullness reminded me of Sunday evenings in boarding school in Wales and brought back words I had not heard for 35 years: the Nunc Dimittis and hymns for evensong. They evoked the same sadness. Do birds feel sad, and cows, or is it just human beings who become subdued at the approach of darkness, the foretaste of the impending night? Out at sea, night after night after night in the open ocean, there was plenty of time to think and nowhere to hide. The ocean is a universe where accidents happen. We were very careful, we did not take risks unnecessarily, but the more I learnt about sailing the more I realised that weather is the most unknown factor. How powerful it is. Even now, I wake at night when the wind howls. During those years I found a joyful, sparse simplicity in living on the edge, not really caring if you have nothing as long as you are still alive when the storm has passed. I didn't want to lose that. I did not want to start wanting anything more than to just be here.

Sailing across the Indian Ocean from east to west, the wrong way, continued to be a hard slog. For three weeks, as we made our way from the Maldives to the Sunda Straits in Indonesia, we had little regular wind and were glad we had stocked up with so much fuel. Most of the wind we did get came from storms. We constantly put sails up and down, reefed and unreefed and worried about how strong the next squall was going to be. It was a time of tension. We were lucky to avoid the edge of a cyclone that Justin, a few days behind us, was battling alone. Perhaps that was why at times we became so silly, out in that ocean a thousand miles from anywhere, as we tried to put up the spinnaker pole so that we could gull-wing, with the main and the foresail out on either side, in the rolling conditions of low wind and still-choppy seas in the lull between squalls. 'We're putting up the poley but it's very very rolly, we call it doing the roly-poly,' we sang, giggling and lurching.

Fear is a potent weapon, one long used by bullies and thugs. When people are frightened enough they will pay a high price, but still 'shit happens', as the graffiti so often reminds us. People lose their jobs, get divorced, have traffic accidents, they are burgled, swindled or mugged. Some people suicide, a few are murdered, some get struck by lightning or die from drinking too much or from prostate cancer or a terrorist attack. We are afraid of losing our lives, our minds, our life savings. We are scared of losing love. The more you think about it, the worse it gets, and if you read the papers, watch television and surf the Net; you can end up thinking about it an awful lot. Fear sells. Fear sells everything from security doors and facelifts to government policies. Fear that we would be swamped by people with funny headgear was selling our government's policies about refugees.

Travelling slowly around the Indian Ocean I had spent most of the time in the countries that border it, and although I had sometimes felt uncomfortable, it was the ocean, not people, that had ever been the real danger. It seemed we were returning to a place that was erecting barriers and creating an atmosphere of distrust and puzzlement. 'Why don't Australians like refugees?' I was puzzled myself. My experience was that average Australians had moved on from the days when kids who ate garlic, cabanossi and spring rolls—the migrants and refugees of earlier eras—were ridiculed in the playground. Yet an election had been fought on refugee policies following the *Tampa* affair, and it showed how easily a population could be persuaded into behaving inhumanely towards people fleeing from persecution. How fragile was our claim to be a civilised nation.

I was trying to prepare myself for getting back. I was looking forward to home but I felt almost afraid. I wanted to believe that if people
in Australia had experienced Third World conditions for themselves
they would be more sympathetic. Before travelling I had still imagined
that refugees were not like me, that the poor, who make up most of
the population in Third World countries, were somehow different. Yet
when I met university lecturers in Indonesia, who courteously welcomed me into their homes that by Australian standards would be
described as hovels, and when I met health professionals in Africa who
earned less money in a week than I spend on my phone bill, I realised
that I did not enjoy a comfortable lifestyle simply through my own
efforts. I did so because I happened to live in Australia, where I had
received a free education, where there are still anti-corruption laws,
laws to protect workers' rights and safeguards to protect the weak and
the sick. Now I was worried that Australian values were shifting. We
were forgetting that it is by helping people in need, both inside and
outside our borders, that we keep our integrity.

A thousand miles from land in any direction, we were tired and
run down. We were lonely. We saw little life, a few dolphins early on in
the passage and occasional birds. When, ten days out from Gan,
Allen said he had seen starry dolphin tracks in the night ocean while
I was sleeping, I made him describe it all to me in detail. I wanted to
believe there was life nearby. And there were the voices. On long passages we often heard things, voices or instruments. On this leg it was
mainly flutes and conversations, but one morning the cello section
seemed to be tuning up. Never so regularly had the rigging sung and
whispered. Was it siren songs or the voices of the drowned? I clung
to every little connection. I talked every day to Justin. We would draw
out our skeds, discussing in detail everything that had occurred in
the last 24 hours, our broken battens, his spinnaker sheet that was

caught round the rudder, the endless 'to fix' list and the nights of storm wrangling.

After two weeks we were only 500 miles off the coast of Sumatra and 200 miles from the Sunda Strait. We began to feel we were almost there, a state of anticipation that stretched time slower and longer. Two days later we picked up the Darwin radio weather report for the first time. But there was still a long way to go and we could not relax, a sumatra was heading our way. When these big storm fronts roll down from the mountains, the whole horizon becomes a looming line of bruised cloud, purple-grey, with spoondrift lashing beneath. As it approached we reefed all the sails and then scudded downwind until the worst was past. During the height of the storm I had sat on the cockpit floor and watched the muscles of my thighs quivering. I no longer registered the fear as an emotion; I just watched it in my muscles, musing, 'Oh, that's what adrenaline does. How odd.' Life was reducing to bare essentials, the texture of the sea, the mood of the sky. I ate little. I slept whenever I was not on watch, and when I was, just gazed into space for hours, six hours each night. Days before, I had craved exercise, clean clothes, a shower, company, music. Now, just so long as the storms were not too ferocious, I was content.

Sailing past the coast of Sumatra, the lightning, gold, silver, pink and a white brighter than stardust, crazed the sky and silhouetted the island volcanoes. The next night we hung around from three in the morning until well after daylight for the rain to ease enough for us to edge our way into the anchorage, a calm lagoon tucked between a small island and the edge of Java at the entrance to the Sunda Strait. We slept all day, surrounded by an ancient jungle, Ujung Kulon National Park, which was home to one-horned rhinoceroses and secretive big black cats. Mists, like so many fires, streamed from among the forested hills when the rain occasionally stopped in the land of the soggy panthers. The next day we went for a walk, or more of a totter, on the small island, where there were tame deer with big velvety horns and extravagant eyelashes as well as grumpy long-tailed macaques picking at shells, and the sweet-smelling mangrove flowers. Then there was all that work to be done, the fuel filters to be changed, the bread to be baked, the pressure pump to be worried over. We still had almost 1000 miles to get to Bali before the winds turned, so we did not want to dawdle, but our bodies had turned to mush and would not allow us to sail for a few more days.

Fuel stops were necessary, first in Jakarta and then at Bawean, a small island in the Java Sea. As soon as we arrived, a local fishing boat full of excitable men came alongside and, despite language problems, we managed to communicate. Within a couple of hours they had filled us up with fuel and guided us to a safer anchorage. In a place full of friendly, curious people one expects visitors. Nevertheless, it was a bit of a surprise later in the afternoon to see an unfamiliar face peering down to where we were sitting, rather scantily clad in the heat and supposed privacy of our home, watching a VCD on the computer. It was a local high-school English teacher who had brought a boatload of school children to visit us. Allen agreed to talk to them at their school the following afternoon, but declined to have twenty teenagers come aboard to gaze at us.

A couple of days later we again heard voices outside; a group of teenagers had come out in a sampan without their teacher to practise their English. We went ashore and they took us on their motorbikes to visit their English teacher. (Never ride pillion with a sixteen-year-old boy. I kept thinking, 'I've made it all the way across the Indian Ocean and now I'm going to die in a motorbike crash.'). These students were from another school, an Islamic school, and their teacher was evidently rather devout. He was taken aback by my name, telling me

Rhydwen (Ridwan) was the name of the angel of heaven. He seemed to find it auspicious, which probably helped temper his defensiveness—he had heard that Westerners were brainwashed into believing that all Muslims were terrorists.

Fifty-three sunrises at sea after leaving Tanzania, we arrived in Bali. Within days, I was sitting on the balcony of my room looking out over a courtyard garden of an intimate little hotel where the two swimming pools nestled in among the frangipanis, bougainvilleas and myriad lush, leafy things. There was the sound of gamelan and fountains, birdsong, someone pruning and, in the distance, the puttering of little motor-bikes. It was gorgeous. I had the kind of holiday I have always scorned, lounging around a pool, having massages and occasionally wandering out and buying souvenirs. And best of all, the world didn't move, though my dreams continued to be full of ocean and frustration. My body basked while my psyche made landfall, and we pieced ourselves together ready for the next couple of thousand miles back to Perth. The days had become long; I was amazed how much I could do before lunchtime. It made me wonder whether, at sea, our metabolisms went into a kind of semi-hibernation in order to endure the demands of that strange combination of vast boredom and the need for constant alertness. It would not be long before we returned to real time, but not, I hoped, quite real life. Already we were in Western Australia's time zone and, within a few weeks, expected to make landfall at Broome.

After two weeks in Bali we set off eastwards back along the island chain, stopping at Gili Aer, Pulau Lawang and Moyo, the islands we had visited when we had first left Australia. I realised on returning that the cruising around those islands east of Bali was some of the best we had experienced. Although over-fished—as everywhere—this part of the archipelago is mountainous and does not support a large population. The water is so clear that, anchored, we could see coral and fish and the bottom at 20 metres. It was perfect. We snorkelled around coral gardens, walked along the shoreline greeting the few local people we saw—'*Selamat siang!*'—hiked in the tawny hills of Komodo amid herds of deer, and just lolled about in the sea, using our lifebuoys as floaties while groups of little stripey surgeonfish clustered round as if we were boats or reefs. But the weather decreed we needed to keep moving.

As winter approached, the winds would become even stronger and more easterly and I had been worried that if we left too late we would be blown right past North West Cape and have to keep sailing eastwards, back to Africa. As it was, we could not maintain our heading towards Broome. I fought an urge to rant and weep. I wanted to come home somewhere lovely, not a grotty old mining town. No matter that Broome was a difficult anchorage and had proved less than welcoming on our previous visit, I had a vision splendid of homecoming that accorded more with the brochure-enhanced Broome of my imagination than the pedestrian reality of rural Western Australia.

Dampier was our first landfall, a week after leaving Komodo. This land is so flat. I had forgotten. There was nothing to see until we were almost within cooee of the shore, but then we had to anchor off and spend a day vacuuming, watching VCDs on the computer and gazing at Australia, waiting for Monday and the working week. Then, as we drew alongside in the strong winds, we were glad the officials were there to catch our lines and help us tie up.

Quarantine, immigration and customs came aboard, giving us the most thorough search we ever experienced, swabbing down our power-point switches.

'Why?' we enquired.

'For traces of drugs.'

Perhaps we should have pointed out that we had not touched our switches since leaving Australia. Without access to 240-volt on-shore power sources, we had not been able to use them. The drugs would have been on the light switches, which ran on battery power.

They sliced open any wrapped parcels, poked around the fridge and charged us lots of money but were quite friendly. The only remaining problem was the form we had to fill in to prove we had bought the boat in Australia. Since we had proof that it was an Australian boat, registered in our names prior to leaving the country, it seemed odd to have to prove we had not bought the boat on our travels overseas but apparently it was necessary for us to pay another A$54 to fill in an incomprehensible form. The answers were all coded, so we were told, 'Put QZ here' and 'Write 54932 there'. No wonder most of the overseas yachties we met had complained that Australia was the most bureaucratic and expensive place they ever dealt with. If anywhere else on our travels we had gone through the process of having to pay to fill in a form to which only the officials could supply the answers, to prove the boat we had left Australia in was an Australian boat, I'd have been convinced it was evidence of official corruption. Here it was a more pathetic sin: bureaucratic bungling and inflexibility, the same kind that meant that we could not re-establish our health insurance because we did not have tickets or boarding passes to show we had re-entered the country. A few dollars or a bottle of rum to lubricate the entry into a country was looking like an easier and cheaper way to do business.

But it was comfortingly familiar back in the land of grubby little corellas sitting around in couples preening each other, even if the Internet machines were coin-operated and cut out just as you were about to send the email you'd spent nine-and-a-half minutes writing, and the region's major tourist attraction, the ghost town of Cossack, reverted to ghost town again when you drove there hoping for lunch. Hey, it was a bit frustrating but it was familiar frustration and there was no malice in it, just down-to-earth, honest slackness. The other side of easygoing was that the Dampier post office chairs were all slung with post bags doing duty as pouches for baby kangaroos. The postmistress doubled as a wildlife rescuer and the whole office was draped with jostling sacks from which long legs poked.

Within a few days we sailed to Exmouth via Serrurier Island, where we stopped for a couple of days and feasted on painted cray, the vegetarian crays that are not attracted to baited pots, and some kind of sea perch we caught on a nerve-racking snorkelling expedition stalked by sharks. The thermometer recorded a temperature of 29 degrees, the first time it had been below 30 degrees, day or night, for as long as we could remember. We wanted to leave as soon as possible but we were waiting for some mail to arrive and by the time it came a front was forecast, so we stayed to wait out the weather.

It came. It rained all day, turning the marina into a muddy pond. When the rain eased in the late afternoon we walked around to find the road into town was flooded; we were marooned. A furious brown river of water was rushing into the marina. The floodway from the hills behind the town fed directly into it just where the whole of the fishing fleet was moored. Everyone else in the marina had taken the chance to go for a walk too, so we were all gathered around, commenting on the strength of the water pressing against the boats, when there was a loud thwang as the mooring ropes snapped and the first boat keeled over, filled with water and sank within minutes, bumping into the next, which then tipped and sank too. Meanwhile, on the other fishing fleet trawlers, people were frantically throwing off lines and heading out to spend an uncomfortable night in the horrendous open seas—a better option than staying safely in port and sinking. No one was aboard the boats that went down, but it was a grim lesson to see how fast and how easily they did and how helpless we had been as we stood and watched.

The next day one of the trawler crew gave us a lift into town. He had been on one of the boats that escaped out to sea.

'How was it out there?'

'Vicious. I'm on my way to the bottle shop now. I need a carton to help me recover. Bloke on one of the other boats told me he was watching our prop spinning out of the water at times, and we're 98 foot long, so it gives you an idea, dunnit?'

With a huge swell and continuing strong wind warnings up and down the coast we were going nowhere. We wandered disconsolately around the marina jetties, rescuing the lizards and snakes that were clinging to the wreckage of the floods. Weather had become the dominating force in our lives, and we listened to every report, searching for signs that might let us scurry south.

After about ten days we were able to make a dash for Carnarvon, two days sail away, and that was how we progressed down the coast for several more weeks: waiting in harbours, then scuttling south as fast as we could. Each passage was squeezed between storm fronts. Sometimes they were so close together we had to wait for a week or two and it became obvious how Australia's history has been shaped by this weather. Most of the Indian Ocean had been regularly visited by trading vessels for centuries, but the coast of Western Australia, especially below North West Cape, is inhospitable with few safe anchorages and relentless, contrary winds. Heading out of Shark Bay past the Zuytdorp Cliffs, we were even forced to turn around and, after 24 gruelling hours, were back where we started.

All the way up and down the west coast of Australia we had listened to the voices of the people in Perth who read the weather reports. You could even call up for a repeat of the report and they provided a check-in service so that, each day, you could tell them your position and planned route. We had grown to know these anonymous voices, but at the end of June they were sacked and replaced by a computerised weather report. It came out in a dalek voice with no change in intonation for storms or sunshine, no special emphasis to make sure a difficult message was understood. There was no one there. In the past, small craft benefited from the services that were provided for major shipping, but with use of sophisticated technology increasingly available only to big ships, the safety of small vessels was in danger of diminishing.

At Geraldton some irresistible urge took me back to the bookshop with the grumpy man in the cardigan.

'Can I point you in any particular direction?' he asked after watching me read all the category labels: Romance, Thriller, War, Sci-fi.

'Well,' I said, 'I'm not exactly looking for a category, I'm looking for—how shall I put it?—a good book?'

He laughed. 'You have to find those for yourself.' But after watching me for a while he said, 'You might like to look in Various.'

I found four books.

'Thats twenty-six dollars' he beamed. 'You've made my day. Twenty-six dollars.'

It was that easy. He was just poor and it made him miserable. I'd have bought something the time before if I'd known.

The whole journey was like that really. I'd go somewhere and try to make sense of it, attach labels and then move on, but so much of the time I probably got it wrong. Only rarely did I have a second chance, a chance to revisit and stumble on it all differently.

By the time we had reached Africa I was already addicted to travelling slowly enough to bump into people and places that would change the way I experienced the world, change my mind—sometimes many times. I had observed that most people are poor, a very few are exceedingly rich, corruption is normal, clean water is precious and good people everywhere are doing what they can. Then, as I stood on the beach in Tanga on 11 September 2001, the event that would change our world occurred and I knew it was more urgent than ever to become familiar with the unknown, to meet with people and tread in places we are constantly being reminded are alien, dangerous and frightening.

Travelling back across the high seas we were still tucked inside our own little nation, happily beyond jurisdiction, subject only to the laws of nature. Later, a quick glance at the Admiralty and Maritime Law Guide confirmed that it had all been fantasy: as the owners and crew of an Australian-registered ship, we were bound by a multitude of inter-national conventions. Nonetheless, the reality is that, out there, we were effectively on our own and felt free. I loved that about sailing out across the open ocean. There was a sense of being just another animal, like the boobies and terns above us and the mysterious fishes deep below, bound by the rhythms of sun and moon, wind and water, life and death. Each sunrise is a miracle, each playful dolphin or curious mollymawk a companion on the journey, and as we drew closer to home I feared losing all that.

We moved over the ocean, that last great wilderness of the soul, at the speed of wind and waves, the speed of things that fly and swim and walk upon the earth. Evan, the man everyone in Tanga called bwana, had taken us on a drive in the hinterland between the town and the distant hills. 'Look,' he had said, with uncharacteristic wistfulness as he gestured towards the sisal plantations he had managed, which supply the automotive industry, 'When I was a young man there were ele-phants here, and leopards and lions.' A shadow passed across his face. 'I used to shoot them in those days.'

Everywhere people have enclosed, reshaped, chopped and dirtied this ground of our being, displacing our co-inhabitants. Too busy to stop, we need electricity and fast food, cars, tools to help us whiz through our lives as fast as we can, achieving as much as we can and always muttering like the White Rabbit, 'Oh dear! Oh dear! I shall be late!' Our bodies can be transported fast, we can stay awake longer in our electrically illuminated nightworlds, and our computer-enhanced intellects can leap across time and space, but our emotions, they still move at the same speed they have always done. We cannot cry faster and grieve more efficiently. Anyone who has tried high-speed love will know it leads to all kinds of trouble.

Once I had imagined I was getting somewhere, going forward, making progress and not noticing that we are always and forever stuck (if you look at it that way) or right at home (if you look at it the other way) in this very moment. Now it no longer mattered that we would have to part with *White Cloud* and find ways to make a living on land. Travelling slowly was no longer a manner of locomotion, it was a way of life.

ACKNOWLEDGEMENTS

My deepest thanks go to everyone who appears in the book named, renamed or unnamed, and to the many people I met during the voyage who are not mentioned but who were part of the reality out of which the book is fashioned. I would especially like to thank all the cruising yachties who welcomed us into that world of marine wandering that, once you experience it, never stops beckoning.

Thanks are due also to my agent, Fran Moore at Curtis Brown, whose calm faith in the project before I even made landfall was infectious and who encouraged me to keep going. Sue Hines, Rachel Lawson and Andrea McNamara at Allen and Unwin helped me navigate from manuscript to book, encouraging me gently and skillfully to jettison unnecessary baggage and suggesting adjustments to the course while leaving me always at the helm.

The cover is based on an idea by Poppy van Oorde-Grainger, an award-winning Western Australian artist. I felt immense pride when someone so young and cool and talented wanted to be involved. Thanks Pops.

Bee Marett and Lucy Rhydwen-Marett read and reread and commented helpfully on the manuscript at various stages, and Kathy Murray listened to me read it all aloud. I am grateful for their forbearance. Brigid Lowry sustained me through the writing and editing with regular emails and Jane Murray did the same by taking me on regular walks.

Without Allen Nash, none of it would have been possible. Not only did he initiate the idea of sailing somewhere but he saw the voyage through to the bitter end, checking my manuscript for factual errors, commenting bluntly on infelicities of style and demonstrating his usual good humour when I refused to change some bits he didn't like much, especially bits about him.

In the end though this is my story, and, in the words of Zen teacher Wu-men, *a thousand mistakes, ten thousand mistakes.*